W0038673

RELENTLESS

A True Story of War and Survival

HOPE

DAVID L. BRITT

with *John Duresky and Vickie Graham*

Copyright 2021 David L. Britt

ISBN (Print): 978-1-09838-539-2
ISBN (eBook): 978-1-09838-540-8

Rights and permissions. All rights reserved. No part of this publication may be reproduced, distributed or transmitted in any form or by any means, including photocopying, recording or electronic or mechanical methods, without the prior written permission of the publisher, except in the case of brief quotations embodied in critical reviews and certain other noncommercial uses permitted by copyright law. For permission send written requests to contact the publisher/author through:

Registered Agents Inc. 7901 4th St N Suite 4000, St Petersburg, FL 333702

Disclaimer. This is a work of actual family history to include letters, diaries, photographs, war crimes testimony, and legends interweaved with historical research and the reported circumstances of several American prisoners of war who survived the brutal and savage treatment of their Japanese captors for over three years. This is a true story not a work of fiction. We sought out and obtained permission to use of materials from other books to tell the story. Many authors and publishers are no longer reachable as the people have died or the businesses are no longer there. We have given credit where it Is due whenever practicable.

This is a first edition work.

BookBaby Publishing designed the cover and overall book, edited the text and handles print on demand orders.

This book is self-published by the author under the name Honor Media LLC. The author can be reached through Registering Agent Inc. as outlined in permissions above or through the LLC website. **www.honormediallc.com**

Ordering information:
Books may be ordered in eBook format through established vendors.
Books in print may be ordered by contacting bookbaby.com who is handling requests for print on demand books which will be shipped directly to the buyer.
Buyers should contact: **www.bookbaby.com**

Trademark name is Honor Media LLC

Author website: **www.honormediallc.com**

Printed in the United States of America

Table of Contents

Dedication

This book is dedicated to my parents Chester K. and
Grace R. Britt, and to his fellow warriors, their friends and
wives who endured sacrifices most can never imagine
to win a war that kept America free.

Dedicated also to my wife, Gail Britt and John's wife,
Judy McLean, who endured separation from us with patience
and embraced our passion for telling this story
as we labored for almost two years in crafting it.

Introduction

When we began researching and writing this book, 78 years had passed since the bombing of Pearl Harbor and America's declaration of war upon Japan. To paraphrase Gen. Douglas MacArthur, the old soldiers are not merely fading away, they are a rapidly dying and disappearing group of heroes. The few who remain for the moments on Earth that God still grants them are a national treasure. If you see a vet from any service, any war, any period, thank them. They deserve it. And if you want to know the real meaning of sacrifice, ask them if they will kindly tell you about their service, but respect them if they choose to keep silent. The pain sometimes can be emotionally overwhelming, too much to expose to strangers or even family.

It's hard to grasp that World War II truly was a war fought around the world. No smart bombs, no drones. It was brutal. It was ugly. And it was very personal. Massive military operations like the Battle of the Bulge, D-Day, Iwo Jima, Stalingrad, and the Battle of Britain are solidly cemented in the world's collective memory. So many battles in so many places with so many leaders who need only a single name to identify them — Eisenhower, Churchill, Montgomery, Stalin, Yamamoto. Other, smaller skirmishes may only be associated with a single country or even town. Others may be only in the memory of a single soldier fighting for his life in hand-to-hand combat — a memory locked away in his mind — too frightening to recall — a heroic story lost forever upon his death.

It is impossible to chronicle the entire war. We are only taking one relatively small, brutal part of that history, starting with a young boy, Chester K. Britt, from the small city of La Crosse, Wisconsin, who became a West Point graduate on June 11, 1940 — married his high school sweetheart the following day. This is their story.

First Lieutenant Chester K. Britt fought in the defense of Bataan, Philippines, after Pearl harbor was attacked, survived the Bataan Death March, was a captive in four POW camps in the Philippines, three Hell Ships in the Pacific, and two prison camps in Japan and Manchuria, respectively. Surviving any one of these horrible, brutal, and savage experiences is, by itself, a miracle. Chester survived them all.

He was liberated from a POW camp in Mukden, Manchuria on August 16, 1945, and repatriated to his hometown of La Crosse, Wisconsin on October 20, 1945. He remained in the Army, after the war and was promoted to captain and then major. But he died young due to injuries he suffered as a POW, one of thousands of "delayed casualties" of the war. Families lost loved ones long after the bombs stopped falling, not just in America but in places all around the world from 1931 to 1945 and beyond.

While this book focuses on my father, then-Army 1st Lt. Chester K. Britt, and my mother Grace, we have endeavored also to honor the many friends who endured alongside them whether they died in the war or survived as he did.

It has been a labor of love to chronicle what they suffered among the thousands who were prisoners of the Japanese. The Bataan Death March, Japanese POW camps, and Hell Ship voyages were the life, and the death, of far too many good men.

We also honor the men and women who served on and below the seas, in the skies, and on the land, while their countrymen were Prisoners of War. Every man and woman who served their country is truly deserving of a book about their own lives.

These are the Americans who swore a solemn oath, put their lives on the line, and saved our nation from an existential threat, preserved democracy, and gave all of us a future.

We will touch upon the incredible contribution of civilians in America, on the home front, who were the engine that drove an almost limitless supply of weapons and material to the various theaters of war. These war-time workers included Lieutenant Britt's own wife, Grace, who worked at a factory producing 20 mm brass shell casings; his and her brothers who served in the military and their parents who kept the home fires burning, helped raise a first grandson on the home front, and delivered war and commercial materials by train, keeping the economy going and generating the cash needed to pay for the war.

This book is dedicated to all the Allied men and women who served in WWII, in all the theaters, in all the services. The collective war history is, in reality, the accumulation of small stories of everyone woven together. We may read of the Battle of the Bulge, but it is really nothing more than the combined efforts and actions of every man or woman on both sides that results in the big picture battles about which we read. The Battle of the Bulge is really the Battle of 2nd Lt. Jesse Morrow (Lieutenant Britt's brother-in-law) or others like him, both officer and enlisted (Grace's brother Pvt. Bill Runice). Countries may win or lose wars, but it is the individual citizens — military and civilian — who live or die. A mother grieves her son even in the victory of her nation. Sacrifice is most intense when it's personal. A slogan from the 1960s said it well, "War is unhealthy for children and other living things."

Be forewarned, this book recounts horrible details of war, worse than we can imagine. The reality of what the POWs endured is unspeakable. We did not change anything to make it socially palatable. Eyewitness accounts are written as they were recorded. Yes, war is hell — and it's on full display in the details of this book.

Many of the photos and images are cherished by the Britt family, which has strong connections to La Crosse, Wisconsin. We incorporated information in news articles from the hometown paper, the La Crosse Tribune, as well as other newspapers from across the nation and included details stored in other archives and official documents, including archives of the Department of the Army and the West Point history department. While the Britt family holdings of physical memorabilia from this time period are extensive, they were not complete enough to tell the whole story. We have used descriptions of conditions the POWs experienced, as written in numerous books by fellow POWs, legal testimony as recorded in official Army documents, including war crimes affidavits and testimony to give readers an accurate description of what our American captives experienced at the hands of their Japanese captors. Our goal was to depict an all-encompassing sense of the men, the time, and the events.

The key relationships of a handful of warriors and their wives — who shared life and death experiences with our Dad and Mom, before, during, and after the war — provide a deeper, richer, more compelling tribute to their courage and sacrifice. Anything less than our best efforts to tell their stories would not be sufficient or acceptable.

CHAPTER 1

Early Years, Future Hope
(1915 - 1940)

Chester Kieser Britt was born June 13, 1915. Friends and family called him Chet. His parents, Archibald Ray Britt (1890-1952) and Hazel Henrietta Britt (nee Kieser, 1894-1990) were married on November 17, 1912, in the small, scenic, rural farming community of Prairie Du Chien, Wisconsin, along the banks of the Mississippi River. Hazel's family home was in Prairie Du Chien, where she lived until her marriage. After their wedding, Archibald — called A.R. by most of his friends — and Hazel lived in a rented house at 1542 Wood Street, La Crosse, Wisconsin. A.R. worked as an engineer on the Chicago, Burlington, and Quincy (CB&Q) Railroad, within walking distance from home.

The first of Chet's six siblings, Dorothy M. Britt, was born March 20, 1917. She would become a good friend in high school and later a great help to his future wife Grace during WWII.

On June 2, 1919, when Chester was just 4 years old, he touched what at that time was a thick telephone wire, which had fallen on some streetcar tracks. The local newspaper, the La Crosse Tribune, reported the incident in a June 21, 1919 article, noting he was nearly electrocuted. This is likely the first time Chet cheated death, excluding any undocumented early childhood illnesses, which killed many children during that time in history.

1915 Chester Britt in arms of his mother Hazel

Brother Edgar R. Britt was born in 1919. He lived in several homes in La Crosse by the time he was 5 years old, but all the homes were in the same neighborhood and only a few short blocks from where his father worked on the Northside of La Crosse. The city runs approximately north to south along the eastern bank of the Mississippi River, and you were either a proud North Sider (aka "Swampies" because of the nearby marshes), or a proud Southsider. Chet's was a family of proud Northsiders. By August 15, 1920, the family purchased a home at 1508 Wood Street. Chet lived there until he left to attend the United States Military Academy at West Point (commonly referred to simply as West Point). His parents still lived there during WWII.

The next siblings to be born were brother Archie (Arch) G. Britt Jr. in 1922, brother Franklin (Frank) S. Britt in 1924, and brother Kenneth (Ken) D. Britt in 1927. The youngest Britt was sister Hazel Jean — called Jean by most people — born on November 6, 1929, a little over a week after the stock market crash of October 29, 1929, which led to The Great Depression. As this book was being edited, Hazel Jean (Britt) Buehler, the last surviving sibling of Chet, passed away at the age of 90 on February 11, 2020. Because of the coronavirus (COVID-19) pandemic sweeping across the globe, Chet's three sons, and no doubt many more family member and friends, were unable to travel to her funeral. As if history were repeating itself, the modern stock market was dropping like a stone, and economists were predicting the pandemic would lead to a recession and possibly a depression comparable to 1929. It was ironic how her life began and ended in a period of great economic turmoil. Irony is a common occurrence in this book. Chet's little sister witnessed The Great Depression, WWII with her four brothers going off to war, the first TV, the Korean War, the Cuban Missile crisis, the first man and the first American in space, the Vietnam war, the first man on the moon, the first smart phone, 9/11 and so much more.

It was a happy, active home full of playful kids who were growing up with supportive parents in a beautiful location with short, hot summers and long, cold winters. The Britt household experienced its share of snowball fights and snow forts built in the winter and rafts slap-dashed together in the summer to explore the flooded marshes nearby. Trips to the banks of the adjacent Black River, La Crosse River, and Mississippi River provided ample opportunities for swimming and fishing.

However, little is factually known about Chet's activities until about 1928, he was 13 years old, when articles in the Tribune frequently began to appear with his name. Back then, local newspapers were the social media of their time, with a great deal of newspaper space devoted to the movements of local citizens, social events, community activities, and local news, which competed for attention with national and international news. Today, it seems quaint to read such mundane things as "The Tom Robinson family motored across town to visit Tom's aunt Betsy where they had homemade pie," but 90 years ago it was of keen interest to subscribers and fun for them to see their names in the paper.

1931 siblings   back L R Dorothy Edgar Chet age 16
front L R Frank Ken Jean Archie

Thankfully, that "small" news captured in those old newspapers offered a bigger and richer picture of the lives of Chet, his family, and friends, and also the many other people mentioned in this book. In a way, the social media of today, where people post photos of the food they make and the places they've visited are the modern-day local news media of the past.

On December 2, 1928, we learned that at some point in his young life, Chet learned to play the bugle. An article in the newspaper that day reported he had called a meeting to order by playing his bugle. The following summer, Chet was appointed the head bugler for the Boy Scout camp at Decorah, Wisconsin. By then, he was a 14-year-old Boy Scout in Troop 1 of the North Side Presbyterian Church. He continued to play the bugle with the high point of his musical career occurring on December 3, 1929. Chet was selected to ride with Santa Clause through La Crosse playing his bugle to herald Santa's arrival. It was a huge honor to be chosen, and no doubt the Britt home was bursting with pride and joy as congratulations poured in for young Chet. Christmas music probably wasn't the Boy Scout song book, but perhaps "Charge" or "Reveille" was sufficient for the task at hand. And we have to wonder if A.R.'s tough, blue collar, railroad buddies asked him if Chet could whisper a few good words for their kids in Santa's ear.

SANTA CLAUS TO ARRIVE BY AIRPLANE; RECEPTION AT HOTEL AT 7:30 TONIGHT

SANTA CLAUS will be here to-night a little before 7:30 p. m. That was the announcement this morning of the merchants bureau of the Chamber of Commerce, which held a wireless conversation with Santa this morning.

Traveling by airplane he hoped to drop in at the municipal airport about 7:30 tonight. He will be brought from the airport to the bus-iness district by automobile, and will ride around the streets of the city, his appearance to be heralded by a Boy Scout bugler, Chester Britt, who will be in the automobile with Santa.

After making his tour of the city, Santa will hold a reception in the lobby of the Stoddard Hotel. He has asked that all the children in the city be there to meet him.

December 3, 1929 article in the La Crosse Tribune, Santa's arrival and Chet the Bugle boy

The four very distinct seasons of La Crosse came and went year after year for Chet. Winter was long, cold, and usually very snowy. It was a time to shovel snow, build snow forts, engage in snowball fights, and go ice skating — if your family could afford skates. As always, spring in Wisconsin came slowly, and then winter would sneak back and reappear just when you thought spring had finally arrived. But the full, glorious spring finally would arrive, and all the barren trees would begin sprouting their leaves. Snow melted down streets and dirt or coal cinder alleys back then. It was not unusual for kids to toss objects in the runoff water and watch them float away. Spring was gorgeous, beautiful, breathtaking as the colors of flowers, leaves and more bloomed everywhere and emerald-green lawns again needed to be mowed with push mowers. They made their own music as the blades whirred, grass flying in the wind. Summer followed, albeit only for about four months. Days were long and full of fun for young kids in La

Crosse, where the three rivers met. Extra daylight offered countless hours of swimming, canoeing, and lots of outdoor games and entertainment.

Back then the area was surrounded by undeveloped land where kids could make forts, explore, chop down trees, hunt, and fish. With all the boys in the Britt household, they certainty did this a lot together and with friends. Finally, fall would come around with leaves from the many elm and oak trees in the city dropping to the ground, then being raked into huge piles to be jumped into by kids who then would pile them up again. Fall colors were everywhere. Kids played endless games of football, ran through the neighborhood lawns, and made-up games on the spot when they tired of hide-and-seek or cops and robbers. The only electronic toy for a kid, if his could afford it, was an electric train. Lionel was the preferred brand.

Thanksgiving family dinners were immensely important, and no less so than in the Britt home which worshipped and thanked God for all they had. Then winter came again, and the cycles of seasons were enjoyed over and over by Chet and his family. The Great Depression greatly impacted the Britt family as it did all families in the nation. A.R. was placed on reduced hours at his primary railroad job, so he took other jobs working construction and selling washing machines. It's hard to imagine feeding a family of nine on part-time wages even with the family yard converted to a vegetable garden. A.R. and Hazel were amazing parents as the family oral history and newspaper articles that feature Chet reveal a family that worked to maintain a sense of normalcy in the most desperate financial times.

Chester loved to build gliders, and on April 13, 1930 he won a contest, triumphing over about 50 other kids. His ROG (Rise-off Ground) glider, powered by a rubber band, flew for 1 minute 28 and 2/5 seconds at La Crosse's Riverside Park on the bank of the Mississippi River. Chester's prize was his first-ever airplane ride at the La Crosse Airport.

He was 14 years old. He flew with the Winneshiek Air Club, which by then owned two WACO 10 biplanes. The pilot sat in the back and there was room for two passengers under the top wing. Another boy won a different contest and was supposed to ride with Chet, but he did not show up, so it was just young Chet and the pilot who likely did barrel rolls and loop-de-loops, much to his delight — and the terror of his parents and probably his sisters. Boys being boys, his brothers were probably laughing and shouting a hearty "neat" or "that's swell" or something like it. Charles Lindbergh had conquered the Atlantic only 11 years earlier, and flying was still in its infancy. When Chet stepped down from the wing, it is easy to imagine he was mobbed by family and friends asking what it was like, was he afraid, what was the neatest thing, and then the next day at school being asked by envious young friends about it. It must have been hard to concentrate on schoolwork for a few days as he replayed the ride in his mind and dreamed of flying again.

WACO 10 like Chet got to ride in for winning a model plane contest

Having experienced the thrill of flying, Chester decided to try making a real glider. He planned to glide from the top of Grandad Bluff and end up on a country club fairway somewhere below, assuming the glider did not plunge straight down onto the jagged sandstone cliffs that drop off precipitously from the take-off point. His brothers helped him get the contraption up the bluff, but when his father heard about what was going on, he raced up the winding roads in his car to stop them before Chet could launch himself off the cliff.

Again, Chet cheated death, this time thanks to his father and no thanks to his brothers who probably got a pretty good earful from their father.

To this day, the view from the top of Grandad Bluff, which overlooks the city, across the Mississippi to the Minnesota bluffs on the mighty river's west bank is spectacular. It was rumored Chet had planned to have his future wife, Grace, ride with him in his glider. Grandad Bluff was certainly a great place for sightseeing, but not for a romantic flight, especially in a 1930 homemade glider.

1929 Chester age 14 with glider he hand-built

Grandad Bluff which 14 year old Chet almost flew from in his hand-built glider until his dad AR Britt stopped him. The plan was to launch in the glider from one of the high sandstone points at the top of the bluff and glide to the bottom, possibly landing in the fairway of the La Crosse County Club about 590 feet below.

In addition to his love of flying, Chet also developed a love of sailing. By November 2, 1930, he had become a member of the Sea Scouts — a group within the Boy Scout organization — where he learned basic seamanship skills on an old, double-mast, 28-foot whaler known as the Sea Scout Ship Malta. He and his fellow budding sailors launched the SSS Malta and enjoyed summer excursions on Lake Pepin, north of La Crosse. Among others in the Sea Scouts were James Mealy, and Weldon "Whip" Whipple (coincidentally the uncle of John Duresky, one of the creators of this book). La Crosse is a small city where a lot of lives interconnect in history. It's too big so that not everyone knows everyone else, but small enough where you know a lot of people, and their lives matter to you. They upheld the tradition of most La Crosse kids: get them near the Mississippi, and they would always find a way to have fun.

1932 Chester tallest in the back row, and brother Edgar front row far right side by flag Sea Scout Drum & Bugle Corps National Champions

The group's leader was Donald E. Field, the principal at Logan High School when Chet graduated from there in 1933. Mr. Field took a leave of absence to serve in the Navy during WWII and after the war, returned to his previous position as principal at Logan. For decades, he was an outstanding educator and principal who helped guide the lives of tens of thousands of young people in La Crosse. (When Mr. Field retired in 1966, Chet's youngest son, David, was a junior at the school.)

On September 18, 1931, on the other side of the world, while Chet was a enjoying a care-free, junior year at Logan, an incident occurred in the city of Mukden, Manchuria. The Japanese deliberately set an explosive by some railroad tracks owned by a Japanese railroad as a pretext for an invasion.

Two days later, Japanese troops invaded the Manchurian region on China's eastern coast off the Sea of Japan. In one sense, the incident was the opening act of WWII, but on the scale of violence in WWII, it was no more than an innocuous event hardly noticed by anyone except the Japanese and Chinese. It is fitting that it happened in the country famous for the Chinese proverb, "A journey of a thousand miles begins with a single step." That first step led to a journey lasting 14 long years, a journey of death and destruction for tens of millions of people. It ended in Tokyo Bay on September 2, 1945, aboard the battleship USS Missouri. On board that day to witness the ceremonial surrender was an honored guest — Gen. Jonathan M. Wainwright, the hero of Corregidor. The arrogant, proud, and cruel Japanese military and government took their first steps to accept responsibility for the loss of life and blood with the signing of their formal surrender.

It is unlikely Chester or anyone else in La Crosse even read an article about Mukden in the local paper, or if they did, they hardly gave it any thought. Japan and Manchuria were almost meaningless to people in La Crosse in 1931. Attending or listening to radio broadcasts of local high school football games took priority over what was happening on the other side of the planet at the time. If it happened on Friday, they were at the Logan High School game. Chester and millions of other kids around the world were just being kids then, playing, having fun, working on family farms, and doing countless other innocent things. Like Chester, many were mere teenagers, all with no hint of what they were destined to face when their young lives would come crashing together in history.

Decades later, Grace Britt would tell her son Don that she and Dorothy Britt walked home from school together almost every day as teenagers in the 1930s. Grace said that she told Dorothy she thought Chester was handsome and consequently Dorothy introduced the two youngsters. Chet and Grace became close friends in high school, though other young women pursued the handsome young Chester. He was tall and lean with a ramrod straight physique he maintained his entire life. A few years later, Chester was accepted to West Point and a long-distance courtship blossomed between them through the letters she wrote. Though other young women wrote him occasionally, Grace was the only one who kept writing him the entire four years he was at West Point.

Her persistence paid off as their high school friendship became more serious and turned to love. A few visits by Chester to visit his family during that time did not hurt their courtship either.

La Crosse Logan High School
Graduation photos
Chet 1933 and Grace 1934

Chester's name appeared numerous times in the Tribune. Stories highlighted events related to the Boy Scouts, the Sea Scouts, and then in the fall of 1932, he was listed as one of the boys trying out for the Logan High School football team. Though he loved football, there are no articles citing his heroics at any game. It could be he was not a star player, or perhaps he got slivers from riding the bench. His name appeared again as one of the young men trying out for a spot on the football roster with the La Crosse State Teachers College team on September 11, 1934. Again, there is no record of any noteworthy accomplishments related to his football skills or lack thereof. Chet was 6'3" and about 185 pounds, so he could have played any position as 185 pounds was average for a lineman in those days. He liked the game enough to want to play, but he was never a standout player.

Chester possessed a natural talent for mathematics and continued to excel in the subject in college. He belonged to a social fraternity and as mentioned earlier, tried out for football, however there is no record of him ever making the team.

Though he took academics seriously, he had a sense of humor too. He loved playing to the camera.

1936 approximate date of Chet hamming up with FDR look

In the photo above, Chet prepares to attend a social event, panning a caricature of President Franklin D. Roosevelt, complete with suit and cigar.

On January 26, 1933, Chester graduated from Logan High School and then enrolled in La Crosse State Teachers College (now the University of Wisconsin — La Crosse). His future wife, Grace Runice, graduated from Logan a year after Chet on January 25, 1934. They continued seeing each other after he started college. Chet's long and active involvement in Boy Scouts garnered him the organization's highest honor — Eagle Scout — on February 13, 1934 at the age of 18. He continued his involvement in the Sea Scouts with, among other young men, James Mealy and Weldon Whipple, both Logan graduates.

Chet Britt grew up in a loving environment, surrounded by siblings. He handled his responsibilities as the oldest brother, grounded in a nice blue-collar neighborhood in a small Midwestern city. He was serious-minded, a trait of many oldest brothers, but a boy of action and activity, playful, and with a boundless desire to try things and do them well.

He played the bugle so proficiently he rode with Santa on his Christmas float. He made gliders so well he flew them. He earned the rank of Eagle Scout, an accomplishment achieved historically by fewer than 5 percent of the Boy Scouts at the time. He was a respected member of the elite Sea Scouts and helped his drum and bugle corps group win a National Junior Drum and Bugle Corps championship.

He was not afraid to take risks — even if his father had to intervene once, which possibly saved his life. His brothers, oblivious to danger as young boys, encouraged his adventurous nature even though they perhaps risked his life in doing so. Clearly, Chet stood out and because of that, and with his academic record, he received a Congressional appointment to West Point.

So, the young man who loved planes and flying, who loved ships and sailing, enters the … Army?!? The wonderful young boy had become a great young man, ready to join those wanting to become part of the Long Gray Line of graduates from West Point.

He was nominated to the prestigious military academy by La Crosse Congressman, Gardner R. Withrow, in the fall of 1935. He traveled to West Point on June 25, 1936, with his younger brother Edgar, and his father A.R. Britt, no doubt a great bonding adventure for the two close brothers and their father. They arrived in time for "Beast Barracks," the traditional beginning of rigorous physical and mental conditioning used to stress candidates and determine who was serious about becoming an Army officer. The six weeks of pressure, learning Army culture and experiencing the discipline expected of future Cadets, preceded every fall semester for new candidates who wanted to earn the title "Plebe" — but first they had to undergo and survive Beast Barracks. Chet passed the mental and physical grind of the daunting training period and began his Plebe (first) year at West Point on September 1, 1936. He was 21.

During the next four years, Cadet Britt faced academic challenges, as did all Cadets, who learned to balance the rigors and discipline of Army life with academic demands. Cadets were NOT allowed to leave campus during the academic year, except for official leave during specific holidays. There were no downtown passes, to New York City and small towns in New York, had few distractions.

Summer camps were real-life Army experiences where Cadets visited active Army units, lived in tents on the post, and received hands on training with all types of military equipment, weapons, and aircraft. At the time the Army oversaw the Air Corps before it became a separate service, the Department of the Air Force, on September 18, 1947.

They spent a good portion of summer camp participating in strenuous physical activities, camping, and planning and practicing military tactics in simulated battle scenarios. They also visited historic military sites such as Gettysburg, where they strolled through the grounds, learning of military successes and failures. Some even went to sea with the Navy.

Fall was especially exciting for the Cadets, with bus trips to football games — especially the last game each year, the coveted rivalry of the Army-Navy game. Cadets could go to all the games, unless they were "walking the area" — punishment for demerits doled out for any number of minor infractions: improper wearing of the uniform, unkempt rooms, un-shined shoes, improper etiquette while eating, poor posture, virtually anything the Academy had deemed worthy of demerits. After accruing a certain number of demerits, Cadets were required to march back and forth carrying a rifle for a certain amount of time in order to reduce the number of demerits they received. They could be expelled from the Academy if too many demerits appeared on their records. The system was designed to instill self-discipline, respect for authority and the ability to follow orders. Walking tours occurred in the center square of the campus and occurred after all other responsibilities were completed. At one time or another, most Cadets walked punishment tours during their four years at West Point. Sleep deprivation was common, especially during Plebe year.

There was little to no free time at West Point. Cadets were authorized some vacation in the summer, but only after their first year was completed. Cadet Britt earned the duties of Quartermaster Sergeant and in his senior year, M Company First Sergeant, selected for both positions due to his leadership abilities. Coincidentally, Chester's great-great-great-great grandfather, (John) Robert Britt born in 1750 in Maryland, was a Quartermaster Sergeant in the Revolutionary War from 1777 to 1789, for the Continental Army's 2nd Artillery Regiment. Ironically, 155 years later, Chester followed in his ancestor's footsteps as an artillery officer. In the classic sense of history repeating itself, John Britt was a little over 26 years old when he began fighting the British in the Colonies, about the same age as Chester Britt was when he began fighting the Japanese in the Philippines.

On June 11, 1940, Chester (Chet) Kieser Britt, of La Crosse, Wisconsin, graduated from West Point Military Academy after four years of intense training and education, and while reading in newspapers and magazines of war in Asia and Europe. Still, at this point, isolationism was favored by most Americans, many of whom were veterans of WWI or widows caused by WWI, which, ended only 23 years before. Many of Chester's instructors were veterans of that earlier World War. (In newspaper articles of that era, WWI was simply referred to as "the World War.")

Overall, the young men in the class of 1940 were young, honorable, patriotic, and wanted to serve their country to the fullest. Little did they know that in 18 short months, their country would call upon them to defend the United States. Some would come home. Many wouldn't.

As America slowly recovered from the Great Depression, Hitler's forces invaded Poland on September 1, 1939.

Japan continued its expansion in Asia, and British and other Allied forces barely escaped annihilation by the Nazis at Dunkirk with an amazing display of English stubbornness and courage by June 4, 1940.

1938 Chet with sister
Dorothy at WEST POINT

1939 Chester Britt at WEST POINT
beside cannon

One week later, on June 11, 1940, Chester Kieser Britt graduated from West Point as a commissioned officer with the rank of second lieutenant. One of his classmates was James Thomas Hennessy who he would not see again until the end of the war, more on that later. As Chet and friends celebrate, in England the Dunkirk evacuees were being treated for injuries, or being buried, and those brave soldiers were extremely thankful for the sacrifices of so many civilian countrymen to bring them home.

Having experienced a European war only 23 years before, Americans were not interested in sending boys to die in Europe again. An isolationist sentiment gripped America, and the country tried to stay out of the European war. Providing what material and moral support it could to those fighting the Nazis, the United States largely ignored the brutal war in the Pacific. On June 30, 1940, the size of the Regular Army was about 264,000. By May 31, 1945, the number would be 8,291,000.

CHAPTER 2

Newlyweds Adventure
(1940 – 1941)

Chester, like many West Point cadets, married shortly after graduation. In Chester's case, he and his high school sweetheart were married the next day in the Cadet Chapel at West Point.

Classmates in the wedding party were 2nd Lt. Edward D. Fitzpatrick, his best man, and groomsmen 2nd Lieutenants Walter E. Gunster, Robert H. Warren, Fred Yeager, and Michael Kuziv. Cadets James I. Cox, Hector J. Polla, Robert E. Panke, and Robert J. Colleran served as ushers. Following the ceremony, the best man, groomsmen, and ushers drew their sabers and formed the customary wedding arch salute to honor the newlyweds.

Following his graduation from West Point and marriage to Grace, the newlyweds enjoyed a month on furlough to rest and relax before Chet was to report to his first active-duty training assignment at Fort Monroe, Virginia.

June 12, 1940 2LT Chester Britt and Grace Runice are wed at the
West Point Chapel the day after he graduates

Traditionally, graduates in the top half of their class received their
operational assignments of choice. Because he graduated rather high in
the class, Second Lieutenant Britt requested assignment to the Coastal
Artillery Corps (CAC) to train on the big guns used in coastal defense, at
that time still a staple of the Army's arsenal. Second Lieutenant Hennessy
also was selected for CAC training and joined Chester at Fort Monroe.
Like many of his classmates, whether in the coastal artillery or infantry,
their stateside training ultimately led them to their first operational duties
in their selected location of assignment, the Philippines. The island nation,

with its warm, tropical climate, naturally attracted young officers and their wives, and was considered a plum location for an overseas Army tour. But Japan would turn their dream assignments into a hellish nightmare.

June 20, 1940 getting gas as they head back to La Crosse.
Grace sips soda in front of brother Bill Runice. Photo by Chester

Following a short trip to tour New York and a visit with his uncle, Edgar Britt, the newlyweds drove back to Wisconsin with Grace's brother Bill Runice helping with the driving. With no interstate highways in 1940 or long, straight avenues to make travel easy, they averaged half the speeds of today. Traversing two-lane roads that snaked through small towns and large cities, their journey lasted 40 hours, a long, tiring journey that made the couple appreciate a third driver, even if they were on their honeymoon.

1932 to 1934 Grace at archery camp

The families enjoyed lots of picnics where they played friendly competitions of softball, football, and archery. Grace and Chet were excellent archers, and both used bows that Chet had carved from local saplings.

Well-rested after four years of the intense academic, physical, and mental challenges of West Point life, the couple returned to the Fort Monroe, traveling through Columbus, Ohio, where they visited A.R. Britt's sister, Aunt Bea Whitacre, and her husband Dr. Dan Whitacre. Chester's great grandfather Bazil (sometimes spelled Basil) Britt and his wife Sarah were buried there in the Union Soldiers Cemetery. Bazil was a "skirmisher" in the Ohio militia during the Civil War, earning the rank of sergeant and serving as personal cook to Gen. William Tecumseh Sherman on Sherman's famous drive through the south to Atlanta and then Savanah, Georgia. A Civil War marker next to Bazil's grave was a cannon at the top, pointing to the sky; perhaps it symbolizes his and Chester's place in heaven.

Normally, artillery training at Fort Monroe required nine months of intense study and hands-on experience. But demand was so high for artillery officers that in January 1940, training classes were condensed to four months. By the time Chester's class arrived, training had been cut to a mere two-weeks refresher as the Army scrambled to get men into the field. Upon graduation from the Fort Monroe CAC school in Hampton, Virginia, Chet received orders to Corregidor, at the entrance to Manila Bay in the Philippines. Grace, as his wife, was authorized to accompany him to the island nation. The couple visited Annapolis, Md., home to the U. S. Naval Academy, a few days before shipping out from New York City for his first operational assignment. War was the furthest thing on their minds as the couple, young and in love, were off on a grand adventure together. After being separated for the better part of four years, they headed off to a foreign land of tropical breezes and cocktails on the beach, enjoying each other's company as they began their new life together.

On September 12, 1940, Chester's parents, along with his sister Jean and brother Kenneth, met the couple in New York City after they had "motored" up from Fort Monroe, according to an article in the Tribune's local news. It was the final family gathering before the newlyweds sailed for the Philippines two days later, and the last time they would see their son and brother until October 20, 1945.

They set sail aboard the USAT (U.S. Army Transport) Grant with several friends from West Point joining them on the voyage. Among those traveling with them were 2nd Lt's. Robert "Bob" Cooper, a bachelor Augustus "Gus" Cullen, John Presnell, Harry Simpson, John M. Wright, Jules D. Yates, Melvin "Mel" Rosen, Robert Ila Wheat, Jules David Yates, and one civilian, Max D. Wait, who would become their good friend.

September 20, 1940 Grace and Chester on USAT Grant relaxing en route to the Philippines

They traveled down the East Coast and stopped in Charleston, South Carolina, on September 16th to pick up other soldiers and West Point graduates including 2nd Lt's. Silvio Emil Gasperini Jr, Herbert "Herb" Pace, Paul H. Krauss, and Frederick "Fred" Jacob Yeager. The ship then sailed across the Caribbean through the Panama Canal, and up the West Coast to the port of Oakland, Calif., arriving on October 2, 1940, less than four months after Chet's graduation. The couple spent six days relaxing ashore before the ship headed west to Hawaii, arriving in Honolulu on October 19, 1940. The ship departed a few days later for Manila, the capital of the Philippines. Like Chester, among the passengers were not only many of his classmates, but their new wives.

As the ship sailed westward, friendships blossomed aboard, as the newlywed couples bonded, recalling their shared life experiences, which mostly revolved around the "Boys School on the Hudson," a term of endearment for the U.S. Military Academy at West Point.

In October 1940 Chet and friend Herb Pace nap on the USAT Grant en route to Philippines. Unknown woman

Other graduates from Chet's class who went to the Philippines at earlier or later dates included 2nd Lt's. Felicisimo Sulit Castillo, and Vicente Gepte, natives of the Philippines, who departed for their home country in July 1940, less than a month after graduation, on the USAT President Pierce; and 2nd Lt. Joseph V. Iacobucci, who arrived in October 1941 aboard the USAT Holbrook. Also headed to the Philippines were 2nd Lt's. John Joseph Murphy, Paul David Phillips, Morris L. Shoss, Warren Curtis Stirling, Walter Israel Wald, and Jerry Geza Toth. By November 1941, 22 West Point officers from the class of 1940 were stationed in the Philippines.

From San Francisco, the newlyweds enjoyed their time together, relaxing in route on the Grant, even though newly minted Second Lieutenant Britt was assigned duty as the Chief of the Mess, whose job it was to ensure everything needed for dining was in order for the general and his wife, as well as the other officers and their wives. Like all the passengers, they took advantage of the chance to enjoy the fresh sea breezes and relax in the warm, tropical sun. At times, Chet and his classmate, 2nd Lt. Herbert E. Pace, snoozed on the deck. Other times, the young officer Britt chatted with his friend, 2nd Lt. Bob Cooper, who had attended high school in Honolulu.

From San Francisco, they sailed to Hawaii and Guam, arriving in Manila on October 31, 1940. Several classmates and wives, as well as the future commander of U.S. Forces Far East, Lt. Gen. Jonathan Wainwright, and his wife also were on board.

A short stay in Guam provided the travelers a chance to socialize and stretch their legs on solid ground. Grace and Chet enjoyed time at the officers' club with their friends, 2nd Lt. Charlie Monteith and his wife Ruth, and Evelyn Cullen and her husband, 2nd Lt. Gus Cullen. Gus, a classmate of Chester at West Point, and his wife Evelyn were married in the West Point Chapel the same day as the Britts; they became good friends from that day forward. More about Lieutenants Cooper, Cullen, and Wheat in a later chapter.

October 24, 1940 Writing on back of photo by Chester after he got home in 1945. "GUS & EV CULLEN & GRACE ON OUR STOP AT GUAM, 1940. GUS KILLED IN ACTION."

On November 1, 1940, the USAT Grant arrived in the Philippines. The Navy was making plans to return wives to the U.S., but General Wainwright said the Army had no intention of evacuating wives from the Philippines. Clearly, concerns about war with Japan already were affecting decisions in the Philippines 13 months before the surprise attack on Pearl Harbor.

After arriving in Manila, Chet and Grace took a shuttle boat to Corregidor to set up their living quarters on Fort Mills. A letter to Chet's parents dated November 12, 1940, described the young couple settling into their first real home, on the second floor of a large duplex. Because the local tap water was not potable, they had to buy water in 5-gallon containers at the base exchange and then muscle it up to their second-floor home.

Their car was shipped over. Grace with the car and the new 1941 MANILA plate. Chester likely took the photo

But they were pleased with their new radio, which allowed them to listen to three stations. During Chet's off-duty hours, he and Grace played softball, cards, honed their archery skills, and walked around the island in the cool evenings, arm in arm — newly married and deeply in love. They played catch sometimes, and Chet played on a battery team that competed against other units; Colonel Boudreau and Captain Massello also were on his team.

Promoted by then to first lieutenant, Chet's first operational assignment was to Middleside Barracks on Corregidor, the location of Battery B of the 60th Coastal Artillery, the only anti-aircraft unit in the Philippines.

But his assignment there was short-lived. Due to his academic excellence in math, Chet's knowledge and skills were in demand at the 92nd CA at Fort Wint where he would teach math to Filipino military officers undergoing artillery training. The fort was located on Grande Island in Subic Bay and used for artillery training and practice. He taught algorithms and trigonometry for use in artillery calculations.

Prior to leaving Corregidor, in December 1940, friends threw the couple a going-away party. Someone in the group of revelers provided entertainment with a short poem about Fort Wint. The author is unknown, but perhaps it was penned by one of several couples assigned to the 60th AA or one of the wives of Massello, Pace, Baldwin, Monteith, Ramsey, or possibly bachelor Bob Cooper, all close friends. The poem below teased the couple about problems with their quarters: a rattling stove, noisy cats, and children, etc., and envied the tranquility of their new quarters on a nearby but secluded island with beachfront homes.

A Poem to the Departing Britts

Robinson Crusoe, you will be, Said the higher ups to Chet, and to a desert island you will go, where palms are high, and land is low.

Where flowers grow and fish are blue, where guests are scarce and trouble too, on this tropical isle that you are going to.

You can save heaps of money you will be glad to know. You will live a life untouched by woe, Tranquil and quiet and peace galore,

no screeching of cats and neighbors' brats, at Fort Wint will make you sore.

So will the Britts pull up their stakes, and leave that kitchen that badly shakes, they are quite content to mind the big boss, but it is Middleside that takes the loss.

They are ready to leave for unconquered lands, they are all set to loll on those seaside sands, and while Chet, in shorts, gives out commands, little Grace will lie lazily in the sun.

So, Saturday morn they'll sail at seven, to get a glimpse of
their tropical heaven,

and with them goes their brand-new furniture, packed with care
by the Quartermaster Corps.

Good luck to you Britts, and bon voyage, we hope all troubles
you will dodge, and we are sure that you'll both be content,
during your future days at Fort Wint.

Six months will go mighty fast, with movies, and fishing, and books to
last, and lazy days are lots of fun, when there are two lazy people, not one.

In all events, we will see you soon, guests were pretty rare, that we are
quite aware, but things will be different when the Britts arrive there."

After 18 months at Fort Wint, Chester was scheduled to return to the
States. But, the drumbeat of war had become louder, and changes in orders
were common. The poem no doubt brought a lot of laughs, but in fact there
was probably no harder working couple than Chet and Grace, and they
were the opposite of lazy.

On Fort Wint, Chet and Grace (back to camera) play cards with
friends Charles and Ruth Monteith. Charles likely took the photo

Clearly, they expected the new friends they had made on Corregidor to visit frequently, as the trip was only a boat ride of a few miles. It was a sleepy, quiet place to live. Best of all, it was remote from the all-seeing eyes of the senior officers on Corregidor, where life and duties were more stressful. Fort Wint, on the other hand, was the junior officers' hidden treasure when they needed to escape for a few hours to unwind.

Sunday March 16, 1941. Chet and Grace on Fort Wint dock, Olongapo is in the background. The Oryoku Maru would be attacked at Olongapo while Chester was a POW in the hold of the ship on December 15, 1944

For the newlyweds, Fort Wint was their first real home. It was located on the north shore of Grande Island, with a breakwater wall in front and beyond that, Subic Bay. They enjoyed a stunning, unobstructed view of Olongapo and the area around them.

The officers' family housing on Fort Wint comprised a small number of houses grouped close together, so close that occupants could see through their neighbors' screens. Their housing area offered views of Subic Bay and

the surrounding mountains for most of the homes; the commanding officer of the 92nd Battalion, Colonel Boudreau, and his wife also lived there.

About February, 1941, Grace with 92nd CAC (Coastal Artillery
Corps) commander Col Napoleon Boudreau and wife Myrtle on
north shore of Ft Wint, Britt home is to the left of Grace

The island was serviced weekly by a rations boat. Other trips off the
island had to be arranged as no regular boat taxi serviced Grande Island.
Officers frequently took friends and family for sailing excursions on the
bay in outrigger-like boats. The shuttle boats were arranged to transport
officers and wives to social functions on Corregidor, site of the nearest officers' club. Grace developed lasting friendships with Evelyn Cullen, Ruth
Monteith and Olga Massello. They were generally content and enjoyed the
mostly casual lifestyle, learning about Philippine culture with their new
husbands.

In letters home, Chester wrote of his students' poor math skills, which
made his job even more challenging. But a little more than six months after
their arrival, everything changed. The Army decided to begin evacuating
family members back to the States due to increasing tensions in the Far
East, the result of Japan's aggressive, military conquests across Asia.

They quickly packed up their household goods for shipment back to La Crosse. Their wicker furniture, among the first items they purchased as a married couple, was well-traveled. Purchased on Corregidor, it was transported to Fort Wint when the Britts transferred and then shipped again to Wisconsin when Grace was evacuated. It remained in the Britt family during the war and after, as they raised their children.

Prior to her departure, Grace copied a poem below penned by Col. Paul Delmont Bunker Sr, commander of the 59th CA, responsible for all defensive artillery support on Corregidor. The West Point men apparently fashioned themselves as poets, and Colonel Bunker was no exception, offering his short poem, "Ode to an Evacuee" as they left for the U.S. and home:

Ode to An Evacuee

The Pennsylvania Station, If what they say is true, Is spraddled over lots of ground, And scrapes the starry blue, But!

Though its large and spacious, Believe me when I say, Its smaller than my quarters since, My Missus sailed away.

The Lincoln Way*, from coast to coast, Is quite a lengthy pike,

From here to Ursa Major, Is not a puny hike

But!

Since the Wife's been sent back home, And days drag on ... and on ...

Our dining table, once so small, Extends to Hell an(d) gone.

The sandy, burning deserts, That stretch around the West,

The steppes of drear Siberia, Are lonely at their best

But!

They are jammed with laughing crowds, And riotous and gay,

Compared with old Corregidor, since you have sailed away.

— Col Paul Bunker, C.A.C.

*The Lincoln Highway was an early transcontinental highway running from New York City's Times Square to Lincoln Park in San Francisco.

About March 15, 1941 Chester at the Olongapo FLEET WAITING ROOM. On the back of the photo was written CHET BRITT SR so we know it was written after Grace returned to La Crosse and had their baby, Chester Jr.

On May 5, 1941, Grace left the Philippines on the USAT Republic. When the USAT Republic sailed out of sight, it was the last time they would see one another until four-and-a-half years later, in October 1945. Once they were at sea, the passengers and crew practiced lifeboat drills in case they needed to evacuate the ship. As she waited to board the lifeboat for the first drill on the USAT Republic, she was overcome with emotion. She was pregnant with her first child and separated from her husband, knowing war could come at any time. Not surprisingly, Grace was tired, stressed, worried about Chet, and hoping she would deliver a healthy son — experiences countless military wives have endured. Now, it was Grace's turn. She was five months pregnant with the couple's first child, a son who would arrive on September 21, 1941. His name: Chester Keiser Britt Jr.

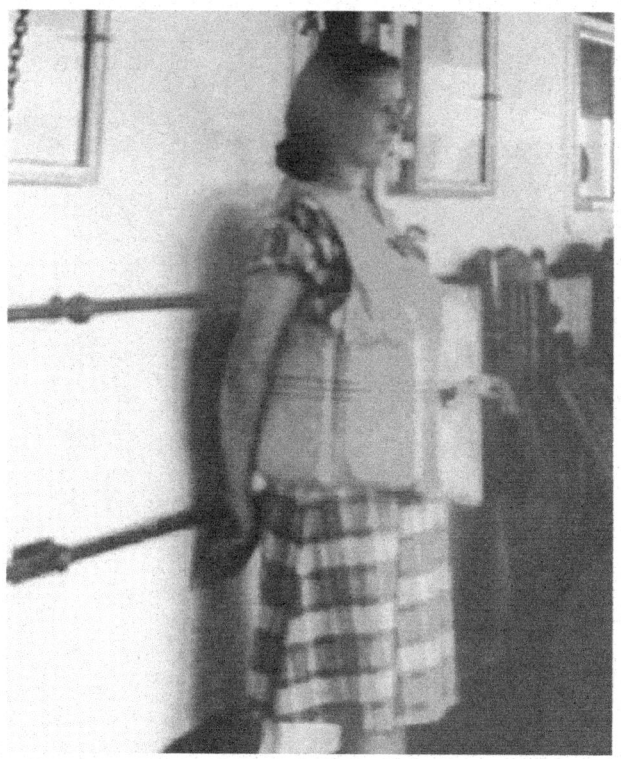

About May 7, 1941, Grace is 5 months pregnant during a lifeboat drill on the USAT Republic. Perhaps two days after sailing from Pier 7 in Manila and seeing Chester for the last time. Worry for her Chet is clearly etched on her normally happy face.

With her on the six-week voyage were many of the wives and children she had befriended during their short stay in the Philippines; they also were ordered to return to the safety of their stateside homes. Undoubtedly, they supported and comforted one another on their journey into the unknown.

The ship reversed the route they had sailed on their voyage to the Philippines — through the Panama Canal and then northward to New York City, arriving on June 11, 1941, one year to the day from when Chet graduated from West Point — and one day shy of their first wedding anniversary. Grace returned to La Crosse, arriving by train in mid-June. Their carefree lives had come to a halt. Chet, household goods gone, moved to quarters furnished by the Army and began to prepare for the fight ahead.

The USAT Republic as it would have appeared arriving in Honolulu beside the Aloha Tower with Grace and the other dependents on board en route to America. The USAT Republic arrived in New York on June 11, 1941, the one year anniversary of Chester's graduation from West Point, and one day before their first wedding anniversary. In the distance is what would be Punchbowl National Memorial Cemetery-Pacific after the war, which today holds the remains of some of Chester's friends.

Throughout the Philippines, the Army began preparations for war in earnest. On Fort Wint, First Lieutenant Britt and his fellow soldiers began preparing for the defense of the idyllic, tropical island, which few in America had ever even heard of, but which sat right at the entrance to Subic Bay — the harbor prize Japan coveted. The same preparations were occurring on Corregidor, nicknamed The Rock. Friends of Chet stationed there included Captains Bob Massello and Chan Baldwin, and 1st Lieutenants Herb Pace, Charlie Monteith, Bob Cooper, and Ken Ramsey to name a few. First Lieutenant Emil Ulanowicz, with the 60th AA on Corregidor, recalled plans to place underwater mines in Subic Bay and Manila Bay to halt or prevent the Japanese advance. Fort Wint was assigned to deploy mines in Subic Bay. The Army mined the shipping channel, while the Navy was responsible for mining the side channels. Preparations called for digging fighting positions and moving weapons, ammunition, food, and medicine to bunker locations so their limited and essential resources would withstand and be protected from attack.

Time passed agonizingly slow for both the soldiers left behind and their families safe at home, some of them 10,000 miles away. Day by day, WWII approached. America was lulled by the current state of peace, even though Europe was in flames because of war. But America was safe, nestled between two oceans. Its citizens largely carried on life as usual, but her leaders and men and women in the service knew trouble was brewing.

By the outbreak of the war, Chet was assigned to the 92nd Coastal Artillery Battalion at Fort Wint. There, he was given several primary and additional duties: battalion adjutant, headquarters company commander; Battery D commander; and battalion communications and transportation officer; one paycheck, but many responsibilities and duties, typical of military life.

Ultimately Fort Wint played little to no part in the defense of the Philippines. Used primarily for training, it had the least amount of armament of the forts guarding the entrance to Manila Bay from an attack by sea: two 254mm guns on disappearing carriages, two 155mm disappearing guns, and four 76mm guns. By comparison, Corregidor, Fort Drum and Fort Frank at the entrance to Manila Bay bristled with many large guns, mortars, and machine guns. After the war, Chet told Grace there was an extremely limited supply of shells needed for the Fort Wint weapons, and they ran out of large gun ammunition early in the fight with no hope of further deliveries.

As a result, military leaders declared the island indefensible in an attack and ordered it abandoned. Troops — and what weapons they could take with them — were repositioned on the Bataan Peninsula and the island fortress of Corregidor before the Japanese attacked and cut off Grande Island. Prior to evacuating the island paradise, Captain Al D'Arezzo sabotaged the fort's guns, removing their breech blocks and tossing them into the bay to prevent Japanese forces from using them against U.S and Filipino forces. (NOTE: In a 1921 study of defenses for the island, officials recommended the installation of defensive barriers, positions, and weapons, but Congress never funded the recommendations, thus leaving the island completely defenseless.)

CHAPTER 3

War Comes to the Philippines
(June 1941 – April 1942)

All wives and family members had been evacuated by early June 1941, and the men moved into bachelor housing to consolidate living arrangements as they prepared for war. The soldiers had little opportunity for recreation but took advantage of what little time they had to themselves. Chester worked and shared quarters with two other men assigned to the same unit, 2nd Lt. Bill Lewis and Max Wait, a civilian armaments technician for the Army; they hunted in the evenings. Armed with pistols, the trio traipsed through the jungle in search of snakes. Their evening adventures served a dual purpose. They protected local farmers, their families, and livestock and provided needed stress relief and recreation for the men. They quickly became fast friends; the bonds they developed proved crucial for survival in the battles to come and their years as prisoners.

Training about 500 Filipino artillery students suddenly became a more serious, high-priority mission, as raw recruits filled the ranks of officers and enlisted men in the Filipino forces. Preparations for engaging the formidable Japanese forces was hurried, and everything took on an air of urgency. The Philippine Army had just begun training and the in-country U.S. Division was assigned the task to get troops up to speed when the war began. This woeful lack of preparation included inadequate food, munitions, medical supplies, and equipment, in addition to nonexistent plans for defending the islands.

1LT William E BILL Lewis   Civilian Max D Wait
Chet's brothers-in-arms and life

Sgt Laurente of the 92nd Coastal Artillery Corps PS (Philippine Scouts) by his home on Grande Island

General MacArthur reversed the decision of a previous commander to keep food, arms, bullets, meds, and other supplies on Bataan because he believed the Americans could not be defeated by the Japanese. He ordered supplies spread out around Luzon — the country's largest island — a decision that proved disastrous. The Japanese advanced so quickly, supplies were lost as American and Filipino forces retreated from the island of Luzon to Bataan peninsula. Many Filipino soldiers had never fired a rifle. Only the Philippine Scouts were combat ready.

Back in La Crosse, Grace gave birth on September 21, 1941 to their first son, Chester Jr. Even half a world away, he was proud and eager to be a dad. With his wife raising a newborn alone, he was concerned about the coming war and wondered whether he would survive to see them again. He found comfort knowing they were at home, out of harm's way. Grace continued to send letters and photos of his new son. Mail delivery was slow, taking a month or more in peacetime.

November 18, 1941 1LT Bob Cooper Christmas Card to Grace

Everyone was focused preparing for war, not paperwork. Lieutenant Britt's promotion to captain, due about the same time Japan attacked the Philippines, on December 8, 1941, actually did not occur until nearly four years later, in October 1945, when he was recovering after the war at Letterman Army Hospital at the Presidio in San Francisco. But he was not alone in receiving his delayed and well-deserved promotion. For all prisoners of war, promotions were frozen for the duration of the war, which added financial hardship and additional stress for their families back home.

Chet, alone at Fort Wint on Grande Island, had good company with the other U.S. Army personnel and their Filipino allies. Grande Island was shaped like a square pork chop, roughly one-half of a square mile in area. Had there been no beach obstructions, Chet could've walked around the entire perimeter in an hour. Five miles to the northeast from his vantage point, the port city of Olongapo and the nearby navy base were getting ready, too. Just a mile away to the east was Bataan province, on Luzon, a peninsula separating Subic Bay and the significantly larger Manila Bay. The peninsula blocked the view of the island fortress of Corregidor on its southeast tip and Manila to the east beyond it.

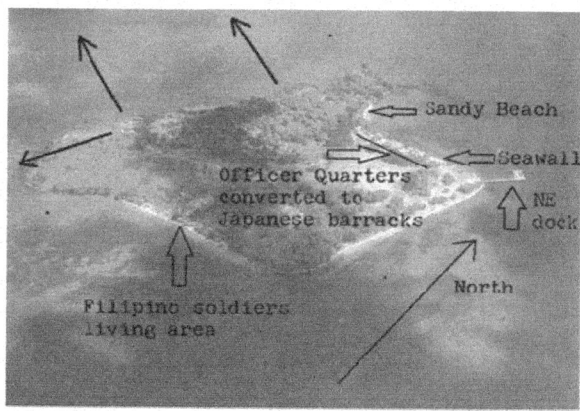

1933 view Fort Wint. Guns point to sea, beaches open to assualt

Grande Island was among the tiniest of the 7,641 islands in the Philippine archipelago, but its location could not have been more strategic — right in the middle of the throat of Subic Bay — one of the first places the Japanese would attack to gain unfettered access to the bay and the American Navy port facilities. It was an isolated, small bullseye in the crosshairs of the Imperial Japanese Army, Navy, and Air Force, indefensible from assault. It was built for a different kind of war in a different kind of world. The men on Fort Wint, Corregidor, Bataan and elsewhere in the Far East hurriedly were preparing for war with a battle-hardened Japan.

While it is true that Filipino soldiers were largely untrained and not ready for battle, the United States was just as equally untrained and unprepared for battle. Most of their equipment — remnants either from WWI or only modestly improved since that war ended — could not possibly compete with Japan's superior weaponry.

Then on December 7, 1941, *"a date which will live in infamy"* as President Franklin D. Roosevelt said in his war declaration, the life of everyone in America changed in an instant. The surprise aerial attack on Pearl Harbor by planes from the Japanese fleet, proved the ultimate wake-up call for America.

The city of La Crosse and nation were now at war, and the newspaper reports coming in about how things were going for U.S. military forces were not good. Perhaps nothing explained the confusion better for the Britt family than an announcement in the local paper two days after Pearl Harbor. Chet's middle initial was wrong, he was listed with the Air Corps instead of the Coastal Artillery and was said to be at Fort Grande in Hawaii instead of at Fort Wint on Grande Island in the Philippines. Such errors were commonplace in reporting of the period as reporters and editors scrambled to try to keep up with an escalating pace of events around the world. There was no time to double-check their facts.

On December 8, 1941, only nine hours after the surprise Japanese attack on Pearl Harbor, the Japanese began their aerial attacks in the Philippines. (Due to the International dateline, these events happened on December 8th in the Pacific and December 7th in the U.S.) The War Department ordered General MacArthur to allow the Japanese to initiate hostilities; Japanese pilots began their assault immediately, destroying almost the entire air force fleet based in the islands. Two days later, unopposed, about 45,000 Japanese soldiers began their assault on the island of Luzon. In the meantime, the U.S. Navy had evacuated its forces to the Dutch East Indies. Twelve days later, on December 22, the Japanese completed their landing of combat and support forces on in the Lingayen Gulf on the west side of Luzon.

At the start of the war, and for many months afterwards, things were in a total state of confusion. The bombardment of Fort Wint was reported to have been fierce but intermittent, with the Japanese attacking infrastructure, specifically electricity and water. The after-action report for forces on Grande Island reported seeing a Japanese landing craft with 30 soldiers attempting to land in early December. But Lieutenant Britt and his fellow artillerymen had other plans. They destroyed the approaching boat and watched it sink into the bay. Not a single Japanese soldier set foot on the island.

Battery Jewel 3 inch gun that hit Japanese barge (landing craft)

After inflicting notable damage on the Japanese attempting to enter Subic Bay, the garrison was ordered to abandon the island when it became impossible to defend. Lieutenant Britt was assigned the task of planning and carrying out the move from Fort Wint on Grande Island across the bay to Olongapo and then onward to the defensive line in northern Bataan.

On the evening of December 24, 1941, Lieutenant Britt orchestrated the clandestine movement of the 92nd CAC to Bataan. A similar withdrawal of 2,000-3,000 troops from Manila to Bataan happened simultaneously as the U.S. consolidated forces in the two most defensible positions, Bataan, and Corregidor. The lieutenant's orders involved moving the entire battalion, including guns, ammo, necessary support equipment, and men, while maintaining communications among all elements. Everyone evacuated the island, including the Filipino trainees who accompanied them to Bataan.

Under cover of darkness and using barges, boats, trucks, tractors, and private vehicles, he positioned the guns and equipment to allow fire support of the 41st and 51st Philippine divisions to repel the subsequent Japanese attacks.

The lighter anti-aircraft artillery guns were moved to Corregidor, with the heavier 155MM artillery guns moved by barge to Olongapo in route to Bataan. They were moved nearly 80 miles in a 24-hour period, across the water and then up increasingly steep grades to their firing positions. Under constant pressure to move guns, men, and materials, Lieutenant Britt's plan needed to remain flexible to respond to any Japanese attack, not knowing when or where it would occur. The big WWI-era guns were powerful and the best weapons available, but ammunition was in short supply. For his actions that night, Lieutenant Britt later received the Legion of Merit, the third highest military honor at the time, ranking just below the Medal of Honor and the Silver Star.

On Christmas Day, December 25, 1941, Lieutenant Britt, Capt. Harry Jimerson and 2nd Lt. Bill Lewis, were transferred from the 92nd Artillery Battalion to the 301st Field Artillery (FA), Philippine Army as battery commanders, overseeing the 155mm guns.

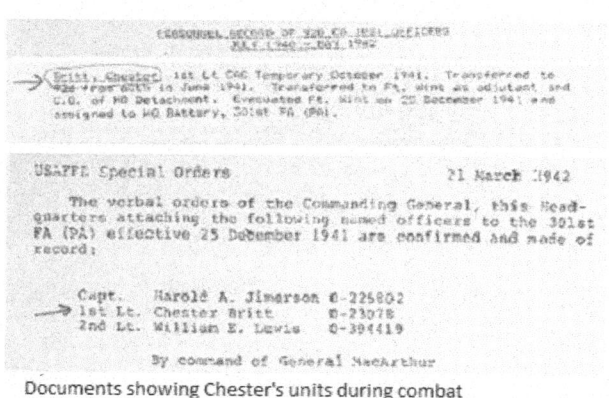

PERSONNEL RECORD OF 320 CO. 1941 OFFICERS
ALL 1940 - Dec 1942

Britt, Chester) 1st Lt CAC Temporary October 1941. Transferred to
320 from 60th in June 1941. Transferred to Ft. Mint as adjutant and
C.O. of HQ Detachment. Evacuated Ft. Mint on 25 December 1941 and
assigned to HQ Battery, 301st FA (PA).

USAFFE Special Orders   21 March 1942

    The verbal orders of the Commanding General, this Head-
quarters attaching the following named officers to the 301st
FA (PA) effective 25 December 1941 are confirmed and made of
record:

    Capt.   Harold A. Jimerson 0-225802
    1st Lt. Chester Britt   0-23078
    2nd Lt. William E. Lewis   0-394419

         By command of General MacArthur

Documents showing Chester's units during combat

The Japanese advanced their attack to the south, capturing Manila on December 29, 1941, a mere week after all their ground troops had arrived on Luzon. Surviving U.S. and Filipino forces had retreated to the Bataan peninsula and created a defensive line there. Captain Jimerson and Lieutenants Britt and Lewis fought side by side until surrender and kept each other alive in captivity. In Chet's words Bill Lewis and he "took care of each other like brothers." The whereabouts of Captain Jimerson was unknown until his name surfaced more than two years later — as a POW in Japan. The other friend in Chester's circle of close friends, Max Wait, received orders for a secret mission — to report to Corregidor as armaments officer. He serviced weapons of all calibers and helped disable the big guns upon surrender. Lieutenants Britt and Lewis didn't see Max again until they arrived at the Camp Cabanatuan prison camp near the center of Luzon island.

Early in January 1942, Chet had re-positioned the 301st FA regiment's 155mm guns, including his battery, as directed, to the west of Abucay, on Bataan to cover the east sector of the Mabatang-Maubang defensive line. It would not be the last time the 26-year-old lieutenant moved the weapons. The Philippine Army's 41st Division faced the 65th Japanese Brigade and the 48th Mountain Artillery Regiment. The 301st's fire power initially decimated the Japanese artillery regiment in an artillery duel but could not stop the Japanese infantry attack on the 41st Philippine Army troops.

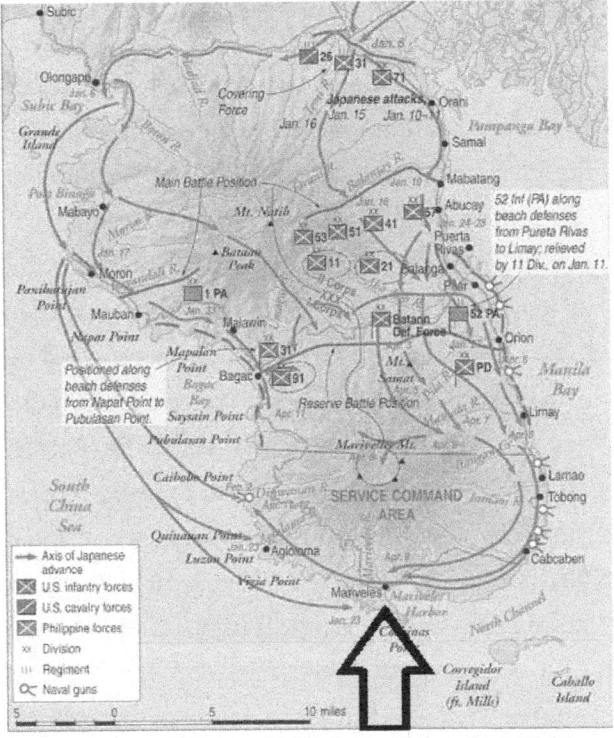

USAFFE Bataan relief map with fighting positions. Gradually the brave Fil-American troops, starved, short of foot and water, sick, and wounded, exhausted from almost nonstop combat, were squeezed into the Bataan Peninsula's southern tip at Mariveles

The well-trained Japanese soldiers attacked through the thick, jungle foliage, avoiding roads and trails to avoid detection. Lieutenant Britt shinnied up a tree to spot the enemy troops to direct fire on their positions. Early in the engagement, he lost a best friend who was standing next to him as they peered at the enemy through binoculars. His friend, whose name is lost to history, was decapitated by an enemy shell.

Lieutenant Britt was assigned an additional duty as the regiment's transportation and communications officer due to his success in moving the battalion. At one point, he was ordered to expose himself to enemy sniper fire at the regimental forward observation post, the most hazardous duty for artillerymen. He called in artillery strikes against a Japanese mountain artillery unit and ground troops attacking them. Due to Lieutenant

Britt's skill and accuracy, his gun battery and the other guns of the 301st, demolished the enemy's artillery unit.

Japanese forces were decimated, forcing the overall Japanese commander to halt the attack and request reinforcements. His failure to force surrender of the enemy in 4-6 weeks as he predicted, resulted in the general "losing face," an unacceptable loss of respect and humiliation in Japanese culture. In fact, the Japanese could not resume their attack for another 45 days because of losses and delays in receiving reinforcements.

General MacArthur had ordered food to be rationed beginning on January 9th in an effort to extend their resistance efforts until at least June 1942, when they anticipated the arrival of a rescue force from the U.S. to provide needed relief and additional troops. Existing on less than one-fourth of their daily rations — a mere 500 calories a day compared to the estimated 5,000 calories a day required for combat — quickly took its toll.

American and Filipino troops were starving. Unknowingly, so were the Japanese, who also were ordered to conserve food. But their sheer numbers could not be defeated. Weakened and moving slowly, the II Philippine Corps (41st and 51st Divisions) could no longer sustain the high tempo of battle and began retreating to the Orion-Bagac defensive line on January 25th. The mountainous terrain and thick foliage made repositioning the 155mm guns difficult. Due to a shortage of tractors to pull the large guns, it took 12 hours to move each one. After three months, the men were sick and too weak to mount a reliable, strong, defensive counter to the Japanese assault.

The Philippine divisions fought hard initially, but they were new recruits with little training, hardly soldiers at all. They suffered from a lack of weapons, ammo, food, and other essential combat supplies. With the loss of officers and informal leaders in their ranks, they broke and ran, scattering in all directions to avoid capture. The majority of the remaining American resistance was isolated on the Bataan Peninsula and Corregidor.

On February 8th, Lieutenant Britt, as transportation officer for the regiment, was ordered to move the guns again and reported the newly established defensive line complete, but Col. Alexander Quintard, commander of the 301st FA Regiment, believed the guns were too close to the front lines. He believed the Japanese were advancing faster than the guns could be repositioned in the rear for support fire.

Although in a support role, the 301st FA continued to engage the Japanese. The Japanese attempted a flanking move by sea using barges to attack the allied rear at Anyasan-Saliim Point. The 301st FA also fought off two other attacks in the rear at two other battles, at Quinian Point and Agoloma Point, known as the Battle of the Points. The Japanese landing forces were destroyed by accurate artillery fire killing about 3,000 Japanese soldiers during all three encounters.

Chester's unit also fought off the Japanese artillery in a duel of guns in the Battle of Trail 2. It was in the center of the main line of resistance (defensive line) where the Japanese focused their attacks. Their first assault failed, but after regrouping, their second attack proved successful in breaking through the defenses of the 51st and 41st Philippine Army divisions. During his post-war trial for war crimes, the commander of Japanese forces in the Philippines testified about the immense losses at Bagac from accurate and devastating artillery fire imposed on Japanese troops by the allied defenders.

In a final letter home before U.S. and Philippine forces surrendered to the Japanese, Lieutenant Britt mentioned the Japanese bomber pilots' inability to hit anything. However, he was wounded by shrapnel in one of the attacks and after the war was awarded a Purple Heart for wounds sustained in combat, as was Captain Al D'Arezzo. Whether the Japanese were good at bombing mattered little as their pilots constantly circled above, looking for artillery positions to destroy. Chet's letters reflected the anxiety Americans and Filipinos artillerymen felt when they saw enemy bombers flying overhead.

On February 17th, Colonel Quintard ordered Lieutenant Britt to move the 301st's guns because the Japanese had zeroed in on their location. So once again, Chet commanded the movement of weapons, supplies, and support equipment.

In early March, the unit's remaining 155mm guns, were repositioned again, this time for action on the slopes of Mount Samat. At 1,787 feet, the peak towered above the bay, providing a sweeping view of the entire Bataan defensive line and the approaching Japanese forces. Because the peninsula was so narrow, from their new vantage point, Lieutenant Britt's unit could fire on enemy forces across both eastern and western sectors.

With the likelihood of the Philippines being overrun, President Roosevelt reluctantly ordered General MacArthur, field marshal of the Philippine Army — along with his wife, family, and staff — to evacuate the island of Corregidor. They departed on March 11th in Navy PT boats, covertly crossing the choppy bay waters, and avoiding Japanese patrol boats. Two days later, they arrived in Mindanao, the most southern island of the Philippines. Upon reaching the safety of Melbourne, Australia, he was named supreme commander of the southwest Pacific area with head-quarters in Brisbane. It was there he uttered his famous three words, "I shall return" in a speech addressed to the Filipino people.

From April 3rd, Good Friday, through Easter Sunday, April 5th, the Japanese artillery shells rained down on the 301st FA. The constant barrage proved an advantage to enemy infantry troops. They overran the American and Filipino forces on Mount Samat, requiring the heavy 155mm guns to move again, this time further into the mountainous terrain to avoid cap-ture as Japanese infantry quickly advanced. After Japanese troops broke through the defensive line, panic broke out among the Philippine's 51st Division and the 301st FA. Desperate to save their lives, soldiers grabbed whatever vehicle was closest to get away from the fight.

As a result, Lieutenant Britt had no vehicles or equipment big enough move all the unit's artillery pieces to the rear. Colonel Quintard's options had been reduced to one. He had no choice but to order their biggest artil-lery weapons left behind and destroyed to prevent use by enemy troops. Lieutenant Britt could locate only enough operable tractors to move three smaller guns; all other guns, equipment and supplies were destroyed before the 301st moved south.

As a West Point graduate, he learned discipline other men did not possess, discipline which greatly contributed to his survival. He knew how to take and give orders, but only one real possibility to survive remained: surrender. An abhorrent choice for a highly trained soldier, surrender became the only viable option for him and the men who had not deserted. He could give them little more than meager encouragement; no positive outcome was possible.

Japanese forces broke through the defensive line and forged across the Lamao River. Despite fierce hand-to-hand combat and against all odds, the Philippine Scouts, and remnants of the Philippine Army's 41st and 51st Divisions disintegrated as a cohesive fighting force due to the enemy's advance. On April 6, Jerry Toth, one of Chet's classmates was killed by shrapnel that had hit a tank directly in front of him, or a projectile that missed the tank but killed him instantly when it struck in the chest.

February 29, 1941 Jerry and Ruth Toth having fun at the beach by the Royal Hawaiian Hotel on the way to the Philippines. Photo courtesy of the Toth family.

The Americans and Filipinos had nothing left to fight with and could no longer withstand attacks by well-equipped, disciplined, and battle-hardened Japanese soldiers who, at that point, had ballooned to an overwhelming force of about 100,000 troops. With no hope of reinforcements, American forces began calling themselves "The Battling Bastards of Bataan." The moniker came from a poem below written by United Press war correspondent Frank, who reported on the war from the news organization's Manila bureau:

We're the battling bastards of Bataan

No momma, no poppa (sic,) no Uncle Sam

No aunts, no uncles, no nephews, no nieces

No rifles, no guns, no artillery pieces

And nobody gives a damn.

On April 7th, 1942, the commander of II Corps (Bataan Eastern Sector) ordered the 301st to remove the remaining 155mm guns to the southernmost point in the Bataan peninsula. The unit was no longer a viable fighting force and retired from the fight to the southern point of Bataan, destroying anything along the way the enemy could find useful in their continuing assault.

A lack of weapons and ammunition forced the defenders to use knives, rocks, sticks and just about anything else they could fashion as a weapon. In the latter days of the fight, hand-to-hand combat was common. When the fighting finally ended, they were exhausted, hopeless, and disillusioned, feeling abandoned by their nation. The American and allied forces in Bataan were defeated and encircled. Their hoped-for rescue never came — and incredulously, never was planned.

The artillery support positions for the big guns and the front line for infantry were one and the same. With Mania Bay to the south and the Japanese occupying the area to the north, the men had nowhere to go — and no hope of avoiding captivity.

Men around a radio on Bataan listening to the VOICE OF
FREEDOM broadcast from Corregidor by Philippine Col Carlos P
Romulo.. This is a wirephoto that was sent out and printed in
thousands of papers around the time Bataan fell. The man on
the left has an M-1 Garand rifle with a broken front stock. Any
weapon was better than no weapon with no resupply coming.
We can't hear the broadcast, or the sounds that might have
been going on around them...men talking, bombs and shells
exploding, machine gun and rifle fire, the natural noises of the
Bataan jungle.

By this time, almost everyone's personal effects either had been lost, destroyed, or buried at the beginning of the Japanese attacks; some were lost early on during their imprisonment. Chet buried his West Point class ring and wedding ring. He bought new ones upon returning home from the war (grandson Chester Britt III has his West Point replacement ring). Chet also buried his West Point saber somewhere after fighting began, but he never ordered a replacement.

The men were advised to disguise their military duties because artillerymen were being executed upon surrender in retribution for the great losses they inflicted on Japanese troops. Lieutenant Britt certainly avoided any mention of his primary duties as an artillery officer and presumably claimed he merely served a transportation and communication officer to his unit. Since it was a true statement, it also would have been easier to remember during any future interrogation, if, indeed, his captors interrogated every prisoner.

Major General Wainwright, promoted to lieutenant general on the day of surrender, could no longer hold out indefinitely without sacrificing every American and allied soldier in the fight. The war for them was over. Colonel Quintard received the surrender order on April 9th and moved the remainder of his unit to a staging area. Chet and his fellow American officers destroyed the few remaining weapons as well as all supplies of food, ammo, and fuel, again to prevent use by Japanese forces against Corregidor, which had not surrendered yet. The men then made their way, as ordered by the overall commander of Bataan, Maj. Gen. Edward King, to Mariveles, where they officially surrendered. General MacArthur's poor judgment and planning resulted in the starving men entering captivity in poor mental and physical condition. Thousands ultimately paid for his error with their lives.

Not surprisingly, Lieutenant Britt — two months shy of his 25th birthday — wondered what would happen next. The same was true for his fellow captives. They had heard of Japanese atrocities dealt to Chinese troops and thoughts of home and survival filled their thoughts. Two men Chet knew wrote of witnessing first-hand the unending, heartless brutality of their Japanese captors. One of them, Pvt. Sidney Stewart, described the horrendous scene of an American soldier they knew — dead on the ground, his torso splayed open from the thrusts of a sharp bayonet, guts exposed to hundreds of flies feasting on death — his hands and feet severed for maximum shock value. Their thoughts and experiences mirrored those of the thousands of American and Filipino soldiers who suffered unbearable cruelty. In the photo below, Americans surrender to the Japanese at Mariveles motor pool.

April 10, 1942 photo taken at Mariveles at the start of the Death March. Chester would have been close to this location. The man on the far left in the center row is Jack Merrifield, next to him William Gentry, both members of the 192nd tank corps. Most of these men were tank crews. (tanker info from Jim Opolony)

Private Stewart, in his book "Give us this Day," described the wait for the Japanese army to take his group of fighters into captivity:

"No one dared speak for fear of letting loose a chain of emotions within himself. Each man sensed the fear within his companions. We had a horrible feeling of loss and loneliness. Loneliness for death we knew was coming, and death strikes each man as an individual. You are alone no matter how many (people) are there ... By now we were surrounded by thousands of other men. Their faces showed wide eyes and mouths tight with fear. None of them knew where he was going but cattle-like followed the man ahead."

Such horrific scenes were commonplace; Lieutenant Britt and his fellow soldiers often wondered if they would be next to the slaughter. Capt. Manny Lawton described his thoughts about the fall of Bataan in "Some Survived," his eyewitness account of the Bataan Death March and the men who lived through it. Surrounded on three sides, he wrote:

"There could be only one area of temporary security. It would be better to assemble there and wait for them to come to us, than to run head-on

59

in the jungle into ruthless troops filled with the excitement of battle and the smell of victory. Escape was impossible and further resistance would be suicide … I had visions of individual enemy soldiers or groups of them, bayoneting or clubbing to death any of our group … set up machine guns to slaughter us by the hundreds. There was nowhere to go and no way to avoid whatever might be ahead. In such a helpless situation, I am convinced that the dread of the unknown is much more unnerving than the terror of battle itself."

On the day of surrender, Captain Lawton described the captives' emotions:

"Each man stared silently at the sky, clutching his own thoughts, examining his own soul, waiting for what the sun and the day and (what) the Japanese Army would bring."

The Japanese considered the soldiers "captives instead of "prisoners of war." The Emperor and the Imperial Army considered the American and Filipino surrender to be dishonorable, a distinction that cost many men their lives. There were no international rules for "captives" in 1942. As such, Japanese soldiers were informed they were not obligated to comply with the humanitarian treatment of prisoners of war as codified in the Geneva Convention. Although Japan had signed the document, they failed to ratify it — even though in 1942, they had promised to abide by its terms and indicated they would observe the rules of the Hague Convention of 1907, which was among the first formal treaties to include international laws regarding war and war crimes.

CHAPTER 4

Surviving Death March; Prison Camps
(April 9, 1942 – December 1942)

When word of the American surrender of the Philippines reached the States, Grace, Chester's parents, his siblings, and many relatives and friends wondered where Chester was, what kind of shape he was in, and if he had survived. They furiously sent letters and cards seeking any tidbit of information, but most were returned as undeliverable, were lost in the mail, or were never delivered.

Undaunted by their circumstances, the Britt family continued to support the war effort. Chet's younger brother Edgar joined the Navy and became a pilot. Archie continued his schooling in medicine, and Franklin joined the Army Air Corps, becoming a B-24 tail gunner in 1943. Ken, who was a bit younger, graduated from high school and joined the post-war Army of occupation in Japan as a dental hygienist. Grace's brother, Bill, joined the Army and went to Europe to fight. The Britt family patriarch, A.R. Britt, continued working as a railroad engineer. Railroads were vital to the war effort moving materials and equipment for the military and keeping the economy going to fund the war.

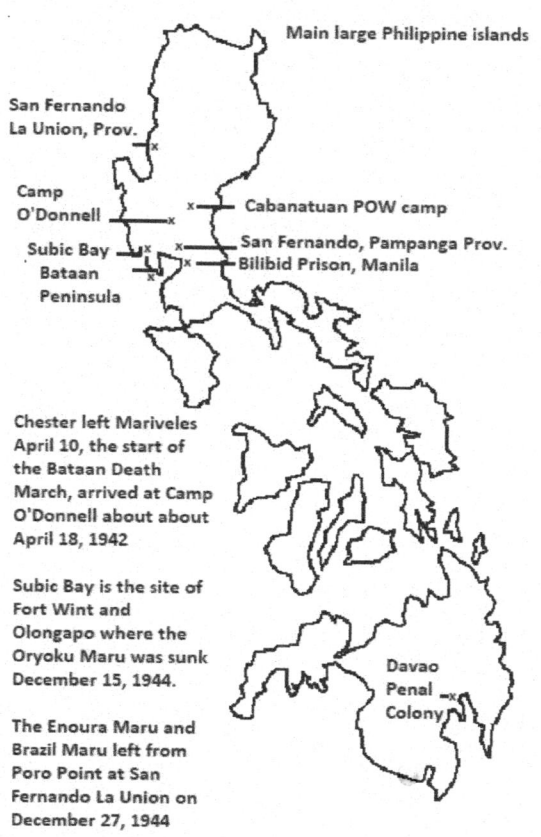

Main large Philippine islands

San Fernando
La Union, Prov.

Camp
O'Donnell — Cabanatuan POW camp

Subic Bay — San Fernando, Pampanga Prov.
Bataan — Bilibid Prison, Manila
Peninsula

Chester left Mariveles
April 10, the start of
the Bataan Death
March, arrived at Camp
O'Donnell about about
April 18, 1942

Subic Bay is the site of
Fort Wint and
Olongapo where the
Oryoku Maru was sunk
December 15, 1944.

The Enoura Maru and
Brazil Maru left from
Poro Point at San
Fernando La Union on
December 27, 1944

Davao
Penal
Colony

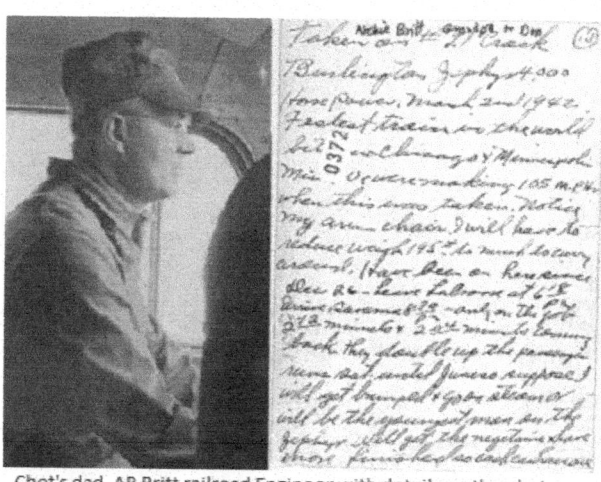

Chet's dad, AR Britt railroad Engineer with details on the photo.
Railroads, and the men and women that worked for them, were a
critical part of the war effort to get troops, materials and supplies,
and weapons where they were needed on time across the country.

Both grandmothers, Hazel Britt and Hilma Runice, helped Grace with Chester Jr. Grace took a job at Northern Engraving, a local manufacturing company in La Crosse, where she worked a variety of jobs making 20mm brass shell casings. See her awards at the end of this chapter. In addition to fulfilling her duties as bread winner, wife, and mother, she joined an organization that supported POW families seeking information about their loved ones. She prayed continuously for Chet's health and safety. Their love was reciprocal and connected despite the miles separating them. While he was away at West Point, Grace had patiently waited four years for her love toward Chet to be fulfilled. This time, her patience would be tested time and time again as she realized the stark reality of life interrupted by the war.

On April 9, 1942, when the Bataan Death March began, the will of American and Filipino POWs was about to be tested as well. Unbeknownst to his family, Lieutenant Britt, was among of them. He had begun the ultimate battle — for his life.

The 70+ mile forced march was the beginning of 41-months of savagery, torture, and endless cruelty. Those who could not maintain the pace were shot or stabbed and left to die in the road. Some were buried alive with only their head and hands protruding above ground; they begged for help as prisoners stepped over them. Anyone stopping to render aid faced certain death. Prisoners had no option but to trample on the corpses. Walking around them resulted in severe punishment — usually a well-placed rifle butt slammed into their heads or ribs — or worse, depending on the guard's mood at the moment.

Exhausted and malnourished, many were clothed only in remnants of ragged uniforms, torn, and tattered from five months of unrelenting jungle warfare. They were the lucky ones. Most wore only shorts or "G-strings" made from scraps of cloth draped around their already emaciated waists. Few had combat boots to protect their feet on the pebble-strewn road.

Along the route, Filipino civilians tried to ease the prisoners' agony by sneaking water and food to them. Those who were caught usually met with immediate execution. Starved, denied water, beaten, clubbed with rifle butts, stabbed with bayonets, decapitated by swords, and shot, the bodies of 1,000 Americans and more than 6,000 Filipinos littered the mostly dirt road from Mariveles to Camp O'Donnell, the location of their first POW camp. Temperatures at mid-day reached 110 degrees, and guards threatened to kill anyone who sat in the shade or wore a hat during the few rest stops each day.

Colonel Irvin Alexander described the forced march in his book, "Surviving Bataan and Beyond":

"Exhausted, sick, traumatized men who are malnourished, wounded or injured found the walk difficult and some impossible. Only the more fit men survived the march, with many senior officers and men dying from a wide variety of causes in route to Camp O'Donnell. Many of the younger men had little self-control and died from drinking bad, untreated water from ditches and streams, where carcasses of men and animals lay rotting. The Japanese guards were merciless in driving the prisoners northward. Prisoners that could not stand or walk, were murdered on the spot, with the Japanese bayoneting, clubbing, and shooting many to death. Men who tried to help others get up to walk were beaten for slowing down to help the weak … Men died of dehydration and sun exposure as they walked under the blazing sun and anyone who broke from the marching column to drink filthy water from a ditch, or a stream faced serious punishment or death. When water was provided at a holding place along the route of march, it required the men to line up at a single water spigot and wait their turn to get a little cup or spoonful of water. The heat and lack of water took many lives along the march."

On the sixth day of relentless torture, the men reached San Fernando at mid-day. They were herded into a holding pen near the rail head where they waited to board a train to Capas, the closest station to Camp O'Donnell. On the march since just before sunrise, they were given no water or food and were packed together so tightly there was no room to sit. They stood in the blistering sun for two hours before boarding the train. When it was time to depart, 150 men were crammed like cattle into half a dozen rusted, WWI-era box cars designed to hold no more than 50. With no ventilation and no room to move, it was impossible to sit. The bright sun beating down on the enclosed steel cars quickly raised the temperature inside to nearly 130 degrees. It was like being baked alive in an over-sized oven.

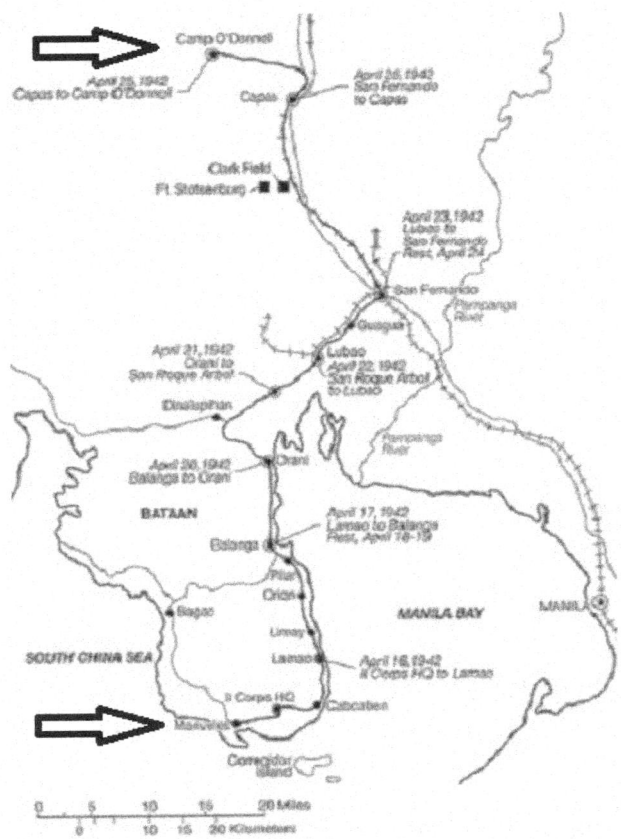

Bataan Death March for Chester, Mariveles north to Camp O'Donnell

Many passed out during the two-hour journey; they remained upright only because there was no space to fall down. Forced to relieve themselves where they stood, the stench combined with the heat became unbearable, causing several POWs to vomit what little they had eaten earlier in the day. The prisoners were squeezed in so tightly those who had the misfortune of ending up in the middle of the cars died on their feet from lack of air. When they reached Capas, those who survived tumbled out of the cars as fast as they could, the 100-degree air outside feeling cool on their skin.

They had been marching at a fast pace for nearly a week, on their feet from before sunrise to well after sunset with little time to rest or eat. But they still had nine more miles to traverse on foot. Thankfully, their new cadre of guards took pity on them and slowed the pace on the final leg of their journey. They reached Camp O'Donnell in late afternoon.

The men and their captors covered the 70+ miles to Camp O'Donnell in 6 days, some days walking as many as 20 miles. Prisoners received less than a cup of water a day and were given a mere cup of rice the entire journey. Surviving with barely any food and scant water, the prisoners were forced to stand in formation for the camp commander's "welcome" speech. A frightened, young, Filipino interpreter translated, while following the smug, irritated captain around the elevated stage and mimicking every gesture and vocal inflection to avoid his wrath. In his book, "Some Survived," Capt. Manny Lawton noted the intense hatred the Japanese commander, held for Americans:

"De captin say you are not honorable prisoners of war … You are captives … As captives you have no rights. De captin say Americans and Japanese are enemies forever … Nippon will build a greater Asia for the Asiatics … You will be used as laborers in this project … He say if you try to escape you will be shoot kill … even to go near de fence will be cause for to shoot."

Capt. John S. Coleman, an Army Reserve signal corps officer, described the camp as a new kind of hell. In his book, "Bataan and Beyond" he said malaria and dysentery were rampant. There was little sympathy and no medicine. The hospital comprised two buildings, one for the sick and one for the dying, known among the men at as Zero Ward. He wrote:

"Thirty to 50 men died every day. At first the prisoners stood and saluted as their comrades' and friends' emaciated bodies were carried out for burial. Soon the burial details became so common place that no one seemed to notice any longer, as a sad indifference to death overtook the prisoners."

Coleman also recalled the camp commander's hatred of his American captives. He enjoyed the life-or-death power he held in his hands and lectured the POWs incessantly, forcing already weakened and sick men to stand in the unbearable heat as he frequently scolded and threatened them with his hostile rhetoric:

"You are mine. You are the enemy. You should be grateful to the great Japanese Imperial Army for sparing your lives. Our children will fight your children for hundreds of years and we will banish the white man from the Orient. You will die from old age under our command. We have laws here that you must obey. Anyone involved in attempting to escape will be given the death sentence. We have drinking water, but it is a death penalty to use water to bathe ... Japan and America will be enemies forever ... therefore you will be treated as enemy captives — not as honorable prisoners of war ... you will be made to work hard to rebuild a New Philippines in a New World Order of Asia ... free from the curse of Anglo-American Imperialism."

Prisoner drawing of Camp O'Donnell burial detail
Cemetery and mass graves

The drawing above is from Colonel Eugene C. Jacobs book, "Blood Brothers."

Lieutenant Britt and his fellow POWs were adjusting to the brutal actions of their captors, who starved and tortured them physically and

67

mentally every day during their confinement at Camp O'Donnell. In his book, "The Naked Flagpole," Col. Richard C. Mallonee wrote:

"... I found out one thing at O'Donnell: when a man doesn't want to live it is pretty easy to die. Many gave up and did just that, although suffering no more than the rest of us. Others like Luther Stevens, you couldn't kill. We left him behind almost dead two or three times when we changed camps, but he was still alive and kicking at the end."

Filipinos who survived the Death March were released after a brief "re-education period," but more than 28,000 of their fellow countrymen had paid the ultimate price according to Chet's war crimes testimony.

Meanwhile, Japan was unleashing its full military might on Corregidor. The enemy, in full control of the Bataan peninsula, focused all its resources and used its strategic advantage to shell Corregidor. However, the Japanese paid dearly for their ultimate victory.

One of Chester's friends from his West Point class, 1st Lt. Herbert E. Pace, was killed at Corregidor on April 28, 1942, just nine days before the fall of the island fortress. An artillery round landed directly on his fighting position on Corregidor, instantly obliterating the lieutenant, his men, and their artillery.

Capt. Bill Massello, who played softball with Chester and Colonel Boudreau on Fort Wint prior to the war, was ordered to Corregidor from Bataan before Bataan was surrendered. His 60-man unit was assigned to operate four, WW1-era, 12-inch mortars. Unfamiliar with the big guns and with no training, they still achieved great success. Near the end of the battle for Corregidor, every one of his men was either wounded or dead. Desperate to carry on his mission, Captain Massello pressed the unit's cooks into action in order to load the one remaining mortar in his depleted arsenal. Because of its condition, the mortar was in danger of exploding when it was fired. After ordering the cooks to take cover, the captain — though wounded himself — pulled the lanyard to fire the last shot, some believe, from Corregidor before the surrender.

The Japanese bombed and shelled Corregidor continuously to soften its defenses before the final assault. Japanese landing forces were annihilated in their attempt to come ashore on Corregidor losing two-thirds of the landing craft to artillery fire, resulting in more than 4,000 dead — a high price for control of "the Rock."

With hope gone, and to avoid the inevitable slaughter that awaited, General Wainwright surrendered Corregidor on May 6, 1942, completing the official and total surrender of all allied forces to Japan. Due to a lack of communication among American and Japanese forces, independent commanders on Mindanao and other on other islands were unaware of the surrender agreement. It caused a delay in surrendering in some areas and the unnecessary death of untold allied forces. One unit already had stacked its weapons as ordered by their Japanese captors only to be attacked by another Japanese unit, which slaughtered the disarmed fighters. In another instance, Colonel Bunker lowered and destroyed the American flag on Corregidor before it was captured but managed to cut and hide two swatches of the flag from America's most treasured symbol.

Captured senior officers — colonels to lieutenant generals — usually were separated from the men they commanded, although four men on General Wainwright's staff were allowed to remain with him throughout his captivity. Their treatment was somewhat better, and the vast majority survived the war after being imprisoned in Formosa and then Manchuria.

The Japanese adhered more closely to the Geneva Convention when it came to more senior officers. The rate of survival was significantly higher than all ranks below colonel. At war's end, 230 senior officers survived and were rescued in Manchuria.

Robert W. Levering, a civilian lawyer who handled contracts for the War Department in Manila when the war started, elected to join his military colleagues in battle. He was among the last to depart the besieged capital city. When surrender was imminent, rather than live out the war with other civilians in relative comfort at Santo Tomas University in Manila, he opted to stay with his fellow fighters. He survived to become a U.S.

Congressman from Ohio in 1959, and recorded his POW experiences in his book "Horror Trek":

"Hell is not a place, but a condition … The living lived because we were able to adjust ourselves to the gradually worsening situation. A man's spirit is subject to great fluctuations, the extent of which are unknown until put to the test. This test was greater than ordinary fear, love and hate. Many men, in their attempt to avoid the rugged impact of realities against their lives, simply gave up and died, because that was painless, while living was terrible … I marveled at the varying degrees of determination with which men held on to the thin thread of life, which seemed to swing over a bottomless pit of despair … To want to live with a mad desire was the *sine qua non* of survival."

There was a single water spigot for 9,000 men at Camp O'Donnell, not enough water to drink and certainly none to be used for cleanliness. The men were caked with their own filth from dysentery, diarrhea, the Philippine dust, and their sweat caused by the hot sun. The stench from the filth, combined with the odor of gangrenous wounds and the ever-present smell of death caused the men to heave and vomit. Conditions at Camp O'Donnell were horrendous; the dead were stacked along the perimeter inside the wire fence just outside the hospital ward, bloating and rotting in the sun. The bodies reeked so badly the Japanese camp commander finally relented and allowed the dead to be buried. But the prisoners were so weak, they physically were unable to bury the corpses deep in the soil. Summertime monsoon rains constantly washed away the dirt covering the dead. Ever-lurking predators — stray dogs and birds — tore the decaying flesh off the dead warriors.

A month after General King surrendered his troops on Bataan, General Wainwright surrendered his troops on Corregidor. They were in better physical shape than the group transferred from Camp O'Donnell. The Corregidor POWs were marched through Manila in order to humiliate them before the Filipino citizens they tried to defend. However, they avoided the horrors of a forced march to Camp O'Donnell, traveling instead by train. Upon arriving, Lt. Col. Art Shreve — one of the Corregidor POWs — was appalled at the sight of those who had surrendered just a month earlier on Bataan. He wrote in his diary:

"A few of them had arrived before us, to help get the camp set up for our arrival. Of course, on Corregidor we had heard that the boys on Bataan were not faring well. But now, seeing them for the first time was quite a shock. We began to notice these guys, a captain, and a lieutenant, who had been on Bataan. And, oh man, these guys had a vacant stare in their eyes. When you started to open a can, they would just stare at the food. You could see their mouths watering. Either they couldn't believe you had a can of food, or else they were afraid they weren't going to get their share. They were frightening. I don't believe I'd ever seen anything like that. It was more than I could handle."

A common trait of those who survived the brutality came down to one word — optimism. In the several books written by survivors of the Japanese imprisonment, optimism was critical to coming home. According to Manny Lawton, "Despite conditions of their incarceration, the prospect of a better day tomorrow buoyed their spirits. Hope was the sustaining asset. Those who blindly clung to it lived, those who lost it gave up and died … there was no room for despondency."

This was true of Chester, as well as others who became experts at survival. The Japanese had total and absolute control of their lives. They understood early on their current situation was temporary. This realization gave them strength to hang on as long as necessary. Day by day, hour by hour, minute by minute, the POWs focused their minds on what they could control. They concentrated on positive memories, which brought them comfort and fueled their will to live — memories of love, family, faith, and an unrelenting yearning to return home. It was especially true for Chester. His desire to be reunited with Grace and meet his first-born son sustained the lieutenant during his most desperate times.

Reminded of the Japanese belief that soldiers who surrender should die, Captain Lawton recalled, "Maybe so, but I don't plan to die, things will improve one of these days." It was that kind of spirit the men needed to survive.

One National Guard unit, the 200th Anti-Aircraft (AA) Regiment, consisted of 100 men from New Mexico, 80 of them Native Americans. They experienced an inexplicably high death rate. Only nine of them survived; no one ever determined the reason. It quickly became evident the war had impacted every village and town in America.

On the home front, the Adjutant General of the Army sent a letter to Chet's mother, Hazel, dated May 22, 1942. In it was the official notification that Chet was missing in action (MIA). The Japanese indicated they would comply with the Geneva Convention regarding prisoners, although in fact, the Japanese had no intention of following it. The letter also said his pay and allotments would continue for a year, and at that point, the Army would determine whether to end his pay and allotments if they received evidence that he was deceased.

Hazel, Grace, and the entire family obviously was relieved Chet had not been declared killed in action. But that still could've meant he was dead. Maybe the Army just hadn't located or identified his body yet. Still, the family held out hope. But one fact remained: they didn't know if he was alive or dead. That, perhaps, was the hardest part. Waiting was unbearable. Faced with the prospect of no husband and a new son to raise alone, Grace agonized over whether the love of her life was alive or dead. Questions swirled in her head. If he was alive, where was he? Had he been wounded? Had he miraculously escaped? Had he been captured? Tortured?

In June 1942, after two months at the hands of their sadistic captors, 60 per cent of those who survived were transported 39 miles northeast by train to Camp Cabanatuan. Upon arrival, they quickly realized conditions at the new camp weren't much improved, except for one thing — water. Cabanatuan provided an adequate supply of drinking water with several spigots. There was enough water not only for drinking, but for bathing and cleaning, which gave them hope of better days to come.

By this point, everyone was stricken with malaria and a variety of other debilitating diseases. They were exhausted from the continuous stress of battle, surrender, and imprisonment. They were fighting to live — just to take one more breath. Starved since January by their own Army and then again by their captors, the Death March survivors were emaciated, many having lost 30-40 per cent of their body weight. At graduation, Chester was a strapping, athletic 6'3" and weighed 185 pounds. In just four months, his weight had dropped 50 pounds. Like all of his fellow prisoners, he looked haggard and gaunt, with sunken eyes and protruding cheek bones and ribs.

Escape from mosquitoes in the humid, Philippine climate was impossible. Malaria permeated the entire camp, impacting nearly every prisoner in Cabanatuan. Chester was no exception. By war's end, he suffered through 66 malaria attacks, more than one a month. Prisoners who had no one to help them when they were sick fared poorly. Malaria led to malnutrition, and those incapable of feeding themselves had to rely on someone else.

Scurvy, pellagra, and beriberi often followed the frequent bouts of malaria. Supplies of quinine, the drug needed to treat malaria, had been depleted long ago. The only remedy was to stay warm and rest, but blankets and sleep were in short supply as well. Hydration was less of a problem for prisoners in Cabanatuan than Camp O'Donnell, but still a challenge for corpsmen in the hospital or friends who had to fetch water for their fellow prisoners. Chet took care of his friend Lieutenant George Pearcy who had Beri-Beri and could not walk, so he brought him canteens filled with hot water to ease his pain.

Prisoner drawing of Cabanatuan Camp cemetery with cross showing burials by June 2, 1942

In June we were moved by truck to Cabanatuan and combined with most of the Americans from Corregidor. Here conditions were better, but still insufficient food and medicines given to us Col. Brietung, Col. Biggs, and Lt. Gilbert (USN) were captured in an attempted escape and were executed after being beaten all night and tied to fence posts in the sun all day.

One evening a Japanese column marched by camp carrying two Filipinos heads on bamboo poles near the guard house. Several times Americans were tied to fence posts to suffer in the sun for trying to get food into Camp via Filipinos on the outside. Our dead were buried in large graves, 25 to 30 in a grave, officers and men mixed. I left Cabanatuan on a detail to Mindano in October 1942. The total dead at Cabanatuan in 1944 was approximately 2400 Americans.

Above from Chester K Britt's post-war affidavit to be used for war crimes trials

Several of Chester's friends were taken to Camp O'Donnell and Cabanatuan. Second Lieutenant Bill Lewis and Army civilian Max Wait — the men he hunted snakes with at Fort Wint — were there. Chet and Bill fought together on Bataan and kept each other alive on the treacherous Death March. Chet, Bill, and Max were each other's lifelines. Reunited in Cabanatuan prison camp, they tended to each other's needs. In essence, they became brothers, united in a singular desire to survive. They quickly learned those men without close friends usually died. Two other close friends of Chet, Captain Lawrence "Chan" Baldwin, from Fort Wint, and 1st Lt. Augustus "Gus" Cullen, from West Point, were at the camp, too.

Throughout the summer and autumn of 1942, the Britt family received no further communication regarding Chet's status. He was still listed as MIA. That, at least, was the best news possible at that point. With each passing day, the odds grew in their favor that Chester might still be alive. Alive! But where?

Grace encouraged Evelyn Cullen, Olga Massello, Ruth Monteith, and other Army wives — friends from her short time in the Philippines — as they exchanged letters to lift each other's spirits. Their men were all listed as missing. But they understood life continues. There were kids to raise, bills to pay, and a lot of prayers to be uttered.

Waiting to learn of Chet's fate was excruciating. The Runice and Britt families wrapped their arms around Grace and Chester Jr, supporting them emotionally and spiritually. The combined families felt God was testing them, and strongly believed He answered prayers and kept His promises. Faith gave them hope and comfort in the midst of their despair.

The same was true for the prisoners. Many sustained their hope for survival through their faith. They read Bibles and shared them with guys who didn't have one. Protestant and Catholic services were conducted, and a Jewish cantor sang for the camp, according to Col. Ben Skardon, a survivor who was 103 on July 14, 2020. In an interview, he recalled how he loved to hear the cantor's voice rising above the din in the camp. It had a calming effect, he said, and he recited everything he could remember from his upbringing — creeds, the Ten Commandments, anything that would help lift his spirit above the insanity around him. His father, an Episcopal minister, had taught his son well. Colonel Skardon attributed his survival to being optimistic, refusing to die — and luck.

On October 28, 1942, Chester, along with 1,000 selected prisoners, was moved from Camp Cabanatuan to Manila. There, they boarded a 5,400-ton Japanese cargo ship, the Erie Maru, and covertly maneuvered through the islands to avoid U.S. Navy submarine patrols. Their destination: the Davao Penal Colony (DAPECOL) on the island of Mindanao. For the next 18 months, the prisoners were assigned to an agricultural work detail, returning to Cabanatuan in June 1944.

The POWs smuggled bananas and other vegetables into the camp at the end of each workday. Chet cleverly stashed his food treasures in his hat. Due to his height — 6'3" — the guards refused to look up at him. When he was required to bow, he never bowed low enough for them to see the hidden food. The guards suffered from inadequate food as well. As the lowest-ranking conscripts in the Imperial Army, they garnered little respect or consideration from their superiors in the Samurai military hierarchy. Interestingly, the Japanese didn't eat bananas, yet they wouldn't let prisoners have them outright, so Chet and his newly trained farming buddies secretly snuck them into the camp.

The Geneva Convention explicitly stated that officers weren't required to work. At Davao, however, the men were informed because they were considered captives rather than POWs — those who refused to work would receive no food. Naturally, the decision was an easy one. Although the quantity and quality of food at Davao was a slight improvement over what they'd received elsewhere, many of the men were so ill it was too painful to eat because they were unable to digest it. Declining food, they forfeited their lives. Unquestionably, living under such harsh conditions was hard. Dying was easy.

Like all communities, nothing would ever be the same again for the people of La Crosse as the city started to lose more sons to the inexorable attacks of the Japanese on American shipping and military facilities in the Pacific. The Japanese had joined in alliance with the Germans, and the attack on Pearl Harbor provided President Roosevelt a reason to enter the war in Europe.

In December, the Britt family finally received the news they'd been praying for since they learned Chet was declared missing. He was alive! But they still wondered. Was he being treated well? Was he wounded or injured? Was he getting medical care? Has he been crippled? Although the news provided immeasurable relief, questions and worries remained, questions that would not be answered until the war was over.

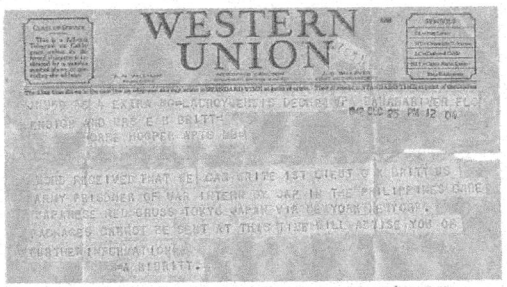

Dad AR Britt's December 25, 1942 telegram to son Lt Edgar Britt
advising that his older brother Chet is a prisoner of the Japanese.
The welcome news that Chet is alive comes more than 8 months
after the fall of Bataan. Such a delay of many months to learn their
loved ones' fate was common for most families.

About the same time, Japan granted official POW status to those held captive. But it really didn't mean much as their treatment improved only a little. Japan continued refusing to provide adequate supplies of the basic requirements needed to sustain life — water, food, shelter, and medical treatment. As a result, thousands of POWs needlessly died in captivity. Japanese commanders, guards, and at least one interpreter repeatedly informed the prisoners they were not honorable men because they had surrendered rather than fighting to their deaths. As a consequence, their captors told the men they should die. And they did. By the thousands. In comparison, 40 per cent of prisoners held by the Japanese died in captivity versus 1.2 per cent for POWs in Germany.

While Chet fought to stay alive, Grace and her workmates supported the war effort making ammunition, receiving awards for their excellent work.

Authority _NND785011_
By _SF_ NARA Date _5/4/P_

SECRET

The group of officers I was with surrendered as ordered in the motor pool area of the 1st Corps in the western area of Bataan on April 10th, 1942. We were told to line up for inspection, on the edge of the road, and that anyone venturing onto the road would be shot. A Filipino came straying down the road to watch the inspection. The Japanese officer shot this young mand throught the head with his pistol. After the inspection we were allowed to transport ourselves with our own trucks and automobiles to Mariveles Airfield where we were relieved of watches, rings and any other articles of value that took the fancy of a Japanese soldier who already had half a barracks bag full of loot. We were forced to line up our vehicles and to take up the march out of Bataan, leaving Mariveles field in groups of about 100 men each. Japanese soldiers everywhere along the way searched us for valuables, cigarettes, and canned food. Some men were relieved of their canteens of water. We marched every day for four or five days and once during the night, never reaching any shade from the hot sun until night. We were forced to assemble for rest periods in the hot sun and made to crowd up closely together with scarcely enough room to sit. Men were suffering from malaria, general weakness, and thirst and hunger. Our group of men was not fed until we reached Lubic, and then only one small ball of rice about the size of a baseball and no salt. Many Americans died along the roadside, I saw also several Filipinos by the roadside, apparently strangled by rope tied around their necks. At various points along the way we were struck on the heads with sticks, and soldiers passing in trucks threw stones and other heavy objects at us; in one case killing the man a few feet ahead of me in the column. We were continually promised food and pushed on without it.

Upon arrival in San Fernando, Pampangi we were put into a stockade, received very little water and food, and left to weather the hot sun and cold rain without sufficient clothing or shelter. After three days we were packed into small box cars, 100 to 150 per car and moved by rail to Capas Tarlac, and then marched to Camp O'Donnell.

The Japanese Captain who received us at Camp O'Donnel told us that all Japanese hated the Americans. He said that Japan would fight the United States and beat her at war even if it took one hundred years. During our stay in this camp our food was insufficient. We received musty rice, little or no salt, token amounts of meat, fish, and vegetables. We needed medicines, especially quinine and sulfa drugs but the Japanese would not give them to us nor would the permit the Filipinos to send in any appreciable quantity of them. Many men died upon arrival in Camp, and a large number each day thereafter. The dead were laid out in the sun behind the hospital and on one occasion I counted seventy of them some already bloated and turning black, having been there three days, before permission was granted to bury them. The men of our camp were too weak to dig graves, latrines, sumps, etc. The dead were in some cases just scarcely covered with gravel in shallow graves. Dysentry spread rapidly and deaths mounted daily. The Filipinos were kept across the road and one day I counted one hundred of them being taken out for burial. During our stay at Camp O'Donnell, a period of about one and three fourths months, approximately 1500 Americans and 28,900 Filipinos died.

October 1, 1945 post-war affidavit by Chester Britt about the Bataan Death March and Camp O'Donnell to be used for war crimes trials

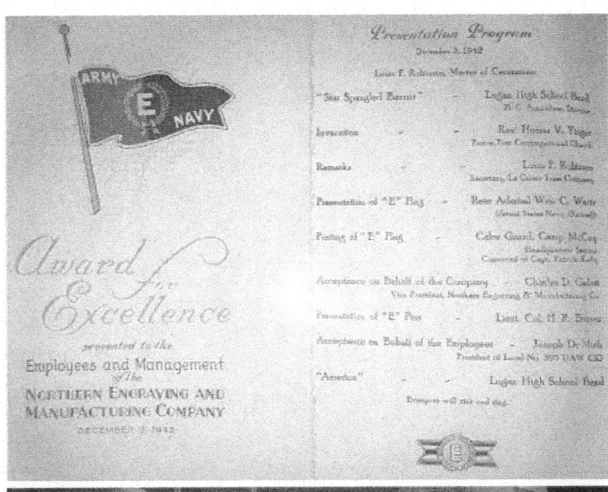

Grace and all the employees and management of the Northern Engraving Corp, La Crosse, received the E Award for production of 20 mm brass shell casings. Music for the celebration by the Logan High School band. Article and program courtesy of the Gelatt family

CHAPTER 5

Surviving the POW Shell Game
(January 1943 - December 12, 1944)

Chester began 1943 still working in the agricultural fields near the Davao Penal Colony. Alongside approximately 1,000 other prisoners from Cabanatuan, he raised food for the Japanese military. Overall, the prisoners found conditions at the penal colony a little better than at Cabanatuan — at least in the beginning. At their former camp, men were dying at the rate of 50 a day. Those who weren't ill were malnourished. More than half were too weak and unable to work when they arrived at Davao.

Another 1,000 prisoners arrived from Malaybalay, about 120 miles north before Chet's group. They, however, had not had the same bitter experiences and barbaric treatment as their fellow POWs from Cabanatuan. To begin with, they had not gone through the five months of strenuous fighting on Bataan and Corregidor. After being captured at their posts in various parts of the southern islands, they were allowed to keep all their personal possessions, such as clothes, money, jewelry, etc. Officers were exempt from work details, and all the prisoners had received sufficient food to keep them in fair health. Not surprisingly, their view of life at Davao wasn't as positive as the men from Cabanatuan. In any event, conditions for all the captives were far below the standards required by the Geneva Convention.

Surprisingly, there was a small library in the camp, available for those who worked on heavy-duty status. Unfortunately, they never had any free time to read, and patients and others who weren't well enough to be assigned to heavy-duty projects weren't permitted to use the library. It remained an idle, mocking gesture of goodwill. Many would have found some measure of emotional escape had they been able to crack open a book occasionally, even if only for a few minutes.

Latrines inside the camp were dug and maintained by the POWs, which ensured a slight improvement in their sanitary conditions. Prisoners were allowed to stay relativity clean with plenty of access to water for drinking and bathing, although soap was a rare commodity. A nearby artesian well supplied the camp's water. It was pumped into three tanks set atop towers within the compound. The force of gravity carried it through pipes to faucets throughout the camp. Although water from artesian wells contains natural minerals essential to good health, it still runs the risk of contaminants found in all spring and well water, and the Japanese weren't concerned whether or not it was safe to drink.

For a short while, the food they were given — which they grew — was fair. It consisted mainly of rice, salt, sugar, and vegetables. The POWs consumed rice three times a day and frequently enjoyed added portions of banana buds, green papaya, mung beans, camote, and jackfruit. Green papaya helped cleanse their digestive systems while banana buds and mung beans were packed with antioxidants and other much-needed nutrients. Similar to a sweet potato, camote provided similar health benefits, especially for bones and heart health. And the unripe, fleshy petals of the jackfruit — which could weigh up to 55 pounds each — provided vitamin C and potassium. Its texture made it a perfect meat substitute in stews. Protein, in the form of eggs, was plentiful as well; the camp also operated a poultry farm. It wasn't a perfect diet, but at least the men were getting barely sufficient nutrition for survival.

On January 29, 1943, everything changed. Each prisoner received one-and-a-half Red Cross packages. They contained canned meats, powdered milk, instant coffee, candy, cigarettes, sewing kits, and other miscellaneous items. A week after the Red Cross packages arrived, some prisoners hit the jackpot, receiving their first mail from home since their capture eight months earlier. Letters from loved ones boosted morale and hope for those who were fortunate enough to receive them. The unexpected deliveries of food and encouragement enabled many men to recover from illness and survive. Manny Lawton, whose POW experiences mirrored Chester's, remarked, "As a grown man, hungry, weak, lonely, and beginning to feel that my comrades and I had been written off and forgotten, the packages had a profound meaning ... they brought a rekindling of hope."

However, that hope was dashed once again, when — as the care packages arrived — the Japanese stopped giving them any food at all. Nor did they resume providing the plentiful fruits and vegetables that helped maintain some semblance of health, even after the Red Cross supplies had been exhausted. Their main diet consisted of rice and whatever they could scrounge and barter for in camp. Chester traded cigarettes and other non-essential items for food and vitamins, exercising discipline in securing needs over wants in an effort to fight off malaria and other diseases.

In April 1943, rice rations were reduced by one-third following the escape of ten prisoners. Movement within the camp was restricted severely, and beatings for minor rule infractions became common in an attempt to maintain a tougher stance. Four months later, rations were reduced again, without any explanation.

For a while, the Japanese established a small canteen where they sold dried bananas, but the enterprise was short-lived. They then decided to sell moldy tobacco leaves, which the prisoners eagerly bought in spite of their condition. Everything had value, and anything could be traded.

To supplement their meager rations and trade for things they might need in the future, Chester and other prisoners began sneaking vegetables and rice from the fields where they worked, carefully slipping their bounty past the less-than-aware guards to avoid suspicion. Upon discovering the crafty plot, the camp commander increased the number of gate guards in an attempt to catch the stealthy food smugglers. If caught, prisoners were beaten mercilessly to the point of unconsciousness. Fellow POWs carried the bloodied and bruised captives back to their shoddy beds hoping they'd survive.

As time progressed, the Japanese commandeered increasingly larger amounts of the food the prisoners grew, which left very little for them to eat. They also were forbidden to consume the wild food that grew nearby. Every prisoner who wasn't hospitalized was forced to work. Usually, that meant manual labor, such as planting and harvesting rice, or work of a more degrading kind, such as building and cleaning the Japanese latrines. Neither officers nor chaplains were exempt.

Prisoners were given access to various movies, newspapers, and athletic activities. They also organized a glee club of 800 voices. It not only helped boost morale but led to comical situations with hundreds of men trying to recall the words and melodies. Humor proved to be an important mental health aspect to survival. However, camp conditions continued to deteriorate gradually. The glee club eventually was forced to disband when the Japanese commander decided the men could no longer gather in groups.

The Bibles, prayer books, and other reading materials confiscated from the prisoners upon arrival eventually were returned to their owners or unwillingly "donated" to the general library. Daily Bible classes saw prisoners poring over the few Bibles they possessed. Faith, for many, was an anchor to hang onto in the midst of an uncertain and fear-centered existence, where POWs were subject to whatever judgment and punishment their captors decided to inflict on any given day.

Although conditions at Davao were somewhat better compared to other prisoner of war camps in the Philippines, the men still suffered unimaginable treatment and punishment. It wasn't unusual for those working in the fields to suffer severe cuts and injuries to their lower legs, some of which penetrated down to the bone. The only "medical" treatment they received was hot water and rags at the end of their workday.

Prisoners who suffered bouts of malaria still were required to work half-days, and on the third day after their recovery, they were required to report for full duty. The protest of two American officers, who claimed such treatment violated the Geneva Convention, were told by the penal colony's arrogant camp commander, "We treat you like we wish."

Elsewhere, others suffered and died. On September 7, 1943, Col. Paul D. Bunker Sr., the man who had written the light-hearted poem for evacuees — including Grace in 1941 — died at a POW camp in Formosa. Fearing he would not survive to see the end of the war, the colonel previously had summoned Col. Delbert Ausmus and sworn him to secrecy. Careful not to attract the attention of the guards, Colonel Bunker retrieved a remnant of the flag he had stashed behind a patch on his tattered shirt — the flag from Corregidor he was ordered to destroy — and asked Col. Ausmus to deliver it to the Secretary of War as soon as possible after he was rescued. Colonel Ausmus took the swatch of red fabric and securely tucked it into the cuff of his shirt. General Wainwright, who was in the same prison camp, sat with the colonel in the final hours before he died, recalling the colonel had been cremated in the rags that held the precious fabric of the American flag he loved so dearly. With his death, only a small piece of the Corregidor flag survived.

At Davao Penal Colony, sick prisoners were hospitalized in a building previously used as a prison hospital, which was part of a civilian prison compound prior to the war. The Japanese exercised general supervision of the hospital but left its administration in the capable hands of a staff of United States Army Medical Corps officers, under the direction of Lt. Col. Dwight Deter. With rudimentary equipment and few supplies to treat patients, the medical staff did what they could to care for the sick, wounded, and injured men. The hospital housed a maximum of 200 patients although under other circumstances, every POW would've been hospitalized.

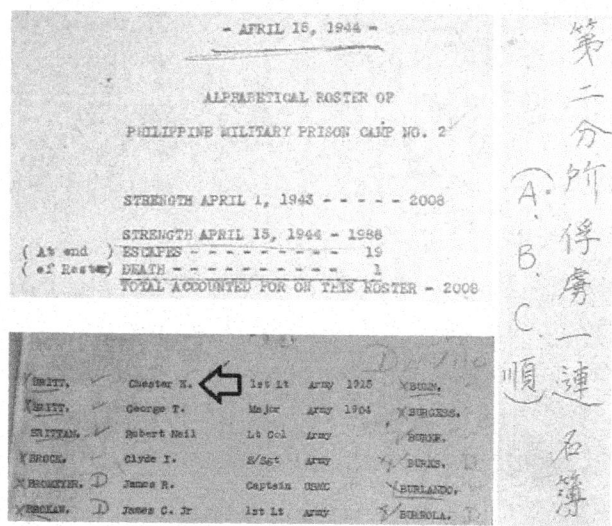

April 15, 1944 TOP and SIDE Davao Penal Colony (DAPECOL)
roster front page BOTTOM Chester Britt is just one of hundreds
of men in this multi-page typed report from the camp

Instead of beds, the patients slept on wooden bunks, most of them
without mattresses. At best, some bunks were cushioned shelter halves —
sections of canvas used to make tents — and stuffed with kapok. It was
similar in texture to cotton and grew wild on trees near the prison. Despite
such dire conditions, the Army doctors and medics performed minor sur-
geries, tended to wounds and infections, and provided much-needed com-
passionate care to those most in need.

On any given day, an average of one-third of the captives were ill
with malaria. Fortunately, there was an adequate supply of quinine available. The hospital's equipment was extremely limited, especially before
February 1944, when a large quantity of medical supplies and equipment
arrived in a Red Cross delivery. An American dental officer took care of
the prisoners' simpler needs, such as extractions and fillings, with his only
equipment being a field-type dental chair and a foot-propelled drill; he had
no capacity to restore or replace missing teeth and used no anesthetics.

February 1944 also saw the second delivery of Red Cross packages,
identical to those the prisoners received eleven months prior. Once again,

morale increased knowing they'd have canned food and other items to regain some of their health and further their chance for survival.

The Japanese ordered that prisoners would no longer be permitted to wear long trousers, shirts, or jackets. The order was intended to prevent smuggling anything into the camp after working in the fields all day. Although the POWs ate fruits and vegetables not consumed in the Japanese diet, the camp commander didn't want prisoners to be healthy enough to escape or fight back. He needed them to be barely alive, but healthy enough to work.

As conditions worsened, daring prisoner escapes, some successful, became more frequent. In March, another escape attempt by eight prisoners resulted in the death of five guards and at least two prisoners. However, six prisoners avoided capture and made their way through the jungle, linking up with Filipino and American guerilla bands. The escape of two more prisoners in early spring further enraged and embarrassed the Japanese commander. He sentenced 12 of those who were re-captured to solitary confinement for 15 days. Later, when ten others escaped, he ordered the execution of the 25 men whose escape was unsuccessful.

Each escape attempt resulted in even more severe treatment for those who remained. The commander ordered more frequent patrols, more limits placed on prisoners' movements, a further reduction in food, and the stoppage of work details outside the camp. With no opportunity to smuggle much-needed nutrients to maintain basic health, the POWs wondered how long they could survive.

By that time, American forces were planning their return to the Philippines, and the Japanese had decided to close the camp. They would move once again, this time north about 1,100 miles from the southernmost island of Mindanao to the island of Luzon.

On June 6, 1944, as the United States was in the midst of D-Day operations in France, Lieutenant Britt was among 1,250 of the able-bodied American prisoners at the penal colony who were inexplicably blindfolded. With their hands tied behind their backs, they were transported by truck to the city of Davao. Those who were too sick and feeble to be moved, approximately 750, remained behind. The men were herded aboard the Yashu Maru, a Japanese cargo ship bound for Cebu. During the five-day voyage, 56 prisoners died from the extreme heat and lack of food, water, and sanitary conditions.

At Cebu, the prisoners were transferred to the rotting and rusted holds of the Singoto Maru #824, another Japanese Army transport. Like cattle in a car bound for the stockyards, the men were crowded on top of each other in the dirty, smelly holds, with no light and scarcely room to move. Each day they were given a very small ration of rice and a little water, never enough to quench their thirst. By the time they reached Manila three days later, most of the prisoners were sicker and weaker, struggling to climb up to the deck. Another POW had died.

They were taken off the ship and transferred to the Old Bilibid Prison, in the heart of Manila near Santo Tomas University in Manila, where allied civilians were held during the Japanese occupation of the Philippines. Bilibid served as a clearing house for POWs moving on to other inland camps on Luzon. It was considered a modern penal institution in its day and was the best accommodations the POWs experienced during their time as captives, although by no means adequate or comfortable in such crowded conditions. Unfortunately, it was merely a temporary transfer point, and the prisoners soon were on the move again. The shell game of moving POWs to various prison camps throughout the Far East continued for the duration of their captivity.

Now down to 1,193 POWs in his group, Chester and his fellow captives returned to the familiarity of Camp Cabanatuan in Luzon where they continued their previous lifestyle of constantly harsh treatment and meager rations. Allied forces, steadily advancing toward the Philippines, decisively recaptured the islands under Japanese control. In October 1944, as American troops closed in on the Philippines, the Japanese were forced to transfer Chester and his fellow POWs and friends back to Bilibid Prison in Manila. There, they awaited a ship bound for Japan.

On the home front, correspondence sent to prisoners held by the Japanese was processed by censors at the Prisoner of War Division in the War Department. Each card or letter could contain no more than 24 words, which had to be typed or block printed and easily recognized in the spaces provided. With such limited opportunity to stay in touch, choosing the right words to convey personal thoughts and information proved challenging and crucial. However, there was no guarantee the correspondence would reach its intended recipient. After approval by the censors, correspondence was forwarded to the Red Cross and was delivered via Switzerland through Tehran and then to Japan. The delivery process alone required more than a month and handling by multiple nations.

Chester's mother received a letter from the Provost Marshall informing her that Chester had been moved to another prisoner camp. The Army only knew this because a card from Chester, which they were processing, indicated a new address. Therefore, the card his mother had sent previously was returned to her. The Japanese rarely informed the U.S. regarding prisoner movements — required by the Geneva Convention — and refused to forward correspondence. Japan's intentional rejection of international law made communicating with loved ones nearly impossible and particularly cruel. Due to outdated addresses and agonizingly slow delivery by ship, prisoners rarely exchanged more than half a dozen cards or letters during their imprisonment. Lieutenant Britt's family received only four, small, fill-in-the-blank postcards during the 3 ½ years Chet was a POW.

In Manila, while waiting for transport at Bilibid prison, Chet made another friend, 1st Lt. Roy Bell, who served as a quartermaster. The duo discovered they had a lot in common as Lieutenant Britt had been tapped to be his unit's quartermaster at Fort Wint, one his many additional duties. They discussed their shared experiences and at one particularly low point, Roy expressed his pessimism regarding his survival chances; he wanted to send a letter home in case he didn't return.

Wall with crosses seen by 1LT Roy Bell from his cell in Bilibid Prison

Another good friend, 1st Lt. Edgar S. Gable, had received a letter from his wife, Marian, in late spring and had kept it hidden from the guards. Getting caught with writing materials — which always were in short supply — was strictly forbidden and those who were caught were subjected to harsh punishment — beatings that resulted in unconsciousness or possible death. By this point, prisoners had become very resourceful at obtaining scraps of paper, pens, and bits of pencils to record events in small diaries or on bits of paper saved and recycled from their Red Cross care packages. Most of the materials were wrapped in their shorts or G-Strings as the Japanese were reluctant to search their disease-ridden captives.

The letter was written on onion skin paper, which was translucent but lightweight and strong. It was popular for sending overseas mail at the time because it allowed more pages to be sent for no additional cost. Realizing Roy's desperation, Lieutenant Gable — in an act of ultimate generosity —passed his treasured 24-word letter to Roy. Using the remaining space on the page, Roy wrote two letters — one to his wife and the other to his parents and family members. His words expressed a deeply moving testimony of love for his wife, Mollie, and daughter, Ann, as well as his immediate family and friends. In them, Roy described his resignation to death as he awaited the upcoming sea voyage to Japan and detailed his medical condition and valiant efforts to stay alive. He hoped, above all, that if he didn't survive, they would be delivered after the war by someone who did. The letters included separate mailing addresses for each recipient and read, in part:

Please deliver in event of Death. If you know for certainty that
we got there (meaning Japan) OK. Please destroy same.

November 2, 1944

My Dearest Mollie and Ann

As tomorrow holds very little for the entire 2,000 prisoners, I wanted to leave a word or two … on October 18th like manna from heaven, we witnessed the first air raid on Manila by our Navy. My God, it was great — they bombed the airports and port area … all the boats in the harbor were sunk. God it was wonderful. Since that time we have had several air raids completely encircling this prison … during all raids we were pinned up in a two-story concrete bldg.— all windows closed — cannot see, only hear the bombs close — in the past few days reliable information has come in we have had several landings on the southern islands, they're establishing air bases — it is a certainty that if the Japanese put us on boats for Japan, the Americans will either bomb or torpedo it and this group of men are ready to die for less than that. The past three years has been hell on earth … it is not possible to write the horrible trials and experiences we have been through — mostly hunger — Mollie dear never allow Ann to be hungry the least bit — we have been on a starvation rice diet since concentration — at present we are eating 200 grams of rice per day = 2 meals only — with salt. In the past two weeks I have lost an additional 8 pounds now weighing 143. I have eaten dog meat, snakes, lizards, bugs, weeds, seeds, potato peelings from their garbage, anything and everything that had only a small amount of nourishment. At present I have Pellagra sores on the back of both hands — my mouth is sore from scurvy and my knees and legs are swollen very much from beriberi. My chest aches and pains continually. It is my opinion that I have T.B. … I really believe it better that I give my life … than return to you and Ann and be a burden the rest of my life. I have thought of you and Ann continuously both day and night and when conditions were rougher than usual, those thoughts and thoughts of returning home is the only reason I want to live … everyone look (s) like walking skeletons, just skin and bones. Harry Glenn and myself are buddies … on the concrete floor together with only one blanket and we are both so weak it is hardly possible to walk up and down the 18 steps to our area … immediately out of our windows are several long rows of wooden crosses of those who have died here either by the hands of the Japanese or starvation … starving is a funny thing, our biggest pastime is talking of meals in the past recalling different foods we have eaten and you know we enjoy those silly things.

Mollie dear, you have been a wonderful and true wife, the kind of wife a man only dreams of. Our daughter is sweet and perfect — God Bless her — keep her that way give her the best education possible and above all do not let her be hungry — as I have told you in the past, my insurance was increased to $10,000 — collect the backpay difference between the allotment — also a claim for $1,000 for personal items lost — all of which you know. All this should help you for a long period of time, use it wisely, and remember always that my last thoughts were of you and Ann — May God bless you and keep you both — I love you even in death. Regards to all my good friends, Don, Margaret, and Mr. and Mrs. O'Donnell — Roy

Lt Bell addressed the second letter to his parents:

Dear Mother, Dad, Sisters and Walter,

To say goodbye under these conditions are hard — I have always loved you all and cherish your thoughts — many, many times the thoughts of you kept me going over a rough spot — and to think after what we have been through over the past 3 years, lived thru this period, and to possibly die at the hands of our own army is not a happy one … but we have all reached the end and (are) ready to go under any conditions for we have ceased to live anymore, only slowly but surely starving to death … we are all very weak and can hardly get up to eat a small amount of rice and salt given 2 times a day — so you can see why we are ready to go. I have always loved you Mother and Dad, Sisters and Walter, however quite often I didn't show it … but in these last moments it is much more vivid than before — May God Bless you all. — Your son, Roy

As Lieutenant Bell noted in his letter, the U.S. Navy was attacking targets in the Manila area by October 18, 1944. The bombing prevented Japanese ships from entering and docking at the harbor without fear of them being damaged or destroyed. The U.S. naval attacks forced Japan to wait longer than planned in order to form a convoy of enough cargo, support, and escort ships to transport thousands of captured allied troops. The ships were headed to various camps in Japanese-controlled territory throughout the Far East, wherever slave labor was needed most.

At Bilibid, there was little or no work to earn food rations. The Japanese were short of food for themselves, and as a result, prisoners in all the camps suffered an ever-worsening situation, leading to starvation. They weren't eager to be transferred to Japan, but they had no control over their destiny.

Waiting for transfer by ship to Japan with little to do and endless time to think about the horrors to come, Chet already had stared death in the face every day for two-and-a-half years. The challenges ahead and his unending will to survive — under even more unbearable conditions than he and his fellow prisoners already had experienced — would once again test the limits of his courage, strength, and mental stamina. His relentless hope for a better tomorrow, his abiding faith, and his ceaseless desire to see his wife and newborn son for the first time had sustained him thus far. But how long could he last under the circumstances of an unknown future? Gathering himself for the next phase of captivity and despite the misery and death that are his constant companions, Chet decided to stay focused on life.

He was disappointed to learn his lifeline — his "brothers" 1st Lt. Bill Lewis and Max Wait — wouldn't be placed in the same group with him aboard ship. However, three of Chet's closest friends, Capt. Chan Baldwin, and 1st Lts. Gus Cullen and Bob Cooper, with whom he had reunited at Camp Cabanatuan, were scheduled to travel with him.

Hunger stalked the POWs continuously. Most conversations led to someone creating a favorite dish or recalling a favorite restaurant. Virtually every discussion mentioned food. Chester fantasized about every possible way to prepare and eat eggs.

By December 12, 1944, the daily diet at Bilibid prison consisted of only 200 grams of rice and a pinch of salt. There was nothing more available for prisoners who didn't — or couldn't — work. By this point, Chester weighed less than 120 pounds. He suffered the afflictions of malaria, dengue fever, and the early stages of beriberi. Along with thousands of other prisoners, Chester was in the poorest physical condition he'd ever experienced.

The Japanese never before had issued any clothing to POWs during their incarceration. But winter was in full force in Japan, located about 1,860 miles due north of Manila, and they'd soon leave warm, tropical breezes and high humidity for freezing snow and ice. For the upcoming voyage, Japan surprisingly issued the POWs one-size-fits-all woolen clothing — and the cigarettes from a recent Red Cross delivery.

Guards kept the remainder of the food and other items in the care packages as they, too, received barely enough food to overpower the weakened and sick POWs. Everyone knew food and water aboard the Japanese ships were rumored to be even worse than at the prison. The same was true for what was to become the prisoners' new "quarters." Before long, they'd be marched aboard ship, where they would experience nearly two months of hell no man ever could imagine — a hell harsher than they'd ever known. Most would not survive.

CHAPTER 6

Surviving Hell Among the Dead
(December 13, 1944 - January 30, 1945)

B efore dawn on December 13, as the prisoners slept on the cement floors of their cells, they were awakened suddenly by the guards and fed their usual meager breakfast — a teacup of rice and half a cup of water. After sunrise, 1,619 POWs were marshalled out the prison gates and marched two-and-a-half miles to a landmark they had seen before — Manila's famed Pier 7, the same Million Dollar Pier that Chet first set foot upon when he and Grace had arrived four years earlier, and where Grace left from on May 5, 1941 to begin her journey to their hometown of La Crosse, Wisconsin. The same emotions would have played out with almost all the men who similarly had come to Manila on many different ships, and if married whose spouses likewise left from that pier. Also, Chester had left there for the Davao Penal Colony and returned there as well. Most of the men were American soldiers, sailors, and airmen, but among the POWs were also 33 American civilians, 1 Australian civilian, 39 British soldiers, 1 Canadian civilian, 5 Czech civilians, 15 Dutch soldiers, 1 German civilian, and 4 Norwegian civilians. Of the total of 45 civilians only 6 Americans were to survive. Time and again, POWs of the Japanese have reported on how important it was to have a few close buddies to help survive, and chances are these outlier civilians were doomed to be almost on their own due to language issues, and other barriers to building up a buddy system.

About 300 POWs were left behind at Bilibid Prison, having been deemed too ill to travel, and unfit for the labor camps where prisoners needed to be healthy enough to work. Those left behind feared they either would be left to starve or shot by their captors. Neither, as it turned out, was true. Ultimately, they were the "fortunate" ones, rescued by American forces as they were fighting to retake Manila just six weeks after the POWs departed for Japan.

Along the march to the port area, Filipinos — lining the streets in front of burned-out buildings — whispered and signaled signs of encouragements as the men shuffled past, ignoring the guards' stern warnings to stay back and not interfere. Most of the POWs were barefoot and barely clothed, with no more than shorts or a loin cloth to cover their emaciated frames. Each man carried a small pack containing what little they possessed along with the shoes, woolen shirt and pants they had been issued the day before. It was the height of the dry season as the monsoons had subsided in October, and the temperature rose quickly after sunrise. The broken pavement of the war-torn streets slowed their advance to the port, but when they arrived, their spirits were lifted by the sight of dozens of Japanese ships — as far as the eye could see — partially sunk in the bay. Even more had sunk completely, settled at the bottom of the bay's murky waters.

When they arrived at Pier 7, the pier itself, with its massive, 3-story-high, concrete archway, was mostly undamaged, spared by Navy bombers for later use when the war was over. At nearly 1,000 feet in length, the pier could accommodate up to four freighters or two passenger ships on either side of its wide loading dock and another small freighter at the end of it. Its entire length was covered by a metal roof held up by steel beams and girders that supported heavy chains and pulleys to facilitate loading cargo from the warehouse facilities underneath. The prisoners were marched into one of the pier's huge warehouses where they were ordered to sit and wait. Large doors on either side of the structure were opened, which provided a welcome breeze and protection from the searing sun for most of the men. There were too many to fit inside, and the overflow of a few hundred unfortunate POWs were forced to sit on the sunlit dock.

As early as January 1942, initially small groups of POWs had been shipped to Japan to be used as laborers. With the fall of Bataan and Corregidor, the small stream turned into a flood of POWs heading to Japan on a variety of ships, some tolerable, many earning the term "hell ship" for their deplorable conditions. By the time the men were about to board their ship, already many of these unmarked ships carrying POWs had been sunk by American or British submarines and American planes, killing as many as 18,000 POWs by 1945.

This ship leaving Manila was to be the last one taking POWs to Japan. The Japanese command knew that MacArthur and his Americans would soon invade Luzon and drive towards Manila, and so this was a last chance to get slave laborers to Japan, and to evacuate their own citizens and military personnel.

Lieutenant Britt and the others soon would learn it was an accurate name, although they could not imagine anything worse than the sadistic brutality, that they had experienced for nearly three years. But they were about to find out just how cruel humans could treat one another.

As Chet and the other POWs watched the flurry of activity around them, they soon focused their attention on what looked like a nearby, converted passenger ship with the name Oryoku Maru painted on its bow. This was their transport to Japan. The ship, built in 1937 for luxury travel throughout the Orient, was just under 580 feet in length and weighed 7,363 tons. Its normal occupancy load was 863 passengers and about 100 crew. In 1943, the Imperial Japanese Navy ordered the ship to be requisitioned and re-fitted for war-time service to transport troops, cargo, and POWs throughout the Pacific theater of operations. On what was normally the promenade deck, two, large anti-aircraft guns were mounted on a reinforced area of the bow and one at the stern. Along the railings on both sides, a line of machine-guns had replaced the area where couples strolled hand in hand to watch the sunset. Teak deck loungers, usually filled with relaxing passengers, were replaced by stacks of ammunition stores for the weapons. The main parlor and passenger cabins had been stripped bare of their luxurious furnishings of overstuffed salon chairs, elegant draperies, and plush carpeting. In their places were the basic, functional necessities required to accommodate Japanese civilian evacuees, Japanese troops, and their weapons. With space at a premium, even high-ranking Japanese troops and civilians had no privileges of station or entitlement. The formerly beautiful ocean liner was now painted an ugly wartime green.

Hour after hour, the men watched the ship being loaded, hopeful they would be traveling to Japan in the relative comfort of the ship's cabins. Most of the cargo being loaded consisted of ammunition, fuel, baggage, four trucks, ashes of 782 Japanese Army war fatalities, and food. One unusual item caught their eyes — Gen. MacArthur's prized Packard staff car — one of the many spoils of war looted by Japanese troops and obviously destined for someone at the top tier of the Japanese Imperial Army hierarchy. With the final pallet loaded into the holds, passenger loading began. The POWs' spirits sank as about 600 Japanese women and children — many of whom were dressed in brightly-colored kimonos — walked past them and boarded. Next came about 1,200 Japanese Army troops and survivors of other ships the American carrier pilots had destroyed. The POWs were the last to board.

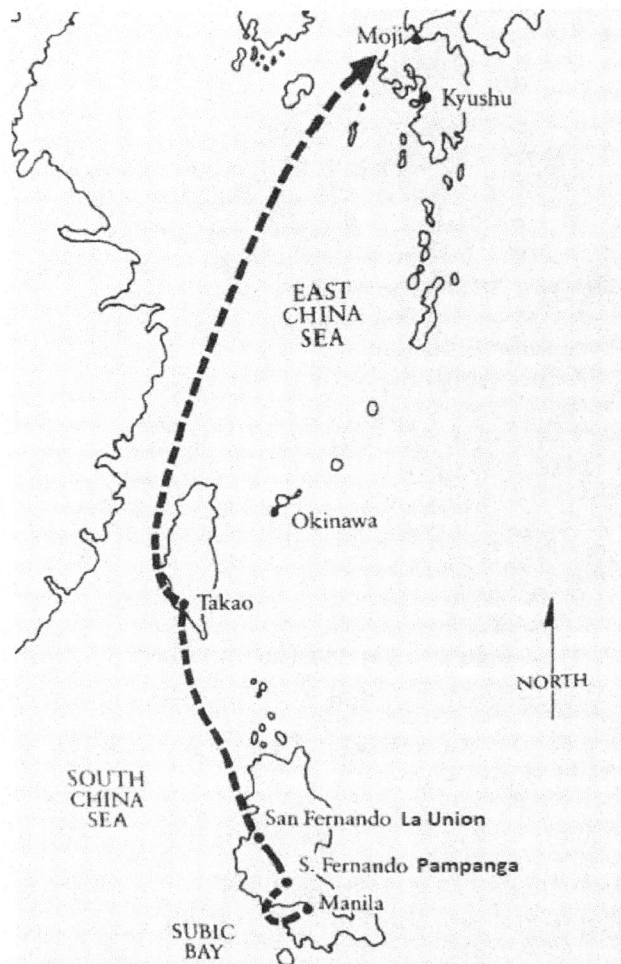

Oryoku Maru: from Manila to Subic Bay. Then overland from Subic Bay to San Fernando, Pampanga Province, then to San Fernando, La Union Province. Board the Enoura Maru and Brazil Maru at San Fernando, La Union and taken to Takao, Formosa. Lastly, the Brazil Maru from Takao to the Southern Wharf at Moji, Japan

Oryoku Maru painting by Kihachiro Ueda courtesy of the SHOKEI-KAN museum in Tokyo, Japan
https://www.shokeikan.go.jp/sub_menu/english_page.html

Copyright © しょうけい館 SHOKEI-KAN (Historical Materials Hall for the Wounded and Sick Retired Soldiers, etc.) The Shokei-kan is a national facility that collects, preserves and exhibits verbal testimony, historical materials, books and information about various hardships experienced during and after the war by sick and wounded servicemen, as well as their families, etc., and provides an opportunity for posterity to learn about those hardships

About 1 p.m., guards separated Chet and his fellow prisoners into three groups and ordered them into the three largest holds below deck. Approximately 600 POWs were loaded into bow hold, 200 in the center hold and 800 in the stern hold. In all, 3,419 passengers were crammed into a ship designed to carry only 843. **Lieutenant Britt was among group of 600 in the bow.** They all were weak and ill, and only one person could be accommodated on the ladder at a time. Upset with the slow pace of loading, guards hit the men with their rifle butts or shovels, often knocking them off the ladder into the holds below, causing dozens of men further injury. At the bottom stood four guards, one with a sword directing prisoners to specific areas while the other three swatted POWs with brooms, poking the men to stand even closer together.

Along the hull and ends stood two levels of cargo bays, each bay about 7 feet by 8 feet. The first prisoners in the holds were jammed into the bays, 20 men to a bay. To squeeze that many men into each bay required each man to sit with his legs splayed apart with the next man shoved against the crotch of the man behind him. In each bay, five men occupied each of four rows with no room to move about, let alone stand. With all the bays filled, the remaining POWs stood on the floor, packed so closely together, it was impossible to fall.

Four 5-gallon buckets were lowered into each hold and placed in the corners to collect human waste. After only two hours, the buckets overflowed, spilling their filthy, foul-smelling contents onto the floor. Several men passed the buckets up the ladder to be emptied, but the guards refused. The prisoners were forced to stand in the waste like rats in a sewer. It was even worse in the bays, where it was impossible to move about; men reluctantly relieved themselves where they sat. To the Japanese, they were nothing more than worthless cargo.

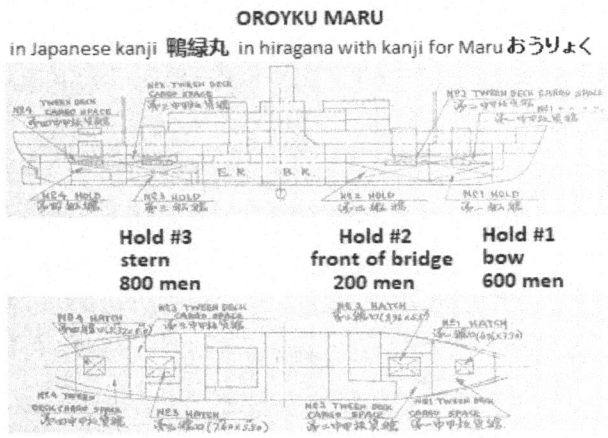

OROYKU MARU
in Japanese kanji 鴨緑丸 in hiragana with kanji for Maru おうりょく

Hold #3	Hold #2	Hold #1
stern	front of bridge	bow
800 men	200 men	600 men

By late afternoon, the POWs all had been loaded into the holds. With outside temperatures still in the 90s, and heat radiating off the metal hull, the men felt as if they were being baked in an oversized oven. Even the hull facing the sun was too hot to touch. Finally, just after 6 p.m., the ship's four, steam-turbine engines belched to life. The Oryoku Maru weighed anchor — and accompanied by the Japanese naval destroyer Momo and submarine chaser No. 60 — deftly maneuvered around the damaged ships, moved out into the bay, and dropped anchor for the night. Sailing during hours of darkness proved too hazardous due to the many sunken and damaged ships in the area. Additionally, submarines patrolled around the clock for moving targets to destroy. It wasn't long before men began passing out due to the heat and lack of fresh air from the single 8 by 10-foot hatch, about 40 foot above, especially for those crammed into the two tiers of bays along the sides of the hold. They began screaming for water and air. The noise became so loud it frightened the women and children above deck to the point where the interpreter from their prison camp days, Mr. Wada, a civilian hired by the Japanese Army, yelled into the holds, ordering the men to be silent. He threatened to open fire into the holds below and close the hatch if they didn't comply. The men settled down somewhat but still begged loudly for water and air. The interpreter, known already among the prisoners as a hateful, vengeful man, dropped the hatch cover and left the men to suffocate, starve or die of disease. It mattered not to him if they lived or died. The chief officer in charge of the POWs on the ship was Lt. Toshino who gave many of the directions to Wada to pass on to the men, and to whom Mr. Wada told about anything that was happening in the holds.

With the hatch closed, the men suddenly were hurled into complete darkness and foul-smelling air. The men quickly started to panic, yelling, grabbing, and cursing at one another. Some lost their tempers and began to fight, shoving and pushing for an advantage they thought would bring them relief. Suddenly a voice rang out in the darkness above the noise, pleading for them to stop fighting and settle down. The voice belonged to a naval officer who had climbed partway up the ladder so he could be heard. He called for those who had shirts to remove them and fan the air towards those in the corners and bays where there was little to no air circulation. His calming voice reduced the panic-stricken men as they began fanning the air. It helped somewhat but wasn't enough for them to survive. He climbed to the top of the ladder, and risking the ire of the interpreter, begged to put those in the worst shape on deck for a while. Surprisingly, the interpreter agreed — but he would allow only four at a time. If anyone tried to escape, they'd be shot. Guards removed the hatch, which brought immediate relief to those below. The unconscious men were passed overhead from person to person and then passed up the ladder. After a few minutes on deck, the fresh air had revived them, and they returned below to be replaced by four others. As a result, dozens of men survived who surely would've suffocated.

As the sun dipped below the horizon, guards lowered buckets of rice and soup into the hold, most of which was spilled before it reached the prisoners. Those with mess kits in their packs scooped a small serving of soup and a couple teaspoons of rice. Those who had no utensils, used their bare hands. Many men got nothing as the rations ran out. Chet was fortunate to get a teaspoon of rice and a bit of soup. No one received water. In the darkness, the POWs settled in for the night, but among them, Lt. Britt could hear shouts and complaints of men who were overtaken by panic and fear. They cursed each other for the slightest offense of accidentally bumping into someone's injured arm or leg, causing unbearable pain. Several men who could no longer bear the heat, the lack of oxygen and the lack of water, lost total control of their senses and became crazed, biting and cutting whoever was closest to them, sucking their blood in order to survive. Desperate to consume any liquid they could, some scooped urine from the buckets with their bare hands and drank it. Other POWs tried to subdue them, but the attackers were relentless in their mission to satisfy their thirst. The only recourse to prevent further attacks was unthinkable. But it had to be done. In the pitch-black darkness, POWs were forced to kill their fellow prisoners, beating them in the head with canteens until they were dead. As Lt. Emil Ulanowicz wrote in his diary the following day, "We had to kill them in self-defence."

Although Chet and his dwindling circle of friends heard everything that was happening, they managed to avoid the harrowing incident, concentrating instead on their own survival, and taking care not to offend. With the men on the verge of losing control, Lt. Col. Howard J. Edmonds, commander of Chet's POW group, ordered the men to stop shouting and fighting. Appealing to their logic, he explained they were using up precious oxygen and energy, which only would make things worse for everyone. The men responded and talked quietly among themselves. Some actually managed to get some rest or sleep.

Already that first night of December 13, the hellish conditions in the ship had claimed the first four victims, and it hadn't yet left Manila. Lives lost for no reason, just the start of many lives to be wasted. Lost to eternity were Lt Col Francis Sylvester Conaty, Major Maynard Goldman Snell, Capt. Mark Twain Goldstine, Jr., and Norwegian civilian Arthur Erik Lindstrom.

At 4:40 a.m. on December 14, the Oryoku Maru weighed anchor and slowly moved southwest with her two escort ships providing protection in case of attack. Her next port of call: Takao, Formosa (Taiwan). Normal cruising speed for the converted luxury liner was 18 knots — the equivalent of about 21 miles per hour. Basically, it was a sitting duck.

At daybreak, Chet saw several men with cuts and bitemarks on their arms and backs. He wondered what had happened in the other holds overnight and whether or not similar events had occurred.

The ship was making slow, but steady progress and by 9 a.m. had rounded the tip of the Bataan Peninsula. It sailed parallel to the coastline to avoid detection and was heading slightly northwest preparing to make a slow turn to the west just past Napot Point. Once the ship had cleared the country's largest island of Luzon on the west, it was to begin its trip north to Formosa. Unknown to the crew, a reconnaissance plane from the USS Hornet CV-12 was flying 5,000 feet overhead searching for targets of opportunity. The pilot spotted the ship and radioed the Oryoku Maru's location. F6F Hellcat dive bombers passed over the ship, went North to do some attacks north of Subic Bay, then came back to attack. About 9 a.m., just as the mess hands were handing out the morning's ration of rice, the Navy pilots located the ship again as it approached Sampaloc Point and began their bombing runs. This began a running series of attacks with no hits registered by bombs, but with multiple hits by rockets.

Note: The full sequence of the attacks is on our website. Our research found gun camera film of the attack at 9AM on December 14, 1944. More information on our website, includes knowledge previously unrecognized of aircraft from a second carrier, the USS Cabot, attacking the ship also. Lt

(USN) John Frank Thompson flying an F6F Hellcat from the USS Cabot was shot down during a divebombing attack at Sueste Point. Information on all of this can be located on our website.

The prisoners assumed they were either going to die, drown or be rescued. Each explosion dislodged tiny chips of rust off the hull, covering the men with a thin layer of reddish-orange metal flakes. The forgotten buckets of rice were covered, too — making it inedible — although eating had become unimportant at that moment. Concussions from the anti-craft guns and bombs rocked the ship with each attack, shaking the men. Pressing their hands to their ears to stifle the noise proved futile. They still could hear the chaos overhead. Children screamed and cried as Japanese officers shouted orders for troops to man the guns and keep firing. Others were ordered to extinguished fires and resupply the gunners with ammunition. At one point, a round from a Hellcat strafing run ricocheted off the frame of the open hatch, striking one of the POWs in the shoulder. Screaming in pain as searing, hot lead tore through his shoulder, he quickly passed out as a medic tried to stop the bleeding.

In the panic and confusion, Chet and his shrinking lifeline circle huddled together on the slimy floor and prayed for mercy. A bomb exploded near the ship, tearing a hole in the hull above the water line. The blast caused a few shrapnel injuries, and the handful of POWs who were doctors and medics, tended the wounded as best they could. The men quickly realized the damage was minimal and surprisingly, a blessing in disguise. The near miss had provided much-needed air and a cross-breeze. Above them, Japanese troops were being slaughtered where they stood as the rockets and bullets pummeled the ship, tearing holes in the deck above. Bodies of Japanese troops and civilians — wounded, dead or dying — were strewn about the deck, and fires raged throughout the galley, salon, and cabins on the main and upper decks. As troops were wounded or killed, others stepped in to replace them in a hopeless effort to defend the ship. Holes in the deck from rockets and machine-gun fire allowed in even more airflow to the holds, which the POWs cheered. But their elation subsided somewhat when blood from hundreds of Japanese casualties 30 feet above them began trickling through dozens of holes, dripping onto the men below.

The planes continued their attacks, bombing and strafing at will. The Oryoku Maru was damaged, and her escorts the destroyer Momo and sub chaser CH-60 left her. The captain then guided the crippled vessel into the west side of Subic Bay and he beached the ship at Sueste Point by 1030. The captain ordered temporary repairs to be undertaken while the ship was beached near Sueste point, close to where the 3" guns of Fort Wint had sunk a troop laden barge in December 1941. It was at this time that the planes from the Cabot attacked, and Lt Thompson was killed by anti-aircraft fire.

The Japanese, with no doctors aboard, ordered the American doctors and medics up top to care for their wounded and dying, who were scattered throughout the dining room, parlor, decks, and cabins. The Japanese, as usual, had not prepared for any medical needs during the voyage. The Americans worked into the night by candlelight, doing what little they could. Once the Japanese commander realized the futility of the situation, he ordered guards to escort the medical teams back to their holds.

They described scenes of horror among the dead and dying, stepping over hundreds of dead and wounded on deck and in the once luxurious first-class cabins. Mangled bodies burned beyond recognition were piled throughout cabins in the upper decks, which were unprotected from the attacks.

The anti-aircraft gun crews had been obliterated by machine-gun fire and rocket blasts. Most of the machine guns along the rails on either side of the ship had been blown off their mounts. Unrecognizable body parts of the gunners had landed atop ammo boxes and were scattered across the promenade deck. Nothing on deck was untouched by the Hellcats' relentless attacks.

BOTTOM PERFECTLY SMOOTH

Above photo DEC 14 1055   Then below photo at 1620

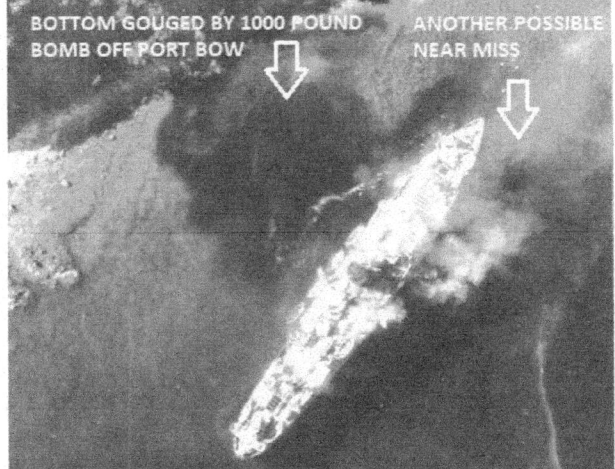

BOTTOM GOUGED BY 1000 POUND
BOMB OFF PORT BOW

ANOTHER POSSIBLE
NEAR MISS

Between the morning photo above and the late afternoon photo below taken by Hornet pilots, the Oryoku Maru was attacked by four F6F Hellcat dive bombers from the USS Cabot (CVL-28) all of which missed with their single 1000 pound bombs. The afternoon photo shows how close at least one 1000 bomb came to hitting the ship. Cabot pilot Lt John Frank Thompson was killed in this attack

That night, the ship backed off from Sueste Point and headed towards Olongapo where it anchored near the seawall. Above the moans of the wounded and dying, Chet could hear Japanese passengers being offloaded for the short trip to shore where they would be safer. At one point, a cable on one of the lifeboats snapped, dumping screaming women and children into the water. Wounded men with blank stares — obviously in shock — mumbled incoherently as they stumbled over those too injured or weak to move out of their way. Emaciated bodies stacked in the corner looked like they belonged in a horror movie. Dried blood caked on their skin, their sunken eyes gazed into an unknown void and their mouths were frozen in twisted screams. We can imagine Lt Britt, perhaps to escape the atrocious madness surrounding him, focuses mentally on Fort Wint, picturing in his mind the wonderful moments he'd spent there with Grace, the lilt of her voice, her loving smile, and the way she looked into his eyes. He thought of his son and wondered if he was healthy and whether he looked more like him or Grace. Doing anything to maintain his sanity in the surreal chaos of the dead and dying that surrounded him.

Before dawn all passengers had been removed, along with the wounded and dead. The only remaining people on board were the guards, ship's crew, and POWs. The prisoners hadn't eaten or had anything to drink in nearly 24 hours, and no food or water seemed forthcoming. The POWs spoke quietly and speculated whether or not they'd actually end up in Japanese prison camps since transport ships were becoming scarce. Perhaps they'd be left behind and be rescued by American forces as they advanced northward. A few men became unruly but were separated from the rest of the men and guarded by fellow POWs throughout the night to avoid a repeat of the previous night's horrors.

As morning broke on December 15, the prisoners were tempted to climb the stairs, but feared being killed by the guards, who had threatened they'd shoot into the hold if anyone tried to escape. Even with the extra air flow, the stench of urine, feces and decaying bodies wafted throughout the hold. The men were hungry, filthy, sick, weak, and wounded. Most importantly, they were in dire need of food and water.

At 9 a.m., Chet and his fellow POWs heard the unmistakeable hum of American planes with their powerful engines circling overhead, preparing to move in for the kill. The men thought they were doomed to die in the holds and steeled themselves for the inevitable. A bomb in the first wave of attacks scored a direct hit, opening a huge hole in the stern, instantly killing over 200 POWs and wounding dozens more. Suddenly, several guards leaned over the hatch opening and shouted excitedly, motioning for the senior officers in the group to climb up to the deck. Wearing only shorts or loin cloths wrapped around their waists, a dozen men scurried up the ladder as fast as they could. More men poured out of the holds with each pass.

The Japanese commander ordered the men to strip off all their clothes, jump overboard and swim to shore. Chet gathered up his canteen and mess kit in his ditty bag, tied the strings around his shrinking waist and waited his turn to climb up the ladder. It was slow going. The wounded were helped up the ladder first, followed by the sickest and weakest. When his turn came, Chet climbed the up as quickly as he could to escape the hell below. As his head cleared the hatch opening, he paused momentarily to take a deep breath and let his eyes adjust to the blinding sun.

Once on deck, he looked around to get his bearings. Stretching his arms as legs as he worked out the kinks from being confined, it felt good to move about and take in deep breaths of clean, fresh air, marveling at the bright, blue sky and thankful for the simple pleasures of life. Chet took note of the long, narrow beach to his left, with its 6-foot-high, concrete seawall, built to protect the low-lying coast. A row of hedges along the top of the seawall were framed by tall palm trees swaying in the breeze behind. To his right, another seawall, this one somewhat shorter, led to a small boat launch and dock at the near edge of the shipyard. He quickly recognized he was in familiar surroundings and did his best to hide a smile.

Chet was a mere 200-300 yards from where he had spent the early days of his short career enjoying weekends at the Officer's Club with Grace and their friends. The boat dock was where they took the scheduled launch back and forth across the bay to Fort Wint.

DOCK

POWs SWIMMING TO SHORE

END OF SEAWALL AND START OF BEACH

TENNIS COURT

December 15, 1944 photo taken at 0900 by a USS Hornet pilot. Chester Britt and hundreds of survivors of the badly damaged and listing Oryoku Maru desperately swim towards the shore

The guards interrupted his thoughts, poking at him with their rifle butts to move along so they could finish evacuating the ship before water filled the holds. He noticed a pile of life vests, an unexpected stroke of luck. Chet snatched one and put it on before guards could object. He struggled trying to figure out how to fasten it when a Japanese guard rushed toward him, adjusted it properly, and connected the straps in a rare act of humanity by his captors. Lieutenant Britt was an adequate swimmer, but in his current weakened state he wasn't sure he could make it to shore. His life vest secured, he was confident as he leaped off the foundering ship and dropped 30 feet to the water. As the cool water washed over him, he felt reinvigorated and more alive than he'd felt since he'd first become a POW, some 918 days before. The filth and grime slid off his body with each stroke as he paddled to the right toward the boat launch area. Many who couldn't swim floundered in the water and drowned. Some men located scraps of wood from the ship floating in the bay, which helped them stay afloat as they made their way to shore. A few accomplished swimmers, even in their weakened state, saved numerous fellow POWs, making several trips between the ship and shore to help those who couldn't swim, including one of the doctors.

While swimming to shore a Hellcat came low and as it saw the men in the water the pilot recognized the men as being Americans. He wagged his wings at the men in recognition and so they were not fired on by the Hellcats.

Determined no one would escape, the Japanese opened fire from a line of machine guns hidden behind the hedge above the seawall. The threat of being shot encouraged those who strayed too close to an invisible line in the water to change course. Some died from the indiscriminate fire while others managed to change course and head toward the boat launch where they joined other POWs gathered in a marshalling area. The remaining crew and guards enjoyed the luxury of returning to shore via a launch dispatched from the nearby shipyard. Typically, the ship's captain was the last to depart. He stood proudly in the launch, dressed in his white uniform, never to be seen again by the POWs.

With everyone ashore, the prisoners were marched about five blocks uphill and herded into a new "cell" — the naval base's outdoor tennis court. A concrete slab surrounded by a 15-foot-high chain-link fence provided enough space for two courts. In the center stood a wooden, referee's chair that had seen better days. Warped and weathered from too many years of exposure to monsoons and triple-digit temperatures, it served as a guard tower from which announcements and roll call were conducted. Guards allowed the prisoners to line up for water at a single tap.

Once everyone was settled in, each man had a few square feet of space to move around, more than in the holds, but not by much. Most of the men were either naked or close to it, and as the temperature rose, heat rising from the cement became inhospitable to bare bottoms and bare feet. With no nearby trees to shade them from the sun, water consumption would prove crucial to survival.

Shortly after noon, the Japanese commander took a count of his captives. Of the 1,619 POWs who had boarded the Oryoku Maru, 1,305 had survived. It was then Lieutenant Britt learned that a friend had been killed in the attacks on the ship. First Lieutenant Dean R. Keating, a friend from the 92nd Coastal Artillery Corps, Chester's old unit, was in one of the holds that sustained a direct hit.

NOTE: The Oryoku Maru actually held more Japanese civilians, as well as injured and sick Japanese military personnel, than the number of POWs, so it was as much of an evacuation ship as a POW ship. It is a mystery as to why the Japanese didn't BOLDLY announce to the Allies that this ship was both holding hundreds of Japanese civilian evacuees and 1,619 POWs, marked it, and lit it up so it would have been assured of safe passage to Japan. Thus, announced and marked, in prewar days, the Oryoku Maru could have easily reached Japan in 10 days with no loss of Japanese life, and even with the horrendous conditions in the hold chances are that at most 200~300 POWs would have died, and those that arrived in Japan would have been in better health and been better slave laborers. However, the U.S. strategy was sea interdiction of every ship that could be used for the Japanese war effort, meaning all shipping was being attacked regardless its use. No ships were spared.

As usual, the Japanese were ill-prepared to deal with unforeseen problems. For two days, as prisoners sat in the unbearable heat, they received no food whatsoever. Finally, at dusk on December 16, the Japanese brought large sacks of unhusked rice. Chet dipped the spoon from his mess kit into the sack and filled his canteen with water. He painstakingly removed the husks from each grain, his thick, untrimmed fingernails hindering the process. Even then, eating uncooked rice increased the prisoners' chances food poisoning — especially considering their current health status. Additionally, the husks were difficult to digest and their sharp, pointed ends could easily nick the digestive tract and colon, causing minor bleeding and ultimately, infection. But they had little choice. Eat whatever little nourishment the Japanese provided — or die of starvation. Some men were too hungry to remove the husks and suffered the consequences of excruciating stomach pain and diarrhea. It didn't take long before a line formed near the open-pit latrine that had been dug just beyond the fence.

Around the clock, doctors and medics tried to ease the pain, from wounds, to no avail. The wounded had enough room to lie down, and a few coats and a worn sheet hung on the fence, provided a few square feet of shade for those most in need. Prisoners with deep gashes or missing fingers were treated with fresh water from the tap and their wounds then covered with strips torn from a shirt that were rinsed and replaced daily. A corporal's severely mangled arm, sustained during one of the attacks aboard ship, had become infected, the dead tissue turning to gangrene. The limb dangled at an odd angle, barely attached to his shoulder. Without intervention, the doctor told him he would surely die. Amputation was his only hope. The corporal agreed. With no anesthesia and no surgical instruments available, two men held down the young corporal against the concrete. The doctor, using a razor blade he'd saved from a Red Cross care package, cut through tendons, muscle, and flesh while his patient screamed until the pain was so intense, he passed out. He died in agony three days later. With proper surgery and treatment, he might have survived.

While the Japanese tried to figure out what to do with them, the men adjusted to their new routine — endure unbearable heat during the day, eat a spoonful of raw, unhusked rice at dusk and shiver all night as temperatures dropped into the 60s. Normally, 60 degrees would be rather pleasant compared to the heat of day, but with little to no clothing or protection from the elements, the now sunburned and blistered POWs suffered around the clock. Chet was glad he still had his stained, threadbare shorts, which provided at least a bit of reprieve from the hot-to-the-touch concrete. Fearing the men would attempt to escape, the guards refused to allow the POWs even a few minutes of respite in the shade of a grove of trees less than a block away. The thought of escaping was laughable considering they could barely walk at a moderate pace let alone try to run away.

Day after day, the men passed the time discussing whether they'd still be shipped out to Japan, returned to Bilibid Prison, or taken into the jungle and executed. Or perhaps by some miracle, American and allied troops would swoop in and rescue them. Periodically, Hellcats would pass overhead, searching for targets. The men could hear anti-aircraft fire coming from the hills above and then a loud boom followed by an eerie quiet. They silently cheered the destruction of yet another enemy target, knowing each attack brought the war closer to its end. At other times, POWs also reported seeing the pilots wave their wings at the men in the tennis court to let them know they were Americans. Although bombing strikes were made nearby on Olongapo no strikes injured the POWs.

On their fourth day of confinement on the tennis court, the Japanese handed out an assortment of used clothing they'd scrounged from who-knows-where. Assorted pants, shirts, socks, and sandals were doled out with those who were completely naked — which was most of them — at the front of the line. There wasn't enough to clothe everyone fully, so no one received more than a single item — a pair of pants, a shirt, a pair of socks or a pair of straw sandals. That was it. Size was of no consequence. The shirts and pants hung on their skeleton-like physiques, but anything was better than nothing. Clothing items ran out before the line of POWs needing them; those who were naked and in better shape received nothing.

Still, the elements took a merciless toll on their bodies. Everyone was sunburned to some degree, with water blisters festering all over their bodies. It was impossible to shield themselves from the burning rays. Several POWs died from heat stroke, exposure, disease, or their wounds. They were buried in shallow graves near the tennis court or along the seawall with no time to mourn or honor their lives. One of them was a friend of Chet's, Captain Rollo D. Winne, who died sometime before sunrise on December 19.

Just after noon, six days after first setting foot on the tennis court, a convoy of trucks roared up to the gate and ordered half the men to get aboard. Lieutenant Britt and his lifeline circle of friends crawled onto the trucks, crammed together closer than even in the holds of the Oryoku Maru. They had no idea where they were headed and held their collective breaths as the trucks trudged over unpaved, jungle roads and up over the Zambales Mountains. Each rut and bump elicited shouts of pain from the severely wounded. Forty miles later, Chet realized where he was — San Fernando in Pampanga Province. Almost three years earlier, he had slogged down the exact same street on the Bataan Death March. It seemed like an eternity as his mind flashed back to that time and all the events he'd survived since.

The convoy came to a stop at the city jail where they were unloaded. Prisoners remaining at the tennis court were taken to the town's movie theater the next day as the jail was overcrowded. Nearly 30 men had died during their week-long confinement on the tennis court, and the men were exhausted and weary, getting worse by the day. Without adequate food, medical care and housing, more were certain to die.

Senior officers and those who were sick or severely wounded were taken into the jail and confined in unlocked cells with guards watching their every move. Everyone else, including Chet, was crowded into the jail yard, a 60 x 80-foot square area with practically no grass, just hard-packed dirt. A 20-foot fence topped with shards of broken glass was designed to discourage escape, and a shallow drainage ditch the length of the fence became their outdoor latrine. Before long, thousands of flies buzzed around the drainage ditch attracted by the odor of human waste.

That evening, the Japanese provided half a cup of cooked rice per man — Chet's first since being aboard ship — and a cup of water. It was a feast compared to what he'd eaten in the past week. Broken water pipes along the outer wall provided all the water he wanted. His shrunken belly felt full as over the next few days, the POW's rations increased to two meals a day. Each included a small portion of rice and one or two camotes — the equivalent of a sweet potato, only purple. Consuming just a little more rice and the vital nutrients from the camotes, the men rebounded, and their spirits soared. But it wasn't enough for Col. Harry J. Harper and Capt. George H Peets (misspelled as Petze in Chet's diary). They both died on the grounds of the jail yard.

The doctors and medics became increasingly concerned about the survival of the severely wounded men. They appealed to their Japanese captors to transfer their most critical patients to a hospital where they could receive the care they desperately needed. They grudgingly relented but allowed only 15 POWs to receive treatment at a Manila hospital, about 30 miles away. The Japanese guard commander, the interpreter and a few guards drove off with the wounded POWs. The doctors, medics and remaining POWs felt relieved. But it wasn't until a year after the war — revealed in affidavits filed for the military tribunals — that Chet and his fellow POWs learned that the commander, interpreter, and guards had no intention of carrying out their orders. Instead, they drove the wounded to a cemetery about 10 miles outside the city of San Fernando. One by one they mercilessly were executed — shot, bayoneted, or decapitated — and buried.

At 3 a.m. on Christmas Eve day, after three more days of "camping" outside in the jail yard, Lieutenant Britt and his fellow POWs were awakened by the guards. Those who didn't respond immediately felt the sharp impact of a rifle butt to now-protruding ribs. Being awakened so early Chet knew something was up, but had no idea what it could be as he'd heard no rumors concerning what the Japanese had planned. The temperature had dropped into the 60s overnight, and he shivered at the stiff, cool breeze assaulting his body. Still wearing only his tattered shorts, Chet, along with those in his group, stomped their feet on the hard ground to get their blood circulating in hopes of getting warm. They knew the temperature would soar into the 90s by midday, but right now, they were cold and mildly upset they'd been awakened in the middle of the night.

Shortly after sunrise, the POWs were escorted out of the prison compound and marched down the city's main street, joined along the way by those being held at the movie theater. As they walked, Filipinos began lining the street, helpless to lend a hand. Many of the men were former Philippine Scouts or guerrilla forces who had fought alongside them but covertly merged back into the local populace when the Japanese arrived.

Dirty, disheveled and some naked, the men shuffled along, staring at the man in front, but stealing a glance at bystanders when the guards' attention was focused elsewhere. The POWs had been through this exercise at least once before. The children stared at them quizzically while women put their hands to their faces and looked away in embarrassment. Some inconspicuously nodded their support and thanks, and Chet occasionally heard the high-pitched voice of a child innocently offering a soft-spoken "Merry Christmas."

About 45 minutes later, they arrived at their destination, which — even though it was now warm — sent a chill through Chet and those who'd survived the Bataan Death March. They were at the San Fernando train station, the same place they'd boarded a train three years before, during the Death March, on their way to Camp O'Donnell. Lieutenant Britt remembered the long, hot, deadly trip and the dozens of men who'd suffocated in the small, crammed cattle cars after enduring the horrors of the deadly march. A similar train now awaited them on a siding, and the men were ordered to start boarding immediately. Chet knew to find a place near the boxcar's entry or along one of the walls of the boxcar and informed his lifeline circle to do the same to ensure they could breathe and keep track of one another.

The train's metal roof and sides were rusty and damaged from years of neglect. Chet feared its rickety roof would prove no match from an aerial attack. He knew a moving train was easily spotted from aerial patrols and an enticing target for American pilots. But the Japanese already had taken Chet's concerns into consideration. They ordered the sick and wounded to ride on top of each car, figuring if enemy pilots spotted the train, the wounded men would wave their arms as the POWs had done on the Oryoku Maru and wave off the attack. If not, they probably wouldn't survive the trip anyway, so sacrificing them might be to their advantage — a problem they'd no longer need to deal with on the voyage to Japan.

A hundred men once again crammed into each box car in a space not comfortable for more than 40. Another 15 to 20 wounded sat or laid on top, their weight slightly caving in the roof over Chet's head. As they boarded, the men learned they were headed to another San Fernando, this one in La Union Province, about 60 miles north. From there, another transport ship would pick them up and take them to Japan. The boarding process was slow, and about 8 a.m., the engineer released the brake on the single steam engine, and the train lurched forward, chugging away from the station at an agonizingly slow pace.

The box cars smelled of cattle, and as the temperature in the box cars rose to more than 100 degrees, sweat rolled off their bodies in large drops. The smell of wet straw combined with human waste and cattle manure, became intolerable. Some men gagged or vomited from the strong, inescapable odor. POWs in the center of the car passed out where they stood and were shifted through the maze of prisoners to the edges where they could get a few moments of fresh air. At several stops along the route to take on water and coal, the men could see bombed-out railcars, some still smouldering from a recent attack.

The train pulled into the station at San Fernando La Union, a short distance from San Fernando bay, just before midnight. The POWs hadn't had any water or food since the night before at the jail yard. After 17 hours of standing, it took every ounce of their energy to climb out of the cramped cattle cars. Chet, completely exhausted, collapsed on the station's platform and promptly feel asleep. Guards quickly realized the prisoners were too spent to attempt escape and stood guard overnight where they dropped. At sunrise on Christmas Day, the exhausted men were marched 2~4 miles southerly (affidavits after the war by the survivors for war crimes trials vary about the distance) to a schoolyard where they were fed half a cup of cooked rice and a cup of water from a nearby, foul-smelling well. Somewhat revived, they spent the day sitting and sweating in the blazing sun. At dusk they were given another half cup of cooked rice and suspicious-smelling water. Several wounded men died in the schoolyard during the day, plus a few more who had succumbed from heat stroke after the long train ride and sitting all day in the 90-plus-degree heat. This short trek for such ill and weak men had become a mini-Death March, but without the bayo-netting, shooting, and bludgeoning that had happened on Bataan. Now they just died because their bodies gave out. In the middle of the night, for no apparent reason, the prisoners were awakened and marched about 3 miles west to the beach near Poro Point. They stopped on the peninsula. On the north was San Fernando bay, and on the south was Lingayen Gulf where the bulk of Japanese troops had come ashore three years earlier and where — unknown to anyone at the time — American forces would do the same in about three weeks. They walked by damaged oil storage tanks which unknown to them had been hammered by planes from the USS Ticonderoga on the day the Oryoku Maru was sunk in Subic Bay.

After sunrise on December 26, they were fed one rice ball each, but no water. Some men were so thirsty they scooped up sea water and drank it, suffering an agonizing death. Chet sat on the dunes on the Lingayen Gulf side with his close-knit friends, covering his feet and legs in sand to protect as much of his body as he could from the offending sun. In late afternoon, Chet's POW group commander, Lieutenant Colonel Edmunds — the man who had encouraged the POWs to calm down during the murderous chaos aboard the Oryoku Maru, died on the beach. He was buried along with Pvt Floyd J Moyer who died that day.

As Lieutenant Britt ate his evening meal of one teaspoon of raw rice and sipped his half cup of water, he watched the sun dip below the hori-zon across the entrance to the Lingayen Gulf and beyond, the China Sea. Watching the last slivers of light, he wondered how long he would spend on the beach and how long it would be until he held his loving Grace in his arms. His last thought at night, and his first thought upon wakening was of Grace. Always Grace. He constantly prayed for blessings on his family as well as his own protection and survival. His determination to be reunited with his wife and meet for the first time his now 3-yr-old son and name-sake, consumed every waking moment.

A full moon overhead cast eerie shadows on the sand as he drifted off to sleep. The sand dunes provided some protection from the increasing onshore winds, but the men still slept on their sides, back to belly to conserve body heat. Sleep was hard to come as they spent another night shivering from dropping temperatures and a moderate, cool breeze.

Shortly after midnight on December 27, the men — now numbering 1,235 — were awakened, divided into groups, and marched to across the dunes to the San Fernando side of the small peninsula. The L-shaped wharf was stacked high with supplies, and the men could see the outlines of several ships at anchor just offshore. The smokestacks of a dozen or more sunken combat and transport ships poked up out of the water at odd angles, their missions cut short by American and allied pilots.

The men walked out onto the wharf, between the supplies. The Japanese were eager to get the men loaded and shouted at the POWs to jump eight feet below onto the deck of a shuttle barge. Those who moved too slowly were pushed off the pier by the guards and many POWs suffered broken bones as they landed awkwardly on the rusted, steel surface. Barges swiftly moved back and forth transferring the men from dock to ship.

The Enoura Maru was the first ship to be loaded. Chester and his buddies stayed close to ensure they'd be loaded aboard together. One of the POWs miscalculated his jump, hit his head on the top edge of the barge and fell into the water, dying instantly. The ship's captain, eager to leave and fearful of being attacked in the harbor, shouted at his crew to get the men up the rope ladders quickly. After 1,040 had come aboard, he signaled he was ready to get underway and weighed anchor before more POWs could be loaded.

The Enoura Maru, built in early 1944 as a cargo ship, weighed in at 6,968 tons. Just under 450 feet in length and 60 feet wide, its four steam engines pushed the fully-loaded vessel through the water at a dismal 10 knots — a little over 11 miles per hour. As far as he could tell, the prisoners were the only passengers aboard other than the guards and crew. There were no anti-aircraft guns or machine-gun mounts, making the ship nearly defenseless except for the rifles carried by the guards and depth charges on the stern to ward off enemy submarines.

ABOVE photo of PORO POINT used for target planning - from FOLD3.com BELOW from a series of pre-war photos used by the OSS for invasion planning showing the L-shaped pier at ground level - from the collection of the authors

Sketch from the book BLOOD BROTHERS by Col Eugene C Jacobs showing boarding barges at the pier, the last place any Oryoku Maru survivorts were on Philippine land as POWs.

All the men were directed into the second hold just behind the bow hold. As the men continued their slow climb down the ladder, Lt. Frederick B. Browne, waiting his turn at the ship's edge, suddenly jumped overboard. Guards opened fire, killing him as he swam away. The excitement of the escape attempt over, Chet was encouraged when he reached the large hatch opening. It would provide more fresh air and perhaps more circulation, and hopefully, reduce the fear of suffocation. But as he climbed down the 30-foot ladder into the hold, an overwhelming stench of ammonia caused him to cough and gag. His lungs burned, and he gasped for air. Stepping off the last rung onto the wooden floor, his eyes adjusted to the reduced light, and he realized the floor was covered with a thin layer of straw that had soaked up horse urine and manure. His eyes began to sting and water, and he wondered how he'd ever survive. The Japanese hadn't cleaned out the hold from its previous four-legged occupants, and Chet now realized why the hatch opening was so large. Horses were a prized commodity to the Japanese during the war. POWs had no status whatsoever.

The hold was similar in size to the one he'd occupied on the Oryoku Maru, but there were no tiers for smaller cargo along the ends. A few buckets for human waste were spread around the hull. The men were once again crammed together with little room to crouch let alone sit. Many of them had suffered injuries jumping into the barges, and the medical teams tried to splint broken limbs with small pieces of wood they found scattered around the edges of the hold. Chet's group maneuvered to a spot along the hull figuring the stench wouldn't be as bad there since its most likely escape route was through the hatch in the center.

They hadn't eaten since they were on the beach, and hunger overtook their better judgment. Someone had found a few grains of oats or barley among the urine-soaked straw and the men — desperate for a morsel of anything close to edible — scrambled to find even a single piece of grain to retrieve whatever had spilled out of the horses' feed buckets. Thousands of large horse flies buzzed at their feet, feasting on the manure while men squinted to pick a grain of half-eaten oats that had landed on the manure. It was a sickening sight, but hunger did strange things to the starving men.

Heading north in the open waters of the South China Sea, a U.S. Navy submarine spotted the freighter and fired three torpedoes, but the captain maneuvered the ship to avoid being hit. The POWs were fed one half cup of cooked rice and four teaspoons of water. As soon as the rice buckets were lowered into the hold by rope, the flies descended on the rice. The flies were so thick the men couldn't even see the rice by the time it reached them. But to starving prisoners, flies were of no consequence. If a fly happened to land on a grain of rice as it was being consumed, it was considered a bonus. As usual, the ship laid up off the coast of one of the islands between the Philippines and Formosa to avoid detection and dropped anchor for the night.

Getting weaker and sicker every day, some of the men openly wished for the ship to be bombed in order to end their suffering. They almost got their wish. On December 29, the ship's air raid warning sounded, and the men could hear planes overhead. Pilot's dive bombed on the Enoura Maru and convoy, but missed their target, and left after just a few bombing runs, most likely low on fuel or ammunition.

As the ship steamed northward, the water temperature continued to drop. Chet could feel cold air coming off the steel hull and drafting down through the partially open hatch. It felt like he was in a refrigerator. He longed for the wool pants and shirt he'd been issued — and the shoes — which would've protected his feet from the half-frozen excrement that now covered the floor. But the heavy clothing had to be left behind in the bombed-out hold of the Oryoku Maru in Subic Bay. The men — most without any clothing or just a G-string or loin cloth fashioned from the remnants of a shirt or pants — contracted pneumonia. They shivered constantly and longed for the tropical weather of the Philippines, which they'd cursed only days before. Huddling together to keep warm was a pipe dream, but they did it anyway if just to make them feel better. Their body temperatures had dropped so low they could no longer see the condensation of their breath when they talked or exhaled. As men died from their wounds or disease, they were lifted up the ladder and their bodies tossed overboard with no more than a short prayer by the chaplain, who was then escorted back into the hold.

To make matters worse, the wind and waves had picked up in the open ocean. The ship, which sat higher than normal in the water due to its relatively light load, caused the men to stumble around the hold, falling over one another, which resulted in even more pain to the wounded. But in one crucial respect, it worked to their advantage. On one occasion, when torpedoes were fired at the Enoura Maru, it was sitting so high in the water the men crouched in fear as they heard the torpedoes approach — and pass right under them.

Whenever the guards weren't looking, we believe Chet updated his diary written on scrap paper and hid these scraps in his loin cloth. The pages had finally dried out from his swim to shore when he abandoned the Oryoku Maru off the coast of Olongapo. When he couldn't document what had happened, he memorized information to add later.

Note: Transferring the scraps to a small notebook, probably did not occur until the Spring of 1945. The 2-inch by 4-inch journal, with its onion-skin pages, was Chet's way of documenting his experiences. He risked and protected it with his life. If the guards discovered it he faced potential execution. It was always close by, tucked in his loin cloth — a place he knew the guards would never inspect — along with a pencil or two from the Red Cross care packages he'd received. Due to the diary's size, Chet kept the words to a minimum, including just the main details — date, location, what he ate and people he knew who had died or sometimes the number of men who had died on a particular day. Many of the POWs had diaries, which became invaluable evidence at several post-war tribunals.

On December 31, New Year's Eve, after five days of sailing north following the island chain to Formosa, the Enoura Maru entered the calmer waters of the harbor at Takao's port (now Kaohsiung, Taiwan). The men received no food that day, only a total of eight spoons of water. The Brazil Maru, the smaller freighter the POWs had seen when they boarded the Enoura Maru, left a few hours after them and dropped anchor on the western side of the harbor. The ship had departed carrying the remaining 195 POWs from San Fernando, La Union. Standing in the filth of the wet straw and the stench from their own waste that had overflowed in the buckets the guards refused to empty, Chet thought about his experiences on the Oryoku Maru and the Enoura Maru. It had been 18 days since he'd left

Manila, and he began to understand what hell was like. He certainly had lived through the most heinous, sadistic savagery known to man. But it was about to get worse.

New Years Day brought no celebration as the weather had become even more brutal and depressing. Covered in grime, and with several weeks' growth of bushy beards and disheveled, unwashed hair, the men were becoming unrecognizable. Eyes sunken into their sockets made cheek bones protrude as much as the ribs in their sunken chests. Lieutenant Britt had lost so much weight he looked like a walking corpse. Several prisoners were near death from starvation, sickness, and exposure to the bitter cold temperatures. Hope was hard to come by in such barbaric circumstances. Two scant meals of rice and water that day certainly was welcome, but Chet and the others knew their current rations couldn't sustain life. They worried how much longer it would take to reach Japan; many knew they probably wouldn't survive the trip unless conditions improved.

The Japanese offloaded their troops and most of the crew. The surviving Dutch troops were offloaded to be transported to an inland POW camp where they would be confined with other Dutch prisoners. A few of the lowest-ranking Japanese guards were left behind to ensure there were no escape attempts. For four days, as the Japanese troops celebrated New Years, the prisoners — basically abandoned — received no additional food or water even though there was plenty available.

They became restless not knowing what was happening above deck.

On January 2, 1st Lt. Boder D. Jordan, part of the medical team, was coming down the ladder, slipped and fell to his death. He landed on 1st Lt. Emil Ulanowicz, which broke several of his ribs. Emil somehow survived and thought how unlucky it would've been to survive the bombings, beatings, and brutality of the Japanese only to die in a freak accident. The following day, Chet noted in his diary that he lost one of the closest friends in his lifeline. First Lieutenant William Roy Bell, who'd written a note to his wife in Bilibid Prison fearing he wouldn't make it home, died from starvation, dehydration, and exposure. His premonition had come true. Like so many others, he left behind a family, and a little daughter who would never see her daddy come home.

First Lieutenant Bell was one of eight prisoners who had died in the past two days from similar causes. The senior officer begged the interpreter for more food but was told that since American submarines were sinking Japanese supply ships, there would be no food.

October 1941 Lt William Roy Bell with daughter Shirley Ann, age 7, taken in Albuquerque, New Mexico. This was the last time she saw her daddy before he left for the Philippines. Such a final scene was repeated too many times in too many homes around the world.

Between January 5 and 9, as the ship sat at anchor, another 18 men died. Among them were two more of Chet's friends noted in the diary

— Commander Warner P. Portz, who died on January 7, and 1st Lt. Gordon S. Benson, who died on January 8. Not wanting to throw the bodies overboard — fearing they would float ashore — they were stacked in a corner of the hold.

During that time, on January 6, about 240 men were moved to the bow hold, which had been emptied of its cargo. It was much cleaner and provided more room for the men in both holds. Another 185 troops who'd survived their journey in the Brazil Maru, were transferred to the Enoura Maru and joined their fellow prisoners in the bow hold.

When he awoke on January 9, Chet discovered the men lying on either side of him had died during the night. Too weak to move them to the increasing pile of those who had died, he stayed where he was; their bodies provided some protection from the cold breeze flowing into the hatch. About 11 a.m., he heard the familiar sound of American planes overhead and braced for an attack. The Enoura Maru had the misfortune of being tied up to a nearly identical tanker at a mooring buoy making them combined a particularly fat target in a harbor full of targets.

He could hear the whistle of a bombs getting louder and closer. The ship shook violently as bomb after bomb exploded just above him. A direct hit on the bow-hold instantly killed about 250 men and wounded dozens more.

A bomb exploded near the aft hold, blasting away nearly a third of the deck directly above Chet. Another bomb exploded as it hit the hatch cover above, sending steel beams onto the men below crushing them to death. Hundreds more were wounded by flying debris. Once the planes had released their load of bombs and rockets, pilots began their strafing runs. As he laid on the feces-filled straw — with planes unleashing bursts of fire from their wing-mounted machine guns — Chet heard a soft voice in his head urging him to move. He was so weak he could barely lift his arm, but he crawled up and over one of the dead bodies next to him. Exhausted, he let gravity take hold and his body rolled back onto the straw, leaving a small space between the dead prisoners. Just as his body came to rest, Chet could hear bullets impacting the deck and streaking into the hold, whizzing not far from his head.

ENOURA MARU

CV12 521 9 JAN 45 U00 9 K 17 12" 8000' TAKAO,FORMOSA CON

ENOURA MARU

KUROSHIO MARU

BELOW bomb hit locations

When the attack ended, the sun was directly overhead, its rays pouring into the hold filling it with bright light. Lieutenant Britt slowly raised his head, opened his eyes — and saw hell. Among the hundreds of men who had been killed instantly when the deck was blown apart, dozens of prisoners had somehow survived among the dead. Trapped under wooden beams and twisted, steel girders too heavy to move, the men cried out in agony for help, but couldn't be saved. Most were missing arms or legs. Others had been decapitated. Blood from hundreds of mangled bodies flowed onto the straw floor forming little pools of red. Several sustained broken backs and pelvises. More beams and metal dangled precariously above his head, threatening to drop into the hold at any minute. Then he saw it — a line of bullet holes had pierced the floor where Chet had lain just moments earlier. The voice in his head had saved his life. To Chet, it was either the voice of a guardian angel or perhaps the Holy Spirit. He had been struck by shrapnel, but he was alive and said another prayer of thanks.

No one, it seemed, escaped injury. The Japanese provided a few bandages and mercurochrome to help prevent infection, but it was woefully insufficient for the prisoners' needs. There was no way to help the severely wounded, and Chet could only watch as men bled to death among the rubble. Bodies and body parts were stacked in the center of the hold providing a venerable feast for the flies.

The surviving medics and doctors used clothing from the dead for bandages and stabilized broken arms and legs with splinters of wood they found among the broken beams. Chet's shorts were used to bandage his shrapnel wounds, and he, too, was now without clothing. First Lieutenant Robert G. Cooper, a close friend and West Point classmate who traveled with Chet and Grace to the Philippines three years earlier, perished in the attack. In all, the Enoura Maru suffered two or three direct hits from bombs. There were so many unidentifiable dead, Chet did not know Lt Bob Cooper had been killed until some time later.

The men remained in the hold without food or water for three days following the attack. Those still alive — barely — were either sick or wounded. Everyone was malnourished and starving. Nearly 15-30 men died each day, their bodies stacked atop the decaying, bloated, and dismembered bodies of those who were killed.

On the second day after the attack, the men were ordered to place the dead in a cargo net, which had been lowered via a rope pulley. When about 20 bodies were placed in the net, it was lifted out of the hold and the mostly unrecognizable remains were lowered into a barge tied up alongside the ship. The chaplain said a short prayer and the process was repeated until about 150 of the dead were removed. They were taken ashore, stacked like cordwood, set afire and their ashes buried in a grave along the beach.

The process was repeated the next day with another 150 bodies, which were buried in a mass grave near Takao's harbor.

The smell of explosives and death still hung in the air, and Chet's chances of survival became slimmer each day. He'd watched hundreds healthy soldiers wither away and die from starvation, battle wounds or torturous beatings. Each time he found himself in a downward spiral, he thought of Grace, which renewed his determination to survive. Instead of focusing on all the bad things that had happened, he concentrated on the positive. First and foremost, he was alive, and he promised himself he'd doing everything in his power to stay that way. He may not have been in the best of health, but he had his Grace. He had his family. And he had his faith. They were his touchstones for survival.

October 1940 (L) Bob Cooper and Chet in happier times chatting on the USAT Grant headed to the Philippines

By early afternoon on January 12th, 900 prisoners began the slow process of transferring to the Brazil Maru. Many were unable to climb the ladder to the deck, so the men used remnants of rope and splintered wood to create a makeshift litter. Those too ill to stand due to dysentery, and men who had sustained broken backs and pelvises suffered excruciating pain as they were hoisted topside. Shivering in the 40-degree temperature, the men were loaded onto a cargo platform in groups of 20, lifted high enough to clear the deck, swung over the freezing water below and then lowered to a tugboat. It then took the prisoners across the harbor to the Brazil Maru. Once they reached the ship, the men had to traverse two cargo barges that were tied up alongside. Some were able to walk, but others needed to be carried. Then it was another 30 feet up a ladder and down into the center hold — Chet's third hell ship. As Chet helped his friend Capt. Chandler Baldwin get into the barge, he wondered if it, too, would be attacked like the others.

The Brazil Maru had been emptied of POWs and Japanese troops to make room for a load of sugar, although mostly it was used to haul coal. As the smallest of the three hell ships, it was 385 feet long, 50 feet wide and weighed 5,860 tons. Its single steam engine and boilers had seen better days and black smoke escaped from holes in its bullet-ridden smokestack. The ship had been lightly damaged in the attack, and the Japanese scrambled to make repairs and shift cargo out of the center hold to accommodate the unexpected prisoners. Once aboard, the men were fed their first meal in three days — a half-cup of cooked rice and a few teaspoons of water.

It was in in better shape than the Enoura Maru, although it had been built in 1919 and had been plying the waters of the Orient for a quarter century. The hold was covered with a layer of coal dust, which kicked up as the men shuffled about to find a place to rest.

Brazil Maru

Sketch by Col. Eugene C Jacobs from his book BLOOD BROTHERS .
Note snow on the deck above the open hatch of the Brazil Maru

Like the Oryoku Maru, the hold was designed to carry cargo, not men and small bays lined its outer edges. Each one was no bigger than 10 feet by 15 feet and about 4 feet high, too small for the shortest of the men to stand. At 6-feet 3 inches tall, Chet could either sit with his legs extended or lie down with his knees drawn up to his chest. Twenty men were crammed into each bay, and even though there remained just over half of the men who had begun the voyage to Japan, being confined to one hold made it impossible to be comfortable. The sick and severely wounded occupied the center of the hold, where doctors and medics could care for them, although little could be done.

At this point, eight people comprised Chet's lifeline circle. Capt. Chandler "Chan" L. Baldwin (West Point class of 1938) and 1st Lt. August "Gus" Cullen (West Point class of 1940 and a classmate of Chet's) had served with Chet since being stationed together at Fort Wint. The others included three of Chet's 1940 West Point classmates: 1st Lt. John Presnell, 1st Lt. Joseph "Joe" V. Iacobucci and 1st Lt. Robert "Trigo" I. Wheat. Rounding out his lifeline circle were Maj. Robert D. Glassburn, West Point class of 1932 and Capt. Harold "Captain Jimmy" A. Jimerson. Finally, the most seriously wounded of the group was 1st Lt. Hector Polla, who graduated from West Point a year behind Chet and had served as an usher at Chet and Grace's wedding. He had been injured during the bombing attack on the Enoura Maru. His wounds had become infected, and signs of gangrene had begun to appear. No longer able to care for himself, the men vowed to feed and care for him despite the foul-smell from his oozing flesh. Without their help, death was a certainty.

By early evening, the prisoners could hear the unmistakable sound of the ship's anchor being raised. The Brazil Maru joined a convoy of half a dozen ships making the little over 1,000-mile voyage to Moji, Japan. The convoy sailed out of Takao Harbor, turned north along Formosa's western shore, and headed for the East China Sea. Since it wasn't overloaded with heavy equipment, the Brazil Maru cruised at only 10 mph, which meant the trip would normally take about four days. But this was war, and nothing was normal. Submarines still patrolled the frigid waters, and to avoid detection, the convoy continued zig zagging between islands during the day and dropped anchor along the coasts at night, just as other hell ships had done.

The prisoners were in the worst condition of their lives, suffering from wounds that wouldn't heal due to malnourishment and insufficient medical care. Mentally and physically, they were exhausted and suffered from dehydration, dysentery, exposure, and starvation. Although the men received two meals a day of half a cup of cooked rice and a few teaspoons of water, their bodies had shed fat and muscle at an alarming rate during captivity, and they had no means of maintaining their body heat. Clothing was practically non-existent for most of the men, and those who died were stripped of their tattered garments, which were passed to the neediest among them. Upon arrival in the port at Moji, Japan Chet at 6'3", weighed 110 pounds and found it difficult to walk.

There was no hatch cover, which had been damaged in the attacks in Takao harbor. A flimsy tarp was the prisoners' only shield from snow, rain, and wind. It didn't provide much protection, letting in frigid air every time a strong gust of wind unlashed one of the frayed ropes holding it in place. A single, 5-gallon bucket was lowered into the hold to be used only by those too weak or wounded to climb the ladder to a "latrine" on deck. It was a waist-high, wooden box that stuck out over the edge of the ship and accommodated two men at a time. Those strong enough to climb the ladder were directed to the box while two men waited at the top of ladder peeking under the tarp to see when the duo in front of them here heading back. With 900 prisoners on board, the latrine always was in use, which meant cold air constantly blew throughout the hold. The coldest area was right below the hatch, and Chet and his lifeline circle stayed in a bay as far away from it as possible.

As they crept farther north, temperatures dropped and so did the men. Deaths averaged 27 a day, mostly from infected wounds or exposure to the frigid air. The temperature rarely hit 20 degrees, and the POWs began to cough and struggle for air as pneumonia attacked their lungs. High fever and delirious, it was a merciful death compared to the agony of the wounded, who with adequate care, would have survived. The dead were stacked beside the dying near the hatch opening. Each morning, one by one, their ankles were bound with a rope and their naked bodies hauled up onto the deck using a winch. Once all the bodies were on deck, a chaplain climbed the ladder and conducted a short service. When he finished, the corpses were thrown overboard like garbage. Scraps of clothing were stripped from the dead for use by the living.

As those who died were moved out of the hold, there was room for the men to move around a little. Thirst was a constant companion, and whenever it rained or snowed, the tarp would be pulled back, and those near the hatch would stick out their tongues to catch a snowflake or raindrop. Every bit of water they consumed was vital to survival.

The prisoners constantly shivered, and Chet huddled together with his friends to maintain their body heat. They realized how crucial it was to maintain their circulation and frequently wiggled their toes, flexed their fingers, and even rubbed their noses to prevent frostbite. Quickly realizing there was a fine line between too much activity and too little, they kept moving, but not enough to use up the few calories they consumed every day. And they knew if they slept for a long period, they could freeze to death. Chet and his friends decided to take short naps throughout the day and night and between times, talked quietly to take their minds off their suffering. Conversations centered on positive topics — trips they'd enjoyed or hope to take, or how many kids they wanted. Other times they'd pose math problems or discuss a book one of them had read.

Chet's shrapnel wounds weren't quite healed, but he kept them as clean as possible; somehow, they hadn't become infected. As the days wore on, the men became quieter as temperatures became colder. Since becoming a prisoner in April 1942, Chet's survival had diminished from day by day and hour by hour to minute by minute and second by second. As he sat in the hold — naked and shivering — his measure of survival had been reduced even further. It was now breath by breath.

First Lieutenant John Finzer Presnell, Jr., West Point 1940 classmate who graduated #3 in the class, one of the men in Chet's lifeline circle, died on January 19. His body was stripped of what little clothing he had and given to a fellow POW most in need. The naked body of the lieutenant was buried at sea the following day along with about 25 other men. It is hard to imagine the man in the photo below and compare that to what he would have looked like as he took his last breath, emaciated, filthy, and freezing in the hold of the Brazil Maru, but this was the fate and condition of all of them. It is a miracle that any survived.

At the Stars Parade Harold C. Brown, 1940's No. 1 Cadet, gets a star. Other honor students are (left to right) Alan E. Gee, John F. Presnell, John W. Burfening.

PRESNELL

2LT John F Presnell graduated 3rd in the 1940 West Point class

During its journey, the convoy came under submarine attack several times, tossing the prisoners about the hold as the captain steered sharply to avoid being hit. Some men shouted for a torpedo to end their misery, but the ship never was struck. The Brazil Maru was slowed to accommodate a damaged ship, in tow, until onboard repairs returned it to seaworthiness.

On January 21, nine days after their departure from Takao Harbor, First Lieutenant Hector Polla succumbed to gangrene from his wounds and was buried at sea. Men continued to die at an alarming rate, but the Japanese weren't concerned for their well-being and continued their inhumane treatment. More than two dozen bodies a day, their eyes staring blankly at nothing, continued to be dumped overboard. Most deaths were due to pneumonia and freezing to death as temperatures dropped into the single digits. For the POWs, their hell actually *was* freezing over.

The daily routine drove some men to delirium. Others simply lost the will to live. There was no escape from the below-freezing temperatures. No escape from starvation and unquenchable thirst killing many from simple dehydration. No escape from watching men die. No escape from the smell of death. Many came to the same conclusion — their only escape was death. And they welcomed it.

As the ship neared its destination on January 29, the Japanese commander ordered a roll call. Of the 900 POWs who boarded the ship in Takao, only 497 were still alive. Barely. Another 72 perished and were thrown overboard before the ship docked the next day — January 30 — in Moji, Japan. A voyage that should've taken a little more than two days had lasted 18 and resulted in the death of more than half the prisoners aboard, most of whom froze to death.

Chet's journey from Manila had taken nearly seven weeks, a trip — under pre-war conditions — that would've required no more than two weeks. Zig zagging between islands and stopping to shelter near island coastlines at night delayed the hell ships' arrivals in Japan causing the deaths of hundreds of POWs who died from wounds, disease, starvation, and exposure. But it was all unnecessary.

Had the Japanese merely painted a red or white cross on the deck or bulkhead — the Geneva Convention's international sign to indicate patients or prisoners were aboard — allied submarine captains and combat pilots would've let the hell ships pass unharmed and searched for authorized enemy targets codified in the rules of engagement. They had no idea they were attacking ships carrying thousands of their countrymen.

Researcher and historian Gregory F. Michino determined that, by the end of the war, 134 hell ships had embarked on 156 voyages. Sixteen of them were sunk in allied attacks. In total, the ships transported approximately 126,000 allied POWs. Some 1,540 men died aboard the hell ships due to starvation, disease, and exposure the to the elements — the result of barbaric conditions in the holds and Japan's refusal to abide by the Geneva Convention as they had promised.

More than 19,000 deaths were due to allied combat attacks on the unmarked ships, many of which could've been avoided if the Japanese had indicated the hell ships were transporting POWs. Of those, many thousands were by drowning in the ocean when the Japanese refused to rescue them or as they simply shot them without mercy. By not doing so, the Japanese also lost thousands of their own troops as well as Japanese civilians fleeing combat areas. The Japanese planned to use the POWs as slave labor to help their war effort, and they certainly didn't want their ships to be sunk. Why they didn't indicate POWs were aboard — which would've resulted in thousands more able-bodied POWs to work in Japanese factories and coal mines, while also saving the lives of countless Japanese troops and civilians — has never been answered.

An error of omission also affected the heavy loss of life among POWs. Allied forces had acquired the ability to intercept, decode and translate classified Japanese messages containing vital information regarding ship movements throughout the Pacific theater. Twice a day, hell ship captains relayed messages to their general headquarters in Japan. They included details regarding cargo loads, departure and estimated arrival dated, routes and interim ports of call. Also listed were the number and category of passengers: Japanese troops — wounded and returning from their combat assignments — and civilians, including the number of women and children. Last in the listing were the numbers of POW aboard.

Allied intelligence units in the Pacific monitored enemy radio traffic and sent it to be decoded at intelligence offices in England, India, and Ceylon (now Sri Lanka). The information was then edited and transmitted via ultra-secret messages, known as Ultras, to theater commanders. They then forwarded the information down the chain of command to allied ship captains so they could plan their attacks. Somewhere along the way, information was edited to include only information regarding each ship's name, location, destination, approximate size, and its defenses. Details regarding passengers, troops or POWs had been deleted. Submarine captains and combat pilots had no idea Japanese troops and civilians were aboard enemy ships let alone American and allied prisoners.

To this day, no one knows why the Japanese refused to paint a symbolic cross on the hell ships or how and where along the messaging chain vital information regarding the POWs' presence aboard them was eliminated. These two factors alone could've prevented massive loss of life — on both sides.

The events below are listed to provide the reader with the context of the total war, as the prisoners fight to survive unaware of the world outside.

Battle of Manila February 3 - March 3, 1945

Battle to retake Grande Island, Fort Wint, January 30, 1945

Battle to retake Corregidor, February 16 - 26, 1945

Battle to take Iwo Jima, February 1 - March 26, 1945

Battle to take Okinawa, April 1 - June 22, 1945

CHAPTER 7

Surviving Japan & Manchuria
(January 30, 1945 - August 1945)

At mid-morning on January 30, a contingent of Japanese military officers — including doctors and medical personnel dressed in gleaming white uniforms and shiny, black boots — stepped aboard the Brazil Maru to take possession of the prisoners. Gray clouds released a light snow, and fog hung in the frigid air. One by one, the POWs emerged, standing in formation on the deck. The Japanese representatives were appalled at the sight of the men barely able to stand before them. Their lungs — filled with deep breaths of fresh, cold air — helped to revive them, even as they stood mostly naked and shivering. Covered in soot and filth with the stench of urine, feces and dysentery wafting over the deck, the POWs were so thin, it looked like their skin had been draped over a hangar at the shoulders. The clothes of the few POWs who had them were covered with sweat stains, blood and human waste, and their hair and beards had become matted like an abandoned dog. Without adequate food, water, and hygiene during their seven-week journey, the men might as well have been beggars on the street. As a group, they were barely alive; one of the men collapsed and died on the deck before he could even get off the ship. In short order, the men were sprayed with a de-lousing powder and slowly began to disembark onto the dock, with many POWs needing help to navigate the gang plank.

From the dock, the POWs marched about three blocks to a theater, which had been converted to receive and process the POWs for transport to various POW camps throughout Japan, Korea, and China. Japanese women and children stood along the street and stared in horror or looked away as the prisoners passed. Many of the women covered their eyes and noses with thick, wool scarves — mostly to prevent gagging from the foul smell emanating from the POWs as they passed. Others were embarrassed to look at their naked, emaciated bodies.

Sadly, one of the men in Chet's lifeline circle, Maj. Bob Glassburn — who had survived the worst conditions ever experienced on the hell ships during his voyage to Japan — died January 30, 1945, as POWs left behind in the Philippines were being rescued. His body was so battered, starved, and diseased, recovery was impossible. Lieutenant Britt's lifeline circle had shrunk to five men, and three of them were in dire condition.

January 30, 1945, Moji receiving facility where Chestera and other POWs were first processed several blocks from the Moji Southern Wharf. Note Japanes army star over the doorway. Post-war Sept 15, 1945 photo courtesy of the POW RESEARCH NETWORK JAPAN

Ironically, on the day Lieutenant Britt stepped off the hell ship in Japan, the POWs left behind at Cabanatuan — who were too ill to travel — were rescued by American Rangers led by Lt. Col. Henry Mucci, with Filipino guerrillas providing invaluable help. In a daring raid deep behind Japanese lines, they liberated 511 POWs. Among those rescued were Army civilian armaments technician Max Wait — who became a "brother in arms" to Chet during their time together at Bataan — and 1st Lt. Jules D. Yates, one of Chet's 1940 West Point classmates.

The heroic mission was part of a hastily organized operation ordered by General MacArthur to be carried out throughout the Philippines upon learning the Japanese intended to execute all allied POWs before they could be rescued. The operation became legendary in the annals of World War II and was considered the most dramatic mission of the war. In 2005, it was the subject of a movie called "The Great Raid" based on a book titled "Ghost Soldiers" by Hampton Sides.

January 31, 1945, the day after the Army Ranger raid to rescue prisoners at the Cabanatuan POW camp. Max Wait in a jubilant crowd of former prisoners.

On the same day, Chester spent his first full day at Fukuoka #3 POW camp

In other action on that day, American and allied forces recaptured Fort Wint — Lieutenant Britt's first duty station. Tragically the operation cost the life of one young infantryman at Fort Wint. He was killed by shrapnel from an explosion 100 yards away from where he was standing, a needless death, as the Japanese abandoned Grande Isle. They, too, had come to realize the tiny island could not be defended.

Late in the afternoon, Chet and the other POWs were issued shoes and wool pants and shirts except for the sickest of the group, who were slated to be taken to Kokura Military Hospital, about five miles from Moji. After they were fed all the rice and water they could eat, the POWs were divided into groups depending on their physical condition. Captains Chandler Baldwin and Harold Jimerson and 1st Lt. Robert Wheat were in such bad shape they were among the 110 POWs loaded into buses and ambulances and taken to the hospital. With a quick good-bye and well-wishes all around as he helped the men onto the bus, Chet's lifeline circle instantly was pared down to two — Lieutenants Cullen and Iacobucci.

Lieutenant Britt and Lieutenant Cullen were assigned to a group of 100 men, including a doctor and medics, and marched to a streetcar for a short ride to the train station for transport to Fukuoka POW Camp #3, about 8 miles to the west. Lieutenant Iacobucci, unfortunately, was in another group of 100 assigned for transport to Fukuoka POW Camp #1, located near the newly built Mushiroda Airfield just east of Fukuoka City. The train stopped at Fukuoka #1 to drop off the group Lieutenant Iacobucci was in before proceeding to Fukuoka #3. Chet's lifeline circle was now down to one, his closest friend — Lieutenant Gus Cullen. Neither were in good condition. They supported each other as they boarded the train and were overjoyed to see well-padded seats in their assigned car. Even though there was no heat on the train, Chet and Gus huddled together for warmth and for the next few hours, felt almost normal — fully clothed and enjoying a ride on the softest surface they'd sat upon since they'd departed Fort Wint. Although exhausted and malnourished, they were grateful to have a full belly and a comfortable seat, at least for the moment. The group arrived well after dark and were driven by bus through eight inches of new snow. At the camp, the men were issued three wool blankets each and given hot coffee at bedtime.

The wooden POW barracks were bleak, but at least the conditions were an improvement compared to the hell ships. Each of the 10 barracks buildings consisted of a single aisle down the middle with double-deck bays on either side. They were built over a hard-packed, clay floor, and a small stove in the center of the room was fueled by coal dust, which provided only enough warmth to heat coffee and tea. Bare light bulbs illuminated the rooms, and the only warmth came from their blankets, which quickly were fashioned into sleeping bags to preserve what little body heat the men generated. Latrines consisted of six wooden stalls, a cement urinal and four sinks with cold water. Soap was a rarity.

The following day, Chet, and Gus — suffering from malaria, shrapnel wounds, exhaustion and starvation and a host of other tropical diseases brought about from a lack of food — were admitted to the camp hospital in critical condition, along with most of the POWs in his group. Work of any kind was out of the question until the POWs regained enough strength and health to do the work they were assigned. They already were near death when they arrived in Japan, barely able to walk and hold themselves upright.

It was the first real bed they'd slept in since surrendering in 1942. They were treated at the hospital by their fellow POW American doctors and medics using a combination of medicine from the Japanese and the Red Cross packages that had been delivered for the Japanese to distribute to them. Although they had begun to receive three meals a days and basic medical care, fatalities continued to mount. Even so, prisoners began to feel like human beings again after being treated like abused animals for three long years. But once they left the relative security and comfort of the hospital, they knew the Japanese guards would continue treating them harshly without regard to their well-being.

On February 3, as the POWs were settling into their new routines in Japanese POW camps, American troops were advancing on Bilibid Prison in an effort to rescue one of the last large contingents of POWs. The fighting raged on overnight and into the dawn as Japanese troops fought in vain to hold the city. First Lieutenant Robert Frank Augur, whom Chet had been imprisoned with at Camp Cabanatuan and Bilibid Prison, scribbled in his diary, "2/4 — Abt (about) 10:00 AM Japs pulled out of compound. Abt 5:00 PM 145th Inf. 37th Division broke the side wall." His sparse words, typically found in POW diaries to conserve space, confirmed that nearly all POWs in the Philippines had been rescued. Only a few small camps remained, and they were barely guarded. The raids to free American and allied POWs proved to be a spirit-lifting success, forcing Japanese forces to retreat in defeat as American troops advanced on their positions.

While liberated POWs were celebrating their new-found freedom on February 4 in the Philippines, the mood was somber at Kokura Military Hospital. Capt. Chandler "Chan" L. Baldwin and Capt. Harold "Captain Jimmy" L. Jimerson, two of Chet's close friends and members of his life-line circle, had succumbed that day to the maladies all POWs suffered — pneumonia, hypothermia, and starvation along with the many diseases and infections resulting from inadequate food and medical care, as well as the cumulative injuries sustained from three-plus years of beatings and torture. Like most POWs admitted to the hospital, the two were deemed of no value and too costly to care for; the Japanese doctors refused to dispense the medicines necessary to treat them, reserving the few medicines and supplies they received for their own troops. The POWs literally were abandoned and left to languish until their last breaths.

At Fukuoka 3 hospital, Chet received a series of B-1 shots, vitamins, plasma, sulfa drugs (to curb and prevent bacterial infections) and atabrine to treat his malaria. The men also were fed three meals a day consisting mainly of cooked rice and hot soup. Periodically, there were vegetables or fish in the soup. Despite finally getting the nutrition and care he needed, Gus had contracted a severe case of pneumonia on the hell ships and was struggling to breathe. Chet, in a nearby bed, could hear his friend's raspy breath getting worse by the day and prayed for them both to survive. Gus did his best to stay positive as he was the guy everyone depended on to lift everyone's spirits, even in the darkest of times. But on February 9, 1st Lt. August "Gus" Cullen drew his last, labored breath. Chet's cherished friend, with whom he served since their days at West Point, was gone.

Chet was devasted. Now alone, he grieved beneath the blankets, remembering the countless friends and brothers in arms he'd lost to the war not as combatants, but mostly due to their torture and treatment as POWs. Had they been treated as well as the U.S. treated Japanese POWs, all most likely would've survived.

Suffering from untreated wounds, infections, numerous attacks of malaria, dehydration, starvation, beriberi, dengue fever, and hypothermia, Lieutenant Britt's 6-feet, 3-inch frame weighed barely 101 pounds — 84 pounds less than he weighed at his West Point graduation. All alone and hovering near death himself, his condition quickly nose-dived. Delirious and unresponsive, doctors feared Chet had only hours to live. Despite the odds against his survival, doctors administered a megadose of sulfa drugs and an infusion of plasma — which was in short supply — in one, last-ditch effort to save his life. They figured he'd be dead by morning. He wasn't. Chet downplayed his near-death casually explaining in a letter to his parents the following August, "I was given up one night in the hospital in Japan last February, but my heart kept going and after receiving many injections and some plasma that was available, I gradually became stronger and was able to hang on." After 18 days of intense treatment at the hospital, Lieutenant Britt was discharged on February 21 and transferred to the POW barracks where he officially entered detention. Still too weak to work, he spent most days in bed covered with his wool blankets.

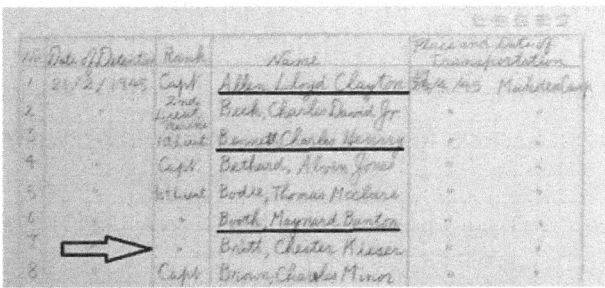

April 29, 1945 part of the transfer roster from Fukuoka #3 to Mukden. Chester arrow, known close friends underlined

Chet later learned the day after his release from the hospital, another of his lifeline circle had died. First Lieutenant Robert Wheat, a West Point classmate who traveled with his wife, Dorothy, with Chet and Grace, succumbed to his illnesses and injuries on February 22 at Kokura Military Hospital. He was left to die after Japanese doctors declared him too ill to care for and withheld life-saving treatment. And on March 14, 1st Lt. Joe Iacobucci died at Fukuoka #1 located near Nagasaki. With Joe's death, the very last member of Chester's closest circle of friends that survived until Moji was gone.

Knowing he needed help to survive the next phase of confinement, Chester joined two other POWs to create a new lifeline circle of friends — men who committed to helping each other survive. First Lieutenant Kenneth W. Ramsey, who had been in Chet's unit at Fort Wint and had traveled to the Philippines on the same ship that brought the Britts to the Philippines, and 1st Lt. George Faulkner, a B-17 pilot who was pressed into service as an infantryman after his plane was destroyed in the initial Japanese bombing raid at Clark Field, promised to help care for and protect each other to improve their chances to survive. Their shared experiences on the Bataan Death March, imprisonment at various POW camps in the Philippines and their treatment on the hell ships cemented their friendship, creating an unbreakable bond.

By the end of February, of the 425 prisoners who survived the hell ships to reach Japan, only 261 were alive. Eight inches of snow covered the ground, and although the prisoners were indoors, it was so cold inside the condensation from their breath filled the air every time they spoke. Men were dying every day due to hypothermia — men they went to great lengths to bring to Japan in order to use them as forced labor to support the war.

Adjusting to his new surroundings in the barracks, Lieutenant Britt discovered yet another enemy. Bed bugs, lice and fleas infested the wool blankets. The pesky insects were a constant source of irritation, and the only refuge from them were the most welcome 10-minute baths every other day in the steam-heated community bath. It was the POWs' only respite from the cold and the irritating insects that had taken up residence in their blankets. The Japanese refused to allow prisoners to boil their clothes to eliminate the infestation and bring some semblance of comfort. Instead, it proved another simple but effective way to torture their captives.

From his arrival at the camp until April 24, the POWs received the equivalent of one-and-a-half Red Cross packages per man per week — of course, after the Japanese had rifled through them and taken what they wanted. Each man received 40 cigarettes per week, which Chet traded for food. He'd quit smoking cold turkey when he was captured, realizing early on the life-saving nourishment he could receive in trade was much more valuable to him than a few, quick puffs on a cigarette. It was a matter of needs outweighing wants — a better chance of survival versus an empty stomach and a possible early death. His West Point training and discipline had served him well so far.

June 28, 1945, photo of Grace with Chester Jr, now almost four years old, in a letter send to FUKUOKA PRISON CAMP
Marked: RETURNED TO SENDER, UNDELIVERABLE AS ADDRESSED

Letters to and from home were like hen's teeth — non-existent. Japan had no desire to inform U.S. officials where American POWs were being held. A letter from the Provost Marshall, dated March 30, notified Grandma Hazel, Chester's mother, that he'd been moved to Camp Cabanatuan in the Philippines. By the time letters from Chester's family reached the Philippines he already was in Japan. With no forwarding address, the letters of love and support were returned, usually several months after they'd been sent. Red Cross packages intended for delivery during Christmas 1944 went undelivered as the men were in transit aboard the hell ships to Japan. Chet's family hadn't heard from him since just after his capture in 1942. The War Department was unable to determine where he was being held or even if he was still alive. The lack of information weighed on the emotions of families and prisoners alike. Loved ones had no knowledge of the POWs' conditions or whereabouts, and the POWs wondered if their families had forgotten them, perhaps assuming they had not survived or possibly were missing in action.

Prisoners were expected to work, and those unable to support Japan's war efforts received reduced food rations. For the first time in more than three years, Chester and his buddies received food on a regular basis. Although it was insufficient to regain or maintain normal health, the food had some nutritional value and was much improved from the lack of food on the hell ships. The three-meal daily ration totaled about 550 grams of grain — rice, barley, maize, and red beans, which were mixed and steamed and served with a soup made of vegetable tops and fish scraps. Although it seemed like a lot compared to rations the prisoners received at previous camps, the diet lacked protein and fats and fell short of the quantity needed to regain and maintain adequate health. Delivery of Red Cross packages helped supplement their diet. Even the small quantity of extra food remaining in their care packages — after guards had helped themselves — was enough to sustain them and save their lives. One of the things the prisoners missed most was salt, which was difficult to obtain. More often than not, it was dirty and not suitable for consumption when it could be passed along by factory workers.

With regular meals and better access to medical care and basic vitamins, Chet's health slowly improved as the weather became milder and temperatures in the barracks increased to a tolerable level. By mid-March, he had begun light-duty work at the Yawata Steel Mill, some five miles from the prison camp. Prisoners who worked received 50 yen per month and could spend it on sundries sold by local Japanese civilians gathered along the camp's fence line. However, purchases of food items were prohibited.

The camp was in an industrial area, near a steam electrical generation plant surrounded by steel mills. It proved to be a highly valuable target area for American B-29 bombers. An aerial raid one night damaged the barracks, shattering windows and blowing-out doors. As this book was being written, Col. Ben Skardon, a spry 103-year-old survivor of the Bataan Death March and hell ships, recalled that during the bombing attacks on the steel mills, he couldn't force himself into the tunnel that served at the POWs' bomb shelter. His experiences on the Oryoku Maru made it impossible for him ever to be in dark, closed-in spaces again. Fortunately, unlike the aerial raids on the hell ships, no one had been killed by their own countrymen. Since the Japanese had shown callous disregard for the prisoners' welfare for three years, they weren't concerned if they lived or died as long as they could extract every ounce of energy from the men until they collapsed and died.

While at Fukuoka #3, prisoners were allowed to write a 40-word radiogram — which Chet took advantage of — but it was never delivered. On March 28, Grace received the first news of Chester since he'd first been captured. A letter from Max Wait, who had returned to his home in Little Rock, Arkansas, indicated Chet's health was very good and that he'd survived the Bataan Death March in good physical condition. Max said Chet had been moved from Camp Cabanatuan in 1944 to go to Manila and then — because American and allied forces were re-taking huge swaths of territory in the Philippines — he had most likely been taken by ship to

Japan. The Army civilian had been taken prisoner on Corregidor and had a very different POW experience compared to Lieutenant Britt, never having been on the death march or imprisoned at Camp O'Donnell. He was taken directly to Camp Cabanatuan and remained there until he was rescued in January 1945. Grace and the family were thrilled with the news, reading Max's letter over and over again, cherishing each word and knowing Chester was alive as of December. The news greatly lifted her spirits and that of Chet's extended family and friends.

March 28, 1945 Max Wait letter to Grace regarding Chet

In late April, the prisoners were notified they'd be moving once again, which raised tensions among the men. American forces were advancing north, and the assault on Iwo Jima and Okinawa forced the Japanese to move the POWs farther inland, away from possible rescue, so their captors could continue forcing them to work for the Japanese empire. The prisoners already had suffered so much and were concerned they'd once again find themselves in the hold of a hell ship.

Despite better treatment during their time in Japan, the damage from their epic journey from the Philippines had taken a visibly, mentally, and physically major toll on every prisoner. Of the 100 men who'd been taken with Chet to Fukuoka #3, 24 of them had died. Another three were near death in the hospital, unable to travel and most likely would be left for dead. Although the increase in food rations helped somewhat, conditions at the camp combined with the continued beatings and torture of already weakened and ill prisoners proved too much for them to overcome. The constant and continual attrition of POWs wore on Chet and his fellow survivors. They could never relax or let down their guard and were on constant alert to avoid angering their captors.

A few days before their departure, the men were informed they would be transferred to POW camps in either Mukden, Manchuria, in the northeast region of China, or Jinsen (now Incheon), Korea. Chet and his fellow prisoners were loaded onto trucks early on April 25 and after a bumpy ride on roads damaged from allied aerial attacks, they arrived at the port of Fukuoka. This time however, they were offloaded at what appeared to be a passenger terminal. They were marched through a large processing building and ordered to sit on the wooden dock. The sun, shining brightly in a cloudless sky, warmed their bodies and the fresh, spring breeze blowing inland was a welcome relief from the foul, coal-fired air that belched smoke and soot through the steel mills and swirled through the broken windows of their barracks. Throughout the day they were joined by the surviving prisoners from the original group of 1,619 POWs who had boarded the Oryoku Maru, 425 of whom ultimately arrived in Japan and were taken to various prison camps. In just 84 days in Japan, their numbers had dwindled to 271.

Even though it had been just a few months since they'd been together for what was the most terrifying and horrific experience of their lives, many men found it difficult to recognize each other without identifying themselves. Chester's friend, 1st Lt. Emil Ulanowicz wrote in his diary, "Most of these officers I had known personally in peace time or during war. Here they were just skin and bones. Some were so weak they could not sit up, and they had to be carried by stronger ones. Not one did I recognize without someone first telling me who they were. Maj. Peterson was skin and bones and completely dehydrated. He could barely walk due to wounds and weakness, his speech gone by utter fatigue. He looked not a day under 70 years old."

A large, two-stack passenger ferry pulled up to the dock and began off-loading a few hundred Japanese passengers. They walked hastily past the prisoners without acknowledgement, eager to be on their way. The POWs boarded the ship, but then out of fears of an air raid they disembarked and spent a cold night on the dock, reboarding the morning of April 26th. The prisoners were marched aboard. The room's low ceiling obviously was designed for the relatively short Japanese passengers, and Chet had to duck to enter, constantly leaning over to walk about the area. Fortunately, it was clean with tiled floors, and there was enough leg room to sit on the floor without being cramped. Prisoners on litters were carried a deck below by stronger captives and were attended by POW doctors and medics.

April 26, 1945 The POWs got off either the Shokei Maru (shown this photo) or sister ship the Keifuku Maru, walked past the Customs House, then turned left to go to the theater.

The ferry pulled away from the dock in the morning and steamed northwest past the island of Tsushima toward the port city of Fusan some 140 miles away. The compartment was warm, the seas were calm, and they were fed three light meals throughout the trip. Chet was as relaxed as he'd been in months and began to feel almost human again. With the increase in food quality and quantity since arriving in Japan, he'd regained 21 pounds. He was still skinny and weak, but he knew every pound — every ounce — increased his chances for survival. Like the other POWs, he had no idea what the future held. Still, he felt secure knowing he had friends he could rely on for help. But what always gave him the most hope — and an incredible determination to survive — were his memories of Grace and thoughts of his toddler son, along with family and friends who were awaiting his return.

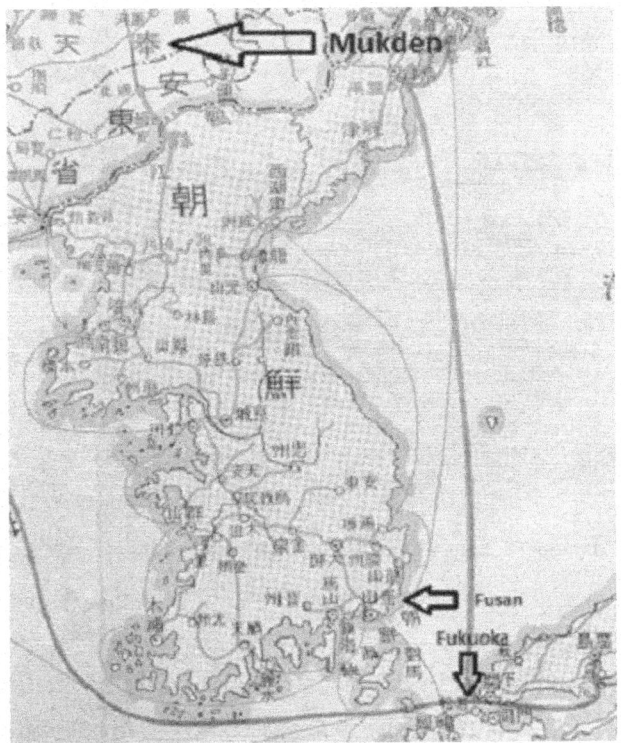

Fukuoka to Fusan by comfortable ferry, then comfortable train up the west coast of Korea, and then northeast by train to Mukden

Sadly, another prisoner died on the afternoon journey to Korea. Major Thomas B. Smothers, the father of beloved comedians and entertainers Tommy and Dick Smothers, who were only 8 and 5 years old when their father died — succumbed to injuries, disease and starvation suffered at the hands of his captors.

TOP Fusan port. BOTTOM Sang Saeng Kwan (Living Together
Theater) in Fusan where the POWs stayed overnight on April 26.
Located about GPS coordinates 35° 5'56.60"N, 129° 2'8.60"E about
0.6 miles west of pier. First known photo identifying this theater,
photo courtesy Busan Modern History Museum
http://museum.busan.go.kr/modern Research assistance from
Steve Kim, Busan citizen, friend of John Duresky

Upon arrival at the port of Fusan, the prisoners were fed a large meal of rice, soup, and fish. The guards were friendly and allowed the men to eat at their leisure. Afterward, they were divided into two groups. Forty men were marched to the nearby railroad station for a train ride to the prison camp at Jinsen, about 205 miles north, just on the outskirts of Seoul to the southwest. The remaining 230 prisoners were marched and carried on litters to a theater about a 2/3 of a mile from the port. They remained at the processing center overnight to await transportation to prison camps in northeast China.

Chester and his newly formed lifeline circle of First Lieutenants Ulanowicz, Faulkner, Ramsey along with the others in their group, including Capt. Ben Skardon, were marched to the train station on April 27 for the 550-mile trip to Mukden. The painstakingly slow train traversed through scenic mountain passes, and the POWs traveled in relative comfort on the commercial train, not stuffed into cattle cars as they'd been in the Philippines. The seats were well-padded and upholstered in a plush red material. Throughout the two-day trip, each man received packed box lunches handed out three times a day by the Korean galley crew, who treated them no differently than the regular, civilian passengers they served. Upon arrival in Mukden, Manchuria, the prisoners were transferred to another, less well-appointed train for a short ride to a station near the POW camp. They marched the final mile or so to their destination, a POW camp officially known at the time as Hoten #1. Chester was the farthest from home he'd ever been — 6,100+ miles due west from his Wisconsin home.

There were two main camps in Manchuria. Lieutenant Britt was held in Hoten #1 outside of Mukden while higher-grade officers — colonels to generals, including their staff members and aides — were confined at Hoten #2, known as Hsian, nearly 100 miles northeast. About 1,200 enlisted POWs were confined at Hoten #1, known as Mukden. (The camp names were used interchangeably, but upon Chet's arrival, most POWs continued to refer to it by its original name, Mukden.) Compared to the group of 230 newly arrived, half-dead skeletons, the enlisted POWs were in good physical and mental shape, although slightly less than normal weight. As Chet and his fellow prisoners stumbled through the gates to Mukden compound, the POWs who greeted them reacted with the same shock and revulsion as the Japanese doctors at the port of Moji.

Mukden barracks #2, Chester was held on the 2nd floor

The POWs were housed in three, 2-story brick buildings, which surprisingly featured electricity, running water and heat — a most welcome improvement from previous camp facilities. Mukden became a "show camp" of sorts in November 1943 in preparation of the first inspection of the camp by representatives of the International Red Cross. It most likely was the reason behind the Japanese guards' more lenient attitude and treatment of the prisoners and their somewhat more "luxurious" quality of life.

After 10 days, the camp commander allowed the prisoners to steam their clothes and bedding, finally ridding them of lice after months of torture. As spring turned to summer, however, the lice were replaced by sand fleas, which were impervious to disinfectant powder. Impossible to eradicate, they infested the barracks, incessantly feasting on their prey.

The majority of prisoners already there worked about a half-mile away at the Manchuria Machine Tool Company Ltd. factory. Under the supervision of Chinese workers who were under control of the occupying Japanese forces, the POWs disassembled machinery into its separate parts. Japanese technicians would then write instructions and draw blueprints for each part and how it should be assembled into the final product. The Chinese supervisors weren't too pleased living under Japanese control and gladly ignored prisoners who sabotaged the process by pocketing or hiding small parts, such as screws, gaskets and washers, which were ultimately excluded from the drawings. Any effort to reproduce the complete machine proved futile. Others raised crops or worked on construction projects. At every turn, they attempted to undermine Japan's objectives.

Lieutenant Britt's weight gain — he tipped the scales at all of 122 pounds when he arrived at Mukden — proved to be lifesaving. Between inspections, food at the camp was insufficient in quantity for those in his group to maintain their weight. Due to their poor condition and inability to work, their rations were even less than those who worked. Most lost an average of five pounds a month.

Chester added two more prisoners to his lifeline circle, befriending two Annapolis graduates in his barracks. Lieutenant (jg) John J.A. Michel and Marine Lt. Charles H. "Bitch-bitch" Bennett. Following the war, Lieutenant Michel wrote of his experiences as a naval officer and published "Mr. Michel's War." They passed the time discussing boats and sailing, with Chet reminiscing about days gone by as a Sea Scout back home.

On May 23, Chet noticed an obvious swelling in his legs. His weight had increased to 128 pounds and fearing he'd contracted wet beriberi — caused by long-term malnutrition — he contacted the camp's medical staff. Upon examination, doctors also found an infection in his neck near his jugular vein. They informed the lieutenant he needed immediate surgery. Without proper instruments, anesthesia, or a sterile place to perform the procedure, several men held down Chester while a doctor used a kitchen knife — sharpened on a rock — as a scalpel to lance the infected area. The crude incision was then irrigated with water to wash out as much of the infection as possible. It was then covered with a piece of cloth wrapped around Chet's neck. Doctors and medics monitored him closely, frequently cleansing the incision and changing the cloth bandage around his neck to absorb the drainage. Without any medication to prevent further infection or stitches to close the incision, it somehow healed. The primitive surgery saved his life.

Swelling in Chester's legs, however, remained a concern. Wet beri-beri, caused by a lack of thiamin — vitamin B-1 — found in grains, cereal, beans and beef, wreaked havoc on his already precarious health. His legs, feet and stomach became swollen, forcing his heart to work harder to pump blood to his extremities. The combination of water retention, excess strain on his heart and all the other maladies he'd endured quickly could lead to an agonizing death. Doctors had exhausted the few remedies available and advised him to consume as much thiamin and protein-enriched food as possible. His only hope was his lifeline. They fed him, carried him to the bathroom and cared for his every need. When grains or soybeans were available, they ensured Chet received a share of their rations.

On May 31, about 320 senior officers — colonels and lower- grade generals — from Hsian were consolidated with the Mukden prisoners. They reportedly refused to work, citing international regulations against senior officer POWs serving as forced labor. The arrival of more POWs impacted the prisoners' rations, and the already insufficient food was reduced again, endangering lives with the threat of starvation. Several POWs were nearly or already blind from lack of proper nutrients and vitamins, an irreversible condition if left untreated.

Throughout the summer, Chet's condition fluctuated between dire and critical. Too weak and incoherent to scribble even a few words in his diary, a missed meal could've been fatal. Finally, at the beginning of August, the swelling in his legs started to subside. Slowly, he became more aware of his surroundings and regained enough strength to help care for himself. Thanks to the unrelenting help from his friends, Chet's date with death had once again been postponed.

CHAPTER 8

War Ends, Free Again!
(August – September 1945)

Throughout the summer, Japan was losing territory to advancing Allied forces who were planning an all-out assault on the Japanese mainland. The war in Europe had ended on May 8, just seven days after Adolph Hitler committed suicide. Russia then turned its attention to the Far East and began repositioning troops and equipment along the northern border of Manchuria knowing Japan was in retreat. However, Japanese forces still posed a significant threat to peace in the region. To avoid the possibility of hundreds of thousands of American and Allied fatalities in an attack on the Japanese homeland, on August 6, President Harry S. Truman — in office only 116 days following the death of Franklin D. Roosevelt — ordered the Army Air Force to drop an atomic bomb on Hiroshima to force the Japanese to surrender.

Sixteen hours after the atom bomb was dropped on Hiroshima, President Truman reported on the bomb to the world. In his statement he said, "… It was to spare the Japanese people from utter destruction that the ultimatum of July 26 was issued at Potsdam. Their leaders promptly rejected that ultimatum. If they do not now accept our terms they may expect a rain of ruin from the air, the like of which has never been seen on this earth. Behind this air attack will follow sea and land forces in such numbers and power as they have not yet seen and with the fighting skill of which they are already well aware...."

The military leaders of Japan did not accept the terms they were given, setting the stage for the final acts of violence of WWII.

With troops positioned at the border with Manchuria, the Russians declared war on Japan on August 8, notifying Japanese leaders in Tokyo that Russia had rescinded its joint Soviet-Japanese Neutrality Pact. Two minutes past midnight on August 9, Soviet forces crossed the border and launched the Manchurian Strategic Offensive operation in a colossal land grab to gain access and control of vital minerals and natural resources needed to expand Soviet domination. Later that day, American pilots dropped a second atomic bomb on Nagasaki. The two bombs killed between 129,000 and 226,000 people, mostly civilians.

Six days later, on August 15, Emperor Hirohito announced on the radio to his millions of stunned citizens that Japan had surrendered. Most Japanese troops immediately laid down their weapons although there were a few, small pockets of resistance throughout the Far East. Of course, no one in Japanese-occupied countries and territories were aware of what had happened at that point. It would take the better part of a day for word to reach the most distant of their military commanders.

None of the POWs, in Manchuria, were aware of the air strikes and surrender agreement but they had been hearing rumors that Japan was near defeat. Nor were they aware of Japan's order to kill all POWs before they could be rescued. Japanese military leaders were concerned all the POWs they held throughout more than 150 prison camps in the Far East could be turned into a fighting force if they were rescued, a ridiculous notion considering most prisoners were starving, seriously ill and could barely get out of bed.

A year before the end of the war, the Japanese War Ministry issued written orders to all prison camp commanders ordering them to prepare for the "final disposition" of the POWs in their control. The translated order read, "Whether they are destroyed individually or in groups, or however it is done, with mass bombing, poisonous smoke, poisons, drowning, decapitation or whatever, dispose of them as the situation dictates. In any case it is the aim not to allow the escape of a single one, to annihilate them all and not to leave any traces."

The orders also applied to civilian prisoners, including women and children. Execution plans discovered in Borneo, indicated the inhumane brutality of their Japanese captors. Women internees, children and nuns were to be fed poisoned rice. Men and Catholic priests were to be shot and burned. POWs were scheduled to be marched into the jungle to be shot or decapitated and burned. And the sick and infirm were to remain at the camp to be bayonetted in their beds. Finally, the entire camp was to be set on fire to destroy any evidence. The orders were to be carried out on August 17 and 18.

Back in Washington D.C., the Office of Strategic Services — precursor to the current-day Central Intelligence Agency — began preparing plans well before the war ended to rescue prisoners to prevent their execution when the war ended because they were concerned how Japanese guards would react to the news. The War Department's goal was to avoid a repeat of the massacre of prisoners at Camp Palawan in the Philippines that took place December 14, 1944. The raid on Camp Cabanatuan in January 1945 happened to prevent a similar massacre prior to the Japanese surrender.

The mission to Mukden was incredibly daring and dangerous. Rescuers needed to avoid being taken prisoner or killed by Japanese forces on one side and being held for hostage by advancing Russian troops on the other. Nine 6-man teams were assigned to rescue and repatriate POWs from various regions. Each team's mission was code-named after a bird, and Operation Cardinal's mission was of utmost importance — to rescue, in particular, General Wainwright and other American and allied senior military men with him, including Britain's Lt. Gen. Arthur E. Percival, Britain's Governor General during the fall of Singapore.

They were thought to be held captive at Camp Hoten #1 near Mukden, the same camp as Lieutenant Britt, after learning some 320 senior officers had been transferred there on May 31 from Hsian, about 100 miles northeast of Mukden. Operation Cardinal consisted of OSS personal from its special operations and special intelligence sections who had specific skills in communications, clandestine operations, medicine and language proficiency in Japanese, Chinese and Russian. The Cardinal team was led by Maj. James T. Hennessy, a 1940 West Point graduate; Maj. (Dr.) Robert F. Lamar, the team's flight surgeon; technician Edward A. Starz, a radio operator; Staff Sergeant Harold "Hal" Leith, a linguist fluent in Russian and Chinese; and Sergeant Fumio Kido, a Japanese interpreter. A Chinese national, Cheng Shih-wu, accompanied the team as an interpreter.

A few days before Japan surrendered, the Cardinal team secretly was inserted into China, landing at an airfield in Chungking (now Chongqing) where the team set up a small area of operations. With the ink barely dry on the initial surrender agreement signed on August 15, a B-24, named Flight Pay, carrying extra fuel tanks, departed the Chungking airfield at 4:30 a.m. on August 16, circled the field and headed north. It was carrying weapons, munitions, a couple of radios and batteries, a half-ton of equipment, medical supplies and 1,300 pounds of rations. Also on board: the Cardinal team. Their primary mission: rescue Lieutenant General Wainwright.

During the 1,250-mile flight, they slept, reviewed their operational plans and discussed potential scenarios that might occur. No one knew how the million-plus Japanese troops still in Manchuria would react — or even if they knew the Japanese emperor had surrendered. Six hours later, on a sunny but windy Thursday morning, the Cardinal team and 17 cargo-laden parachutes dropped out of the sky, landing in a cabbage patch in Mukden, about two miles from the POW camp. The area was patrolled by Japanese fighter aircraft, and Russian troops were only 120 miles away.

Chet could see the parachutes in the distance from a dilapidated, second-floor doorway. He and the other prisoners assumed the Japanese were conducting defense drills. What they couldn't see were the hundreds of Chinese men, women and children who had descended on the drop zone. With Sergeant Leith and Cheng Shih-wu interpreting, a handful of Chinese men agree to escort the team down the dirt road leading to the POW camp. They'd traveled only a half-mile when they were confronted by a platoon of Japanese soldiers, and upon seeing the Japanese troops, the Chinese men fled. Although Major Hennessy waved a white handkerchief indicating he was not a threat, the soldiers surrounded the outnumbered team. The soldiers aimed their rifles at the men's heads, clicking the bolts on their guns in a show of force. They were ordered to throw their weapons on the ground and squat in the dirt, whereupon the Japanese troops began kicking the defenseless men and beating them with their rifle butts.

Major Hennessy tried to explain the war was over, but the Japanese remained hostile and suspicious, unconvinced of the team's peaceful intentions. After all, the Russians had declared war on the Japanese, he said, and the team could be Russians dressed in American uniforms. After several minutes of tense negotiations, the platoon marched the Cardinal Team to his unit's headquarters at the POW camp. There, they were separated, blind-folded and interrogated. The POWs could see the camp commander's office from a window in the barracks' latrine and thought they could see pistols in their holsters. Rumors ran wild that the Americans had taken control of the camp, and although no one was certain what was happening, their spirits were lifted just seeing Americans in uniform.

The POW camp commandant, unsure of the Americans' explanation, sent them to a nearby, walled-off compound in Mukden, the location of a higher-level headquarters. They were led under guard into the office of the commander, and with Sergeant Kido interpreting, Major Hennessy tried to convince the head of the Japanese forces the war was, indeed, over. The headquarters staff admitted they'd heard Japan had surrendered, but the commander refused to believe the Americans until he'd received definite confirmation from Tokyo. He sent the team back to the POW camp under guard while he awaited further information. Finally, after three stressful hours of not knowing whether the team itself would become prisoners, the Emperor's surrender was confirmed by the commander's superiors.

With Japan's surrender announcement on August 15, unbeknownst to Chet and all his fellow prisoners — not only in Manchuria but throughout the Far East — they had escaped a horrible death by a mere 24 to 48 hours. In a letter to his wife, Bettie, Major Hennessy later recalled the harrowing experience, writing, "They treated us like kings after the first three hours, but I wouldn't do that mission again for a million bucks — we all thought we were dead ducks."

When word reached the prison camp commandant, he ordered the guards not to harm the prisoners further and instead protect them. Upon surrendering, Japanese troops, posts, headquarters, POW camps and facilities were subject to looting and physical threats. Everything related to Japan instantly had become targets of opportunity and revenge by Chinese gangs. Being at war with the Russians didn't help their situation either.

Although the prisoners indeed were free, it was safer for them to remain inside the prison walls rather than leave the camp. It was a tense and confusing dilemma for the guards, who had inflicted years of endless pain and suffering upon the POWs. Instead of being captors, they soon would trade places with the prisoners and themselves become captives. They feared how they would be treated once they were ordered to surrender their weapons and be subject to the mercy and whims of the Americans — or more worrisome, the Russians.

Due to the Cardinal team's importance, Major Hennessy and his men were returned again to the walled-off headquarters in the city, where they received increased protection overnight. Japanese leaders had no desire to expose them to unnecessary danger, especially since the war was over.

The following morning, they were driven to the Japanese secret police headquarters where the colonel in charge bowed deeply, said he was surrendering and offered up his pistol and saber. Eager to complete Operation Cardinal, Major Hennessy and the team were driven to the

Hoten #1 Camp to locate and rescue General Wainwright and the other senior officers. Except they weren't there.

After the team's pistols and gear were returned politely by the embarrassed and humbled Japanese commandant, Major Hennessy tried contacting OSS headquarters in China to find out if they had more current information regarding General Wainwright's whereabouts, but the connection failed. He then asked the POW commander to summon the senior American POW to the camp commander's office.

Major General George M. Parker, malnourished and emaciated — and wearing not much more than a loin cloth — meekly walked in a few moments later and began to bow to the Japanese commandant as he'd done hundreds of times as a POW. Upon seeing the general's actions, Sergeant Leith immediately stepped forward to interrupt him. "No sir," the sergeant said gently so as not to frighten him. "No more bowing." And then came the words from the sergeant that General Parker and all POWs longed to hear. "The war is over, sir," he said. "It's over."

Shortly afterward, Chet and the more than 1,600 American, British, Australian and Dutch POWs were ordered to assemble on the prison grounds. With the Cardinal team beside him, General Parker stepped onto a small, elevated stage and gleefully announced that Japan officially had surrendered. Upon realizing the war finally was over, the men cheered, punched the sky with their fists and wept happy tears.

After the announcement, Major Hennessy and his team walked through the mass of ill and starving prisoners to shake their hands and accept their gratitude. Unexpectedly, he recognized one of the men in the crowd who was so weak he needed a crutch to lean on in order to stand. It was Chet. He weighed only 103 pounds, but Major Hennessy knew his friend immediately. Holding Chet at arm's length, the major greeted his fellow West Point graduate with a wide smile followed by a long hug. They had graduated together in 1940 and marveled at the odds of them meeting again under such circumstances. As they spent a few moments catching up on their lives since graduation, Chet noticed Major Hennessy was wearing his West Point class ring and made a mental note to ask Grace to order a replacement for his own ring, which he'd lost after becoming a prisoner.

After the outdoor celebration subsided, General Parker informed the Cardinal team that to the best of his recollection, Generals Wainwright and Percival still were at the Hsian POW camp some 100 miles away. He also informed them that Maj. Gen. Edward P. King, who commanded the artillery during the battle for Bataan, and Maj. Gen. George F. Moore, who commanded the Pacific Coast Artillery during the battle for Bataan — two of Lieutenant Britt's former superior officers — had not been included in the prisoner transfer on May 31 and most likely were with General Wainwright.

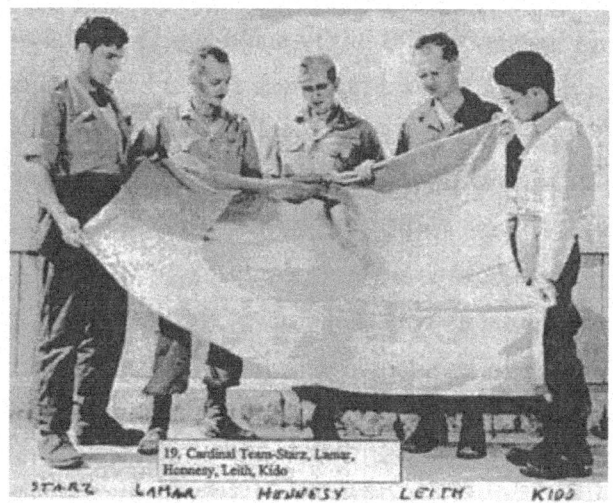

OPERATION CARDINAL OSS team holding a Japanese flag. L-R Tech. Edward A. Starz, radio operator; Maj Robert F. Lamar, physician; team leader and 1940 West Point classmate, Maj James T Hennessy; SSgt Harold "Hal" B. Leith, linguist; Sgt Fumio Kido, Nisei Japanese interpreter.
Not in the photo, Cheng Shih-wu, Chinese national interpreter

Unable to communicate with his OSS superiors in Chungking, Major Hennessy reluctantly decided the best course of action was to split up the team. Major Lamar and Sergeant Leith would travel by train to Hsian along with a Japanese lieutenant who would serve as their interpreter and guard. Meanwhile, Major Hennessy and the others would remain behind to make flight arrangements for the immediate departure of General Wainwright's group and prepare for the imminent arrival of a POW Recovery Team. Their mission was to prioritize and coordinate the departure of the American and allied POWs at Camp Hoten #1, Hsian and elsewhere in the region.

On August 18, as an American plane flew over the city of Mukden dropping leaflets announcing the Japanese surrender, Major Lamar's trio headed out in search of General Wainwright. After several delays and a change of trains, they arrived at Hsian at 3 a.m. on August 19. Following a brief confrontation with the camp commandant, General Wainwright was awakened and brought to the commander's office before sunrise. Major Lamar and Sergeant Leith were stunned when he entered. Dressed in what was left of his tattered uniform, the general was extremely gaunt and had difficulty hearing. "Are you really Americans?" the general asked in amazement. Major Lamar replied, "General, you are no longer a prisoner of war. You're going back to the States."

General Wainwright inquired about how he was perceived back home after surrendering to the Japanese, worried that he'd be called a coward. Major Lamar assured him that was not the case, and in fact, the opposite was true. The general was considered a hero, and — unbeknownst to either of them — already had been nominated to receive the highest honor accorded in the military, the Medal of Honor.

Like the radio Major Hennessy had, the radio Major Lamar carried with him also was inoperable. The advancing Russian troops had cut the telephone lines, leaving no way to inform anyone that General Wainwright had been found. Concerned the general would be kidnapped and murdered by Japanese troops before he could be rescued, the major decided to leave Sergeant Leith with the general while he immediately returned by train to arrange transportation back to Hoten Camp #1 for about two-dozen high-ranking American and allied prisoners.

As Major Lamar made his way back to Mukden on August 19, Chester wrote his first letter home since the war had ended. Paper and pencils were in short supply, but he covered a lot in the two-page letter. He was happy to be able to write whenever, whatever, and as often as he wanted, rather than being constrained to a mere 24 words a few times a year with no guarantee they'd be delivered. Addressing his letter to the entire family, he knew they mostly were concerned about his health. Without going into details and wanting them to know he had not suffered any serious combat injuries such as an amputation, he wrote, "Please don't worry. I feel well and still have a whole body." Of course, he mentioned food, the subject on every POW's mind all day every day. "I've eaten so much in the last 2 days," he said, "that I feel that I'll never be hungry again." He mentioned that ironically, one of his West Point classmates had led the team that rescued him, and that he hoped to be able to be home in time to celebrate Thanksgiving.

Unknown to Chet and his now-free comrades, the first Russian troops landed that day at the airport in Mukden joining advanced units of the Soviet 6th Guards Tank Army who finally had reached the city. They would prove crucial to the POWs' safety, so much so that several Soviet officers subsequently would be recommended for U.S. military decorations for their service to the United States. Just before sunset, the prisoners held a church service of thanksgiving to commemorate their survival. Photo below courtesy of NBC-TV.

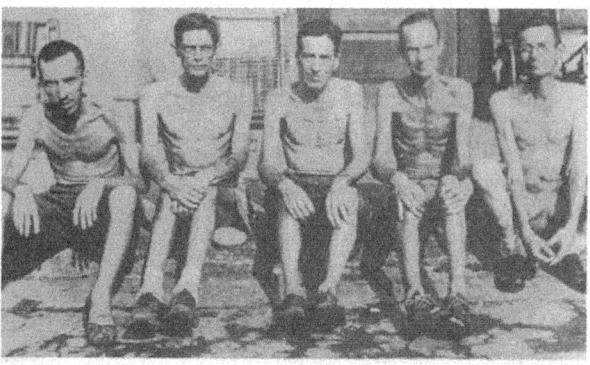

August, 1945, five American ex-POWs immediately after the surrender of Japan

Early in the evening of August 20, the men gathered in the compound for a patriotic songfest to celebrate the war's end. As the men sang a rousing version of "God Bless America," a Russian commander with the Soviet 6th Guards Tank Army entered the compound, ascended the small stage and in a booming, thick accent, shouted in English, "Ve haf come all da vay from Berlin to liberate you. You are FREE MEN!" With that, the Japanese staff and guards were disarmed, and their weapons handed over to the Americans. Chet watched as the Japanese troops — under control of the Russians — were marched out of the compound, never to be seen again.

From his vantage point on the second floor of the barracks, Chet could see the red stars on the Russian tanks surrounding them outside the walls. Though they were free, the city still was unsafe, and the men were advised to remain inside what had become their fortress. Throughout the day and into the night, they frequently heard gunfire nearby. Ironically, they were kept safe by the same walls that had imprisoned them just days before.

OPERATION CARDINAL OSS team Left, Major Robert F. Lamar, physician; Russian soldiers at Mukden, and the team leader Maj James T Hennessy, West Point 1940 classmate of Chester Britt

With the airport secured by the Russians, an American B-24 Liberator arrived on August 21 carrying additional supplies and equipment to support the Cardinal team, including much-needed radios to complete its mission. Of utmost importance was the repatriation and evacuation of the most critically ill and injured men as quickly as possible. Nearly 260 men required extensive and immediate medical attention or critical treatment for a multitude of serious illnesses that threatened further decline. Doctors had prioritized the men according to their medical conditions. The B-24, emptied of its cargo, quickly was converted to accommodate 18 critically injured POWs. They comprised the first flight of evacuees from Mukden directly to hospitals for life-saving care.

While exploring areas in the prison complex formerly off-limits to them, the remaining men discovered thousands of letters addressed to the POWs during their captivity, but which the Japanese had refused to deliver. The letters had been stored in hundreds of boxes in a locked storage room along with thousands of boxes of Red Cross packages that had been ransacked for food and other small supplies of value to the Japanese.

None of the letters, however, were addressed to Lieutenant Britt. He hadn't received any correspondence from home since July 17, 1944. The Japanese refused to inform anyone of the POWs' locations and moved the prisoners frequently. Intelligence lagged woefully behind due to higher-priority information, resulting in the War Department sending outdated address information to their loved ones. Most of the letters sent to Chet were returned without explanation, stamped simply with a single word — UNKNOWN.

Sadly, many letters were addressed to men who had died in captivity, never knowing their loved ones had written to them. The mental torture, anguish and abuse imposed upon the POWs by their captors knew no bounds of mercy or decency. As the men combed through the packages, they traded the items they needed for those they didn't. The letters were read repeatedly until the men could almost recite them from memory.

During the day, Major Hennessy asked the men to write down the details of what they'd experienced since becoming POWs while it was still fresh in their minds. The facts and details they provided from their diaries and memories would become the basis for future military tribunals to hold their Japanese captors accountable for their reprehensible crimes. It was a time-consuming, mentally exhausting task recalling the horrors they'd endured over the past three-plus years and would take weeks to complete.

B-24 FLIGHT PAY with prisoners gathered around. Also, Russian soldiers in the group. Chester's notebook reports they arrived on August 20, so this photo woiuld be on that day or soon after

In a letter to Grace dated August 23, Chet told her that although he was busy writing his official report, he could write every day and hoped that by now she knew he was still alive. Realizing she probably had no idea where he'd been or what he'd experienced since the war started, he mentioned briefly all the places he'd been and generally described what he experienced — leaving out the horrid details so as not to worry her. Chet ended his letter with some startling news, however, mentioning, "Of the 1,619 men who began our trip on Dec 13, '44 we have left only about 250. All the others are dead — so you see how fortunate I am. I shudder to look back." The letter answered a lot of questions regarding where Chet had been. But it was what he didn't say that caused her to weep as she poured over his words, knowing he'd suffered tremendous pain and loss. Though she was a strong woman, she had a tender, loving heart.

Like many wives whose husbands were away at war, Grace worked at a factory that had been converted to support the war effort. Northern Engraving Company, which normally made metal signs and other specialty metal items, was tasked to manufacture parts for large-scale munitions. Grace's job was to produce and inspect shell casings. While she worked, her mother, Hilma, or her mother-in-law, Hazel, looked after Chester Jr. She credited her ability to endure the hardship of not knowing Chet's condition or location to her faith and to her extended family, who supported and sustained her.

In Hsian, Sergeant Leith was unaware that Major Lamar had returned to Mukden on August 21, arriving by train. The Russians had taken control of the city and were in a drunken rampage. They had no interest in helping the Americans at that point, and Majors Hennessy and Lamar were powerless to locate and obtain the vehicles needed to retrieve the general and the other high-ranking prisoners with him. After three days with no word from Major Hennessy — and no one having arrived with transportation for General Wainwright and his group — Sergeant Leith wondered whether Major Lamar had survived the return trip to Mukden. Unsure if transportation was being arranged, he began negotiating with the Japanese commander to obtain transportation for them, but they refused to cooperate. Vehicles and fuel were highly valued and hard to obtain.

The afternoon of August 24, as the seemingly endless negotiations continued, a Russian commander arrived at the prison. He was leading a convoy to Mukden and agreed the POWs could tag along — on one condition. They had to provide their own transportation. Upon hearing the Russian's terms, General Wainwright realized it most likely was their best chance at freedom. He immediately regained his military bearing, asserted his three-star rank — and with Sergeant Leith translating — the general commandeered two rickety trucks and enough fuel to make the trip. The group joined the Russian convoy, and at 6 p.m., began their treacherous journey to freedom.

As the convoy headed south, a B-24 arrived at Mukden and unloaded its belly of more supplies and equipment. Then 32 liberated men, critically in need of medical care, were loaded onto the plane. They comprised the second group of liberated men to be evacuated. Once again being able to communicate, the operation was moving like a well-oiled machine, and Major Hennessy was pleased with the progress. He just wished he knew the status of General Wainwright and Sergeant Leith as well as the other high-ranking prisoners in his charge.

In a letter that night to his parents, Chester wrote it was the first day they were allowed to venture outside the prison. The Russians had secured the city, and it was safe to explore the area beyond the walls. Although at that point he was too weak to walk and unable to lift his foot even four inches, he hoped to join his friends in the coming days. He told his parents it might be best to wait a while before coming home so he could regain his health and fitness. At times, he said he felt lonely because "all my close friends are dead." He attributed his survival to the strong body they had given him and to God's care and guidance. "I guess the bullheaded streak of the Britts' [sic] must have its good points after all, Dad," he wrote. Curious to know about his siblings, he asked about their status, wondering how his brothers were faring and if younger sister Dorothy had married Jesse, the Army lieutenant she'd been dating.

He also wrote a separate note to Dorothy that night, asking her to send Grace a big box of flowers for her birthday, writing, "Pick out the biggest most beautiful bunch you can find." He also inquired about Jesse, asking her whatever happened "to your friend, sweetheart or husband … I hope everything turns out OK for you." Referring again to the nightmare he'd survived, Chet noted, "I'll tell you all the story when I get home. It's horrible enough that you probably will never believe it."

Additional supplies were being air-dropped or delivered every day, which meant more life-saving food and medicines, along with needed clothing and hygiene items. It had been more than three years since they'd seen so much food on their plates. And the American POW doctors and medics in the camp quickly dispensed vital medications, antibiotics and vitamins critical to the prisoners' recovery. Sterile bandages and basic medical equipment — stethoscopes, blood pressure cuffs, scalpels, suture kits and pain medication — helped diagnose medical problems, halted the risk of further infection and helped wounds heal more quickly. Soap, shampoo, toothpaste and toothbrushes were in high demand.

B-29 parachuting supplies to ex-POWs in Camp Hoten.
Chester's barracks #2 is beside the shoulder of man on the right

Once their basic necessities were met, air drops included magazines and newspapers, which the men passed around so much the ink barely was readable. They were stunned to learn President Roosevelt had been elected to an unprecedented fourth term but had died only 82 days after his latest inauguration. Harry S. Truman, his new vice president, assumed the presidency and was now their commander-in-chief. It was he who ordered the atomic bombs to be dropped on Hiroshima and Nagasaki, essentially ending the war. The men also enjoyed sports news and bantered about the St. Louis Cardinals — who had won the World Series twice in the last three years — and the New York Yankees, who had captured the coveted title in between the Cardinals' two victories.

Meanwhile, Sergeant Leith and his high-value charges were having difficulty keeping up with the Russian convoy. Torrential rains had turned the dirt backroads they were traversing into a muddy mess. Frustrated with the slow pace and wanting to rid himself of the burdensome task, the Russian colonel flagged down a three-car train and at gunpoint, forced the Japanese crew to take the prisoners to Mukden. The train derailed a short distance down the track, and the Russian colonel promised to send another train, which forced the group to spend an uncomfortable night on the cramped train. Surprisingly, the colonel kept his word. The following day, another train arrived to take them the rest of the way to Mukden. Arriving at 1:30 a.m. on August 27, Sergeant Leith immediately left the train, located a radio and contacted Major Hennessy, who then passed the good news to his OSS superiors.

At 3 a.m., the major arrived at the train station with several vehicles and met the general, informing him a C-47 and a B-24 were waiting at an airport north of the city to take him and the other POWs to U.S. Army headquarters in the Far East, which was located in Chungking. Sergeant Leith — who was awarded a brevet (temporary) promotion to major — was assigned to accompany the group to expedite and arrange further accommodations and travel. Upon arrival in Chungking, the general was awarded the Distinguished Service Medal. As the citation was read, tears flowed down his sunken cheeks as he realized what Major Lamar had said to him was true. His escort mission complete, Major Leith then boarded a flight back to Mukden to rejoin the Cardinal team.

With the Russian security forces providing protection throughout Mukden, the pace of evacuating injured and ill prisoners increased. On August 29, POW Recovery Team #1, led by Lt. Col. "Wild Bill" Donovan, landed at Mukden to assist the Cardinal team in organizing and processing the remaining POWs. Included in the team were graves registration specialists who were assigned the grim duty of locating, exhuming and identifying the bodies of those who had perished in captivity. Remains would be returned to their next-of-kin for burial close to home. The 19-man team identified each of the approximately 1,300 remaining prisoners at Mukden and provided them temporary documentation, immunizations and clothing. They prioritized and determined each man's route home based on his individual medical needs while taking precautions to avoid exposure to the various contagious diseases the prisoners had contracted.

Once the recovery teams were in place, the return of POWs began in earnest as more than 1,000 B-29s began flying supply missions to the 157 prison camps throughout the Far East. Each plane carried 10,000 pounds of food and medical supplies, enough to feed and treat the POWs until the mission was complete. In those areas lacking airports or adequate landing strips, deliveries were made via air drops, which sometimes missed their targets. The massive mission was vital to facilitating the return of prisoners who had suffered and survived years of unspeakable inhumanity.

The deliveries sometimes included unexpected surprises. Movies, cards, checkers and other forms of entertainment helped the prisoners readjust to freedom and the normal lifestyles they'd soon be experiencing once again. It didn't take long for their stomachs to adjust to a richer diet, and Chet informed Grace that — after dreaming about and craving eggs throughout his three-plus years as a prisoner — for his first "real" meal, he had consumed 15 pigeon eggs.

Finally, on September 2, 17 days after Major Hennessy and the Cardinal team dropped out of the sky, Lieutenant Britt and 28 of his fellow survivors were transported to the Mukden airport. Awaiting them was a shiny B-24 ready to take them on the first leg of their long journey home. With Chet were Captain Skardon and First Lieutenant Faulkner, who also were on the Oryoku Maru. All three had experienced the seven-week nightmare voyage on the three hell ships that took them to Japan. As the wheels lifted off the runway at 10:33 a.m., the group applauded and let out a booming cheer, knowing they really and truly were free.

While they were winging their way 942 miles south to Xi'an, Gen. Douglas MacArthur and envoys of the Japanese Emperor were gathered on the deck of the U.S.S. Missouri, at anchor in Yokohama Bay. They were surrounded by some 200 American warships. As General MacArthur sat at a small table and signed the two copies of the official surrender document — one for the United States and one for Japan — two men stood slightly behind him in places of honor to witness the historic event. When he'd finished signing, General MacArthur turned to the two men and presented

Lt. Gen. Jonathan Wainwright and British Lt. Gen. Arthur Percival the pens with which he'd signed the documents.

At 4:45 p.m., Chet's plane arrived at Xi'an, where the headquarters for U.S. Armed Forces Far East had been relocated upon Japan's surrender. The men were taken to a hotel in the city that had been converted to a medical facility to care for returning prisoners. They were informed they'd received the promotions due them while they were prisoners and would be treated accordingly, although the official, back-dated orders would be presented at a later date. The men were restricted to the hotel, but none were upset. They had all the food they wanted, and beds with a thick, comfortable mattresses.

The newly-promoted Major Skardon recalled how a nurse had ordered him to change in to clean — yes, clean! — pajamas and get into bed. With a sly grin, he remarked she didn't have to tell him twice. They all felt like they were sleeping on a cloud, something they hadn't experienced since before heading into the jungles of Bataan to counter the Japanese attack.

The next morning, the group was driven back to the Xi'an airport where a twin-engine, C-46 transport plane awaited to fly them 744 miles further south to Kunming. They arrived in mid-afternoon and were taken directly to a hospital where they all underwent chest X-rays and blood draws. Receiving negative test results, the now-Captain Britt was transferred to a casual ward where he received additional clothing.

All of the approximately 260 prisoners who were evacuated from Mukden by plane took the same route to Kunming. But at that point — in order to hasten their return and not overburden the processing centers — some were flown west through India and some head east to the Philippines. Chet was routed to the Philippines, but some of his friends, as an example his friend 1Lt Emil Ulanowicz, went home via India.

With everything running smoothly, on September 5, Captain Britt was discharged from the hospital and taken to a Chinese hotel in Kunming to await his next flight, which was scheduled that night. Along with most of the group he'd been traveling with, he was taken by bus the airport, arriving just a few minutes before midnight. The driver pulled onto the ramp and pulled up beside a four-engine, C-54 transport aircraft. The men were helped off the bus and up the stairs to their seats. With boarding complete, the captain revved the engines, rolled down the taxiway, and the plane lifted off the runway at 12:15 a.m. Enjoying the day at the hotel rather than having to wait at the airport for his flight, Chet felt like a VIP. He relaxed in his seat and went to sleep, knowing he'd be in Manila by mid-morning, and he'd be another 1,400 miles closer to home. It was quite a change from his outbound trip nearly eight months prior.

At 9:30 the morning of September 6, as the plane approached its destination, Chet instantly recognized the landmarks below him — Fort Wint, Corregidor, Bataan, Subic Bay and what was left of the Manila sky-line. It was Grace's birthday, and he thought about their happy and sad experiences on Pier 7 and the wonderful times they'd enjoyed at the Subic Officers' Club dances.

Upon landing, the repatriated POWs were considered patients and taken to a processing center where the group was split up and sent to var-ious hospitals throughout Manila depending on the care they needed. Captain Britt was assigned to the 312th Army Hospital for further evalua-tion, testing and treatment for his illnesses and wounds.

Although Chet had sustained injuries in the attack on the Enoura Maru as it was anchored in Formosa, no one authorized to submit the rec-ommendation had survived. He never pursued it, saying he was just glad he survived to come home because so many hadn't. He wasn't alone in not seeking recognition for his service. Like thousands who had sustained combat injuries, Chet just wanted to forget the war as quickly as possible, get home to his family and move on with his life. He didn't need a medal to remind him of the hell he'd survived.

As he received treatment and continued to regain his strength, Captain Britt was debriefed by intelligence officers and continued writing the lengthy report of his captivity, which would be included in the official records used during the war crimes trials.

Prisoners who were not evacuated by air from POW Camp Hoten #1 were transported by train to the port of Dairen (now Dalian). There, they boarded the hospital ship USS Relief to be de-loused, cleaned up, examined and treated for medical and dental needs. Those deemed in the best of health were placed aboard the U.S.S. Colbert, a transport ship that sailed for Okinawa.

On September 19, the mission of the OSS Cardinal team and POW Recovery Team #1 was completed. Camp Hoten #1 was handed over to the Russians. And in perhaps the best possible incidence of karma ever, it continued to be used as a prison camp. This time, however, it would hold 5,000 Japanese POWs — captured by the Russians.

Chet's first letters from Manchuria, Letters 19 and 23 August 1945. These letters are self-explanatory, filled with emotions and yet restrained as though Chet does not remember how to feel, in shock from how quickly it all ended.

Camp Hoten Manchuria
Aug. 19 - 1945

Dearest Grace, Mom, Dad, & all
on folks at home.
At last I can write anything I desire with fair
assurance of the letter reaching you quickly;
+ I scarcely know what to say or where to begin.
We are very happy here — our dream come true at
last. the dream of freedom under our own flag.
It happened suddenly though not entirely
by surprise, for we had sensed the time was
near. We had heard the Russians was in the war
+ that Japan was being blasted continuously
by us. then out of a clear sky on the morning
of Aug 16 dropped several parachutes, which
we later learned landed 6 Americans whose
job was to take over the control of the camp —
the war being over, the leader of the Group
is Major Hennesay a classmate of mine
from dear old U.S.M.A. I saw him yesterday
+ talked with him for a short while. I was
happy to find that he recognized me. I was
afraid I might have changed but he said
not, except for loss of weight. Today we expect
Amer, planes to bring us supplies of food
clothing + etc. the Japs. are still here but the
Camp is now run by us. We are reorganizing +
getting ready to move, although we know not
where or when as yet. For the 1st time since
the beginning of the war we are getting enough
to eat; in fact to much for our present
gastric capacities. The food is local and

August 19, 1945 Chet's first letter home after liberation. page 1
The last letter he sent was while fighting on Bataan March 6, 1942

consists of brown flour buns heavy as lead, corn meal mush for breakfast, and mainly soy beans + potatoes for the other 2 meals. Enough of this place, except to add that today is a beautiful Sunday cool + sunny. Happy birthday Mon. Glad t' to you September 11th Grace + little. het. I can scarcely wait to return to you all + surely hope we may all be together by Thanksgiving. I'll be able to write or Radio to you frequently in the near future and will let you know as soon as I found out where we will land in the States. Please dont worry. I feel well + still have a whole body. I've eaten so much in the past 2 wks that I feel that I'll never be hungry again. My mind is in a muddle so please forgive me for missing things you want to know. May God bless you all + keep you safe. I'll be with you all soon.

All my love to you all

Chet.

August 19, 1945   Chet's first letter home after liberation. page 2

August 23, 1945   Chet's letter home after liberation page 1

In June '44 we were sent back to Cabanatuan in Luzon via Bilibid in Manila. October '44 we went back to Manila awaiting the trip to Japan. Dec 13 '44 we sailed from Manila on the Oryoku Maru and were bombed and sunk in Subic Bay. From Olongapo we went by train to the Northern tip of Luzon and sailed in an old horse freighter to Formosa. In the harbor in Formosa we were bombed again — changed ships to a third freighter, and sailed to Japan arriving in Moji on Jan 30 '45. We stayed in Japan until April 25 '45 and then were moved to this camp in Manchuria. Of the 1619 men who began our trip on Dec 13 '44

August 23, 1945   Chet's letter home after liberation   page 2

we have left only about 250.
All the others are dead — so you
see how fortunate I am. I
shudder to look back.

I must go now hon — I
can write every day now,
and most certainly will.

All my love to you and
to little Chesty

"Chet"

August 23, 1945   Chet's letter home after liberation   page 3

The next two pages provide the group photo for the survivors of the first Hell ship the Oryoku Maru, that were sent to Hoten #1 camp in Mukden, Manchuria.

If you can identify any other men in these photos, please contact the authors as we will continually update this list on our website, if men remain unidentified. These photos and five other high-resolution photos of this group and more men can be found on our website. We hope to eventually be able to identify all the Oryoku men at Mukden. About half the Oryoku survivors were sent to Jinsen POW camp in Korea, but unfortunately no known group photo of them exists.

Survivors of Oryoku Maru rescued in Mukden, Manchuria

Oryoku Maru survivors at Mukden August 19, 1945.

Known men are #8 John E LESTER; #11 Kenneth W RAMSEY; #15 Robert E THOMPSON; # 16 Chester K BRITT; #25 Charles H BENNETT; #29 Allen L PECK; #30 Eugene C JACOBS; #34 Beverly "Ben" N SKARDON; #35 Paul D PHILLIPS; #37 Emil M ULANOWICZ

Survivors of Oryoku Maru rescued in Mukden, Manchuria

Known Oryoku Maru men in this photo are

#34 SKARDON, Beverly N. "Ben"; #35 PHILLIPS, Paul D. ; #37 ULANOWICZ, Emil M.; #41 WERMUTH, Arthur; #51 Doctor Smith; #58 TRAPNELL, Thomas J; #61 BOOTH, Maynard; #64 WILSON, Ovid O "ZERO"

What follows is the actual diary that he kept from the beginning of the Hell Ship experience through the rescue and trip back to Philippines to receive medical treatment before going home. The booklet was from the MKK factory in Mukden, Manchuria where the prisoners were used as slave labor for the Japanese military.

備　忘　録

氏名

滿洲工作機械株式會社

1Lt Chester K Britt diary Oct 13, 1944 through Sept 6, 1945 from time leading up to and including the hell ships Oryoku Maru, Enoura Maru, and Brazil Maru, Fukuoka POW Camp #3, POW camp HOTEN in Mukden, Manchuria, to liberation

Oct 13/44: Departed from Cabanatuan - entrucked to Bilibid Prison Manila - arrived late at night - everything "blackout." 1 cup hot lugao on arrival. (about 250 in our group of officers) Joined "1 group officers Oct 13 - Dec 12 - Bilibid Prison, Manila. Witnessed several air raids. Were sold 5 coccanuts and 20 bulbs garlic, salt (1 pren can). Later ½ pkg tobacco. (cost 30 Pesos). Plenty of water, shower baths available - library books issued. No mosquito bars malaria - denge fevers. Swollen legs - issued vitamin tablets (Red Cross) daily. Other groups joined us raising total to well over 1600 - some entered in hospital as permanent patients. Food very insufficient (about 250 grms rice plus ⅓ cup poor soup daily - put out as 1 cup lugao at breakfast and 1 cup lugao late afternoon with soup). All men lost weight and strength daily. Were finally issued woolen clothing and cigarettes for move to Japan.

Chet Diary Oct 13 to Dec 12, 1944
From leaving Cabanatuan through his time at Bilibid Prison

Departure for Japan - Aboard Oryoku Maru:

Dec. 13/44. Left Manila - 1619 Officers, men - 1 meal, no water.

Dec. 14. Bombed 9AM-dark off Subic Bay - 1 small meal at dark.

Dec. 15. Bombed in Olongapo Bay. Abandoned ship 10AM to Naval Yard. No food all day. Plenty of water.

Dec. 16. In tennis court. 1300 survivors. Bombing + strafing all around us entire day. 1 G.I. spoon raw rice at dark, 1 canteen water.

Dec. 17. Tennis court. 294 casualties estimated. 1 spoon raw rice.

Dec. 18. Tennis court. Hot days, cold nights - no clothing except shorts. 1 spoon raw rice (sent daily issue). 1 canteen water.

Dec. 19. Tennis court. No food. 1 canteen water.

Dec. 20. Tennis court. Doc amputated arm of enlisted man. Capt. Winnie buried. 2 spoons raw rice. Moved by truck to San Fernando. Cooked rice, first since bombing of ship (½ cup per man). Housed in yard of city jail. 1 cup water.

Dec. 21. San Fernando jail yard. 2 small portions cooked rice.

Dec. 22. San F. jail yard. Am. planes over city. Col. Harper + Capt. Petze died. 2 small portions cooked rice, 2 camotes.

Dec. 23. San F. Moved out 15 sick to Manila. 2 meals cooked rice.

Chet Diary Dec 13 to Dec 23, 1944
Oryoku Maru, tennis court, to San Fernando Pampanga

Dec. 24. San F. Waked at 3AM for move. Bitter cold. Moved at daylight by train to San Fernando, La Union. (In box cars all day - no water - no food). Arrived at dusk - Spent night on station platform.

Dec. 25. San Fernando, La Union. Marched to school yard - 2 meals (½ cup rice per man). March to beach in middle of night.

Dec. 26. San F., La Union Beach. 1 rice ball at daybreak. entire day in hot sun (no clothing, hats, or shoes). 1 spoon raw rice at dark, ½ cup water. Col. Edmonds (Inf.) died

Dec. 27. San F., La Union. Boarded horse freighter (2-4AM)

Dec. 28. Freighter off Philippines. Lt. Brown jumped overboard in escape attempt. 3 torpedoes fired at ship (missed). ½ cup cooked rice, 9 GI spoons water.

Dec. 29. Freighter. Air raid (no hits on our ship). 2 men died. 1 meal (½ cup cooked rice). ½ cup water.

Dec. 30. Freighter. Arrived in harbor of Formosa. 3 men died. 1 meal (½ cup cooked rice)

Dec. 31. Freighter. 3 men died. no food. 8 spoons water. Cold weather. no clothes or shoes.

Chet Diary Dec 24 to Dec 31, 1944
To San Fernando La Union, Enoura Maru to arrival at Takao

193

Jan 1/45 · Freighter · 2 meals (½ cup cooked rice each) · 3 spoons water.

Jan 2 · Freighter · 4 died · Jordan fell 40 feet into bottom of an hold · 1 meal (½ cup cooked rice) · 8 spoons water.

Jan 3 · Freighter · 4 died · Air alert (no raid) · ½ cup rice · 6 spoons water. (Roy Bell among those dead today)

Jan 4 · Freighter · 3 died · 2 meals (½ cup rice each) · 6 spoons water.

Jan 5 · Freighter · 5 died · 1 meal (½ cup rice) · 1 cup water.

Jan 6 · Freighter · 3 died · 2 meals (½ cup rice) · ½ cup water.

Jan 7 · Freighter · 2 died (Cmdr. Ports) · 2 meals (same) · ½ cup water.

Jan 8 · Freighter · Lt. Benson died · 2 meals (same) · 6 spoons water.

Jan 9 · Freighter · 4 died · Ship bombed and strafed. About 260 killed in forward hold, many (50) in 2d hold · 1 meal before bombing · no water · Wounded

Jan 10 · Freighter · Holds piled with dead · Many dies dysentry · Many wounded + sick (No medical supplies or bandages) Continued cold weather - no clothes · 2 meals (½ cup rice each) · ½ cup water.

Jan 11 · Freighter · Consolidated in 2d hold · Moved outdoors 224 out of 473 in forward hold · 50 from 2d hold · Moved to 3rd ship · No food · No water.

Chet Diary Jan 1 to Jan 11, 1945
Enoura Maru bombed at Takao, aftermath of the attack

Jan 12 - Jan 29. 2 meals day (½ cup rice). ¼ cup water per day. Cold weather - no clothes. Men died hourly from exposure, starvation, dehydration, dysentry, exhaustion. Rain and snow. Several submarine attacks (no hits). Arrived in Japan (Moji Harbor).

Jan 30. Issued clothing and shoes (except hospital group). Cold rain & snow. Left ship (Moji) - marched to theater (about 450 men left - all in poor shape). Fed in theater (all rice and water we could eat). Split into groups. One group (100 officers ? N.C.E.M.) marched to street car, transported to Camp 3 (arrived at night - were given hot "coffee" before going to sleep).

Fukuoka Camp # 3

Jan 30 - April 24. Cold weather. Poor treatment. Poor hospital. Men died, mainly from run down condition resulting from trip. Lives saved in hospital (B side, vitamins, plus sulphur drugs, etc abroad). Food (3 meals daily - rice and soup). Small amount Red Cross Food (about 1½ boxes per man, spread over entire period) - about 40 cigarettes issued per week. Paid once (10 yen). We were sold few tangerines. Zora gas, clam mashed powder. Food here and bed bugs. Lice terrible. Hot cold baths on arrival. Lice bad.

Chet Diary Jan 12 to Apr 24, 1945
Brazil Maru, arrival at Moji, POW camp Fukuoka #3

each day. 24 men died over this period. Forced to
volunteer to work in order to avoid ration cut.

April 25: 76 (Officers + 3 corp. men) departed the Hdytrs.
camp (via street car, train) had to march about 2 miles
Hdytrs. camp to ship (2 miles). Air raid - stayed on
dock all night - very cold. Combined with other groups.

April 26: Left Japan (Fukuoka), with other groups,
in morning. 3 light meals. Maj Smothers died - Arrived
Korea. (Fusan) late afternoon - to theater for night.
Supper good (Army ration - box rice + side dish) ←→

April 27. Boarded passenger train (250 men)
3 good rice meals. very little water. 2 men per seat.

April 28. On train. 3 good meals (rice). little water.
Treatment good.

April 29. Arrived Mukden (Manchuria) 1 AM.
Changed trains. Breakfast (¾'s bag ration crackers).
Arrived Hoten Camp mid morning - usual ceremony
and admission.

April 29 - May 23. Food good but insufficient (3 small
rns + 1 bowl mush + 2 soups daily. wt 122 lbs on
_____

Chet Diary Apr 25 to May 23, 1945
Ship Japan to Fusan, train to Mukden, life at Mukden

Blood Typing arrived tec. Finally detained.

May 23rd - x Pts 28 lbs - swollen legs. Infected neck gland cut open. Weak and general run down, but gaining little strength. Small wet Fullress food issued over this period.

May 2th Color Commis arrived (about 520 men) Ration considerably lighter.

Aug 16 - Free - parachute troops (Americans) dropped in to Give us aid. take over camp.

Aug 16 Russian gen. visited camp and told us we were officially free. Japs disarmed and put under own guards. Following days B-29s dropped food and supplies by parachute. First mail in camp Aug 30.

Sept 2 - left Mukden airport on B-24. (2 planes - total 30 in party) departure 10:33 A arrived Siam 4:45 P (975 miles).

Chet Diary May 23 to Sept 2, 1945
Life at Mukden, liberated August 16, evacuated from Mukden

197

Sept 3rd Left Sian airfield 10:00 A on
C46 - fair weather, good trip; arrived Kunming
airfield 2:30 P. Entered in hospital; X ray of
chest — Kahn; blood test.
Sept 4 — transferred ward #1, to ward 15.
Sept 5 — clothes issue. taken to both 14 (Chinese Hotel) in
Kunming 2:30 – 3:15 P Left for airport
about 11:50 P.
Sept 6 Left Kunming on C54 at
12:15 A — arrived Manila about noon
passed over Corregidor — saw Bataan, old
fortified islands, etc. Taken to redistribution
camp #29 south of Manila. Afternoon
taken to hospital, east of Manila for
hospitalization, treatment.
Sept 7.

Chet Diary Sept 3 to Sept 6, 1945
To Sian (sic XIAN) to Kunming to Manila. Sept 7, final diary entry

CHAPTER 9

Recovery & Repatriation
(September 1945 – July 1946)

When Chet landed in the Philippines on September 6, officials at the processing center immediately notified the Army Staff that he was safely in friendly territory and a patient at the 312th Army Hospital in Manila. Unlike the months of waiting for any word from Army headquarters, the War Department wasted no time informing the Britt family of his arrival in the Philippines. Within two days —taking into account the International Date Line — a letter was on its way to tell them the good news.

In correspondence dated September 7 and addressed to Chet's parents, Maj. Gen. Edward F. Witsell, acting Adjutant General of the Army, formally stated that Secretary of War Henry L. Stimson had directed the general to inform them their son had been returned to U.S. military control two days earlier and would be returning to U.S. soil in the near future. That day couldn't come soon enough for the Britt family. The letter included an address where Chet could receive packages and letters. This time, there was no limit to how many words they could write. And they knew whatever they sent wouldn't be returned marked UNKNOWN.

Since his rescue, Chet slowly regained weight, but still was physically fragile. It had been a long time since he'd eaten a normal diet and like all POWs, his digestive system needed time to adjust. That, combined with all the drugs he was given to treat his various medical problems, kept him in a stupor most of his waking hours. Additionally, the prisoners were physically and mentally exhausted from the continuous adversity and deprivation they'd faced. Though they talked incessantly of favorite meals and recipes during their captivity, they were unable to consume the rich foods they'd imagined eating and were somewhat disappointed in the not-so-extravagant meals Army dieticians had prescribed — a bland diet supplemented by seemingly endless quantities of vitamins, minerals, and other nutrients to prevent upsetting their delicate and damaged stomachs. They were informed it would be a slow, methodical process to ensure they were able to travel without the need for intensive medical treatment during their return. Not only were Army officials and doctors concerned about the prisoners' health, but they also wanted to avoid frightening their families. Seeing their ravaged bodies — ribs sticking out, sunken eyes and chests, infected wounds, barely able to walk or function — was not the image the Army wanted families to see. And to a man, the prisoners agreed.

On September 11, in his first letter to Grace from the Army hospital in Manila, Chet wrote he was a bad patient because it was late, and he was supposed to be in bed, but "I just had to write to you." His days were filled with a combination of physical therapy, medical tests and exams and taking medications and vitamins. In the evenings after dinner, he joined his fellow patients in the day room at the end of the ward and listened to music, the news or delayed broadcasts of baseball and football games on the Armed Forces Radio station. Some days, medics would set up a projector and screen so they could watch a movie. Then, as often as he could, he ended the day with a letter to his loving Grace.

He asked about his family members, reminisced about the day Grace was evacuated and how sad he was the day she left. He mentioned he had yet another malaria attack, which was delaying his return. He left out details of the many medical problems he was being treated for to avoid alarming her. His condition, he said, might require him to stay for a while at a hospital in San Francisco, and he mentioned he hoped she could visit him there. In reply to an earlier letter from Grace, he said he had not yet seen Franklin, who was stationed about 65 miles away at Clark Field. Chet wanted to see him if possible before he left, but said he was concerned if he visited his brother, he might miss boarding a flight or ship to come home. He was so eager to see her and be with her again, even in his current condition, he added, "I feel like setting out for home on foot right now."

Two days later, the captain wrote he had recovered from his latest malaria attack and had passed a test indicating he was in remission. As a result, his name had been added to the list of patients cleared to return to the States. His mind was "foggy" from the medications he required, and his mood was melancholy as he listened to the rain on the hospital's tin roof. He mentioned he'd not been sleeping well, perhaps because he couldn't unsee all the horrific things he'd endured while he was a prisoner, recalling them once again for the reports and affidavits the Army sought in order to pursue war tribunals against Japanese troops who had mistreated their captives. The nights were especially difficult to navigate as images of the past few years haunted him whenever he closed his eyes. He mentioned again how much he missed Grace and how desperately he wanted to see her, hoping that she might be able to visit him in San Francisco.

Due to the 13-hour time difference between La Crosse and Manila, Chester Jr. was celebrating his 4th birthday on September 21 as Chet was having breakfast the morning of September 22 in the Philippines and thinking about what he'd write in his letter to Grace that night. As he listened to music on the radio, his mood seemed upbeat. "The moon is beautiful tonight," he wrote "and the radio is playing, 'Let's Take the Long Way Home' — reminding me of those evenings long ago when I escorted you home from the library (the long way)." Franklin had managed a 2-day visit, he said, which most likely was responsible for his improved state of mind.

Seeing his brother after so many years apart had lifted his spirits, even though he lamented his life "had been filled with goodbyes" alluding to the sorrow he felt by the needless loss of so many friends. Frustrated he had not been able to return to her, he wrote, "I can't understand the cause for the long delay. As I've told you, my name was submitted some time ago to headquarters to be evacuated. I hate to spend any more time away from you dearest — even a minute."

The frustration he felt at not being able to return as quickly as he wanted to be returned was due to a flood of 70,000 seriously wounded troops who needed extensive medical care available only in the States. The main holdup was a lack of reliable aircraft to move them across the Pacific Ocean. Planes had been flown beyond their maximum safety parameters during the war and needed to be repaired and serviced. Air and maintenance crews — already over-extended during the war — worked around the clock to get planes ready for the long flight over water.

Monsoon season was in full swing as well, and ships and planes were dependent on calm seas and favorable winds. Most of the wounded returned by ship, but the most seriously wounded were evacuated by air as the weather permitted. Former POWs with the longest time in captivity received priority to travel by air with the sickest men departing first. On September 13, Captain Britt received his medical release to travel, which was the biggest hurdle to clear in going home.

Waiting his turn further prolonged the agony of separation. It was constantly on his mind as he expressed his frustration and sadness in a letter the next day. "The big moon tonight makes me very lonesome," he wrote. "I want so very much to be with you, hon. It's so very disheartening to be free to come home and no way to get there." He then told her he'd learned three of his close friends, who also had been POWs with him, had survived and were at a replacement center about 30 miles away. His colleague at Fort Wint, Capt. Al D'Arezzo; a West Point classmate and one of his groomsmen, Capt. Fred Yeager; and one of his closest friends (like brothers), 1st Lt. Bill Lewis. He hoped to be able to see them before returning home as they had kept each other alive during captivity and had formed a bond that couldn't be broken.

He also recalled particular moments they'd spent together in high school and while he was in college, saying, "I thought of all those times over and over these past few years. I have those mental pictures constantly before me and remember them all, hon. … If this war had gone on for many more years I should have got through somehow." Those memories and images had sustained him through the darkest hours of his life, encouraging him to take another breath, to endure another hardship, to do whatever was needed to live to spur him on and see him through the next challenge.

Sadly, he informed Grace their good friend and classmate, Gus Cullen had died in February 1945 after the brutal voyage on the hell ships. He had reached Japan, but due to his poor physical condition, was unable to fight off the pneumonia he'd contracted in the freezing hold of the Brazil Maru as it headed to Japan. Of the 21 friends and West Point graduates in his 1940 graduating class who were stationed in the Philippines during the war, only 11 had survived. An astounding 84 per cent of his friends and graduates had made the ultimate sacrifice, their common experience being the Hell Ships.

Their loss brought up feelings of sadness, reminding Chet of the pain and torture they'd experienced — and the guilt he experienced as a survivor. He had witnessed so much suffering and death as a young man and felt a kinship even with those he didn't know. The shared experiences of military life — the separation and loneliness of being far from home away from family and friends — brought men and women in uniform together to form a close-knit, surrogate family of sorts to cope with the missed birthdays, weddings, graduations, holidays, and milestones in a family's life. The hopes, dreams, pain, and joy of one was felt by all.

Chet was filled with excitement in his letter on September 25. The monsoon season was coming to an end, and he'd heard rumors a hospital ship might be leaving in a few days, which meant he could be back in the States in a few weeks. He was hopeful yet cautious as he'd heard similar rumors before only to be disappointed. Still, in the event he'd be boarding a ship soon, Chet told her he'd wire her his location when he reached the West Coast hoping she would come to see him. "Oh! I can scarcely wait,

Gracie!" he wrote. "Perhaps in the next three weeks I'll see you again. It hardly seems possible — you'll have to keep pinching me all the time, so I'll know it's not just another dream."

The next day, Capt. George Faulkner, who was with Chet in Manchuria and also a patient at the hospital, managed to obtain a car for a day-pass away from all things medical. It was their first taste of true freedom, a chance to be on their own for several hours to relax, enjoy themselves and tour the familiar sites they knew. They drove past the bombed-out buildings that were nothing more than rubble. They drove by the harbor and Pier 7 — from which they'd departed in the hell ship for Japan 10 months earlier — and saw all kinds of American ships bringing in supplies and loading freighters with combat equipment to be returned stateside.

George Faulkner, second from right with arms behind his back
pre-war photo with other B-17 pilots

They ventured into the countryside, driving over roads that had been shelled in an attempt to cut off the city. Not a single city block had escaped some measure of destruction. Buildings still standing were pock-marked by bullet holes and shattered windows. It was yet another reminder of the devastation the Japanese had wrought upon the once beautiful island country in a futile attempt to expand their empire.

Upon their return, Captain Faulkner hoped to arrange for another car the next day for a trip to Clark Field so Chet could see Franklin one more time before heading home to Grace. Unfortunately, another monsoon had drenched Manila overnight, and the trip had to be cancelled. Chet had received a typhoid shot that morning and was feverish by late afternoon. Heavy rain and strong winds throughout the day had quashed any hope of planes or ships leaving Manila. Delays had become all too common, and the former POWs had no idea when they'd be able to go home. Morale was sinking among the patients, and their false hopes were wearing thin on frayed nerves.

On September 28, Captain Faulkner obtained another vehicle, but instead of driving to Clark Field, they visited several headquarters office seeking an answer as to why they had not left for home yet. They were told a British aircraft carrier was leaving in four days, which might have room for them. Pressing for more information, they were informed the condition of the U.S. aircraft fleet was still in such poor conditions that passenger service had been suspended for three weeks in order to repair the planes for the long overseas flight. However, that turned out to be inaccurate.

The problem, it seemed, was on the West Coast. After every major combat operation in the Pacific, seriously wounded troops were evacuated to Letterman Army Hospital in San Francisco. In the month before the war ended, the hospital had received, processed, and treated 9,000 wounded combat troops. Recovered American Military Personnel or RAMP patients — the term used for former prisoners of war — had to wait until after the wounded combat troops could be transferred to other hospitals near their homes. Only then could the hospital accommodate the RAMP patients and provide proper care.

On October 3, Captain Britt sent Grace the happiest letter he'd written since being rescued in mid-August. He was coming home! And he was leaving later that afternoon! His few belongings had been packed for days in anticipation of the trip, a three-day trans-Pacific flight to San Francisco. They were scheduled to stop in Guam and Hawaii to refuel and change flight crews, and he was due to arrive on the West Coast on October 5, allowing for the date change as he crossed the International Date Line.

Of course, he'd arrive weeks before she received the letter, and he'd already have talked to her by then, but it didn't matter. Chet was so excited to be going home he had to write and tell her how much he looked forward to being in her arms again. "I'm so excited, hon," he wrote. "I can scarcely believe that I am actually coming back …. Don't be surprised if I can't say anything when I first see you, because seeing you again after all that has happened will be the greatest thrill I shall ever have."

Soon after he'd arrived at Letterman Army Hospital on the grounds of the Presidio in San Francisco, Chet called Grace and learned she would not be able to visit him. She needed to continue working and caring for Chester Jr. It was wonderful to finally hear her voice, but they talked only for a short time as other returning troops were waiting to call their loved ones as well.

RAMP patients well enough to travel to hospitals near their homes remained at the California hospital an average of three days, mostly to complete administrative paperwork and update their records to reflect promotions and medals they'd earned. During the month of October 1945 when Captains Britt, Faulkner, Skardon and their group arrived from the Philippines, the hospital received, examined, treated, clothed, and processed more than 10,000 patients for transfer to hospitals throughout the country. On one day alone, 1,841 wounded troops — half of whom were RAMP patients — arrived for processing and treatment evaluations. Depending on their medical needs, patients with more serious injuries and illnesses remained longer.

They received additional therapy and treatment for disabilities ranging from loss of sight or hearing, amputations, and mental health problems. Intense physical and occupational therapy along with educational and reading assistance were provided to those needing extra care to adapt to their new realities. A library with more than 1,000 books helped to pass the time in the evening after a day of treatment, which helped distract patients from the lingering memories of combat.

Chet remained at Letterman Army Hospital about 10 days, undergoing further tests, treatment, and evaluation. He was still underweight, but progressing, and the remaining symptoms from the many tropical illnesses he'd suffered were nearly gone thanks to nearly two months of a regimen of sulfa drugs, thiamine, Vitamin C and a diet high in protein, vitamins and fiber. He underwent mental health treatment to help overcome the emotional damage, depression and stress caused by more than three years of torture, abuse, and the threat of death.

About October 15, 1945   Captain Britt receiving treatmen at
Lettermen Hospital in San Francisco

While at the hospital, Captain Britt — along with all the other RAMP patients in his group — participated in a mass promotion and award ceremony to recognize their achievements and sacrifice throughout their imprisonment. Chet received his official promotion orders to captain and was awarded a Purple Heart for wounds sustained in combat and the Legion of Merit, the seventh highest military decoration and awarded for exceptional meritorious service and achievement.

What follow are copies of the actual letters which Chet wrote from the hospital in Manila. We provide them so the reader can get the sense of his mental and physical condition directly from his words.

With a final medical check completed and receipt of new uniforms indicating his new rank and decorations, Captain Britt was declared ready for discharge and travel. He sent a telegram to Grace on October 13 notifying her he would be traveling to Vaughn Hospital in Chicago for a stay of three or four days. Once there, he would undergo a series of final medical evaluations before being released on convalescent leave at home. As he traveled on the three-day train ride, all Chet could think about was his wife, son, and family. He imagined the reunion at the train station and how his son would react to seeing daddy for the first time. Excitement built up inside him with each mile, and the train couldn't move fast enough.

Chet easily cleared every test at the Chicago hospital and was discharged to begin convalescent leave. He notified Grace he'd be in her arms on Saturday, October 20, sometime in the afternoon. Stepping off the train in his dress uniform on the crisp, fall day, he was greeted to a hero's welcome. Grace and Chester Jr. rushed to meet him on the platform along with his parents, extended family, and friends. A photographer from the local paper captured the moment Chet held his son for the first time. Until he held his namesake in his arms, fatherhood hadn't been real. But the look on the captain's face in the photo was inescapable. Chet was a dad. A very proud dad.

Chet joined Grace and Chester Jr. at his parent's house, where Grace had been living since her return from the Philippines. Readjusting to a life of peace didn't happen overnight, even though Chet had been rescued more than two months prior. The memories of the horrors he'd seen and experienced weren't far from the surface, especially at night, and sleep didn't come easy at first. His days, however, were filled with laughter and

joy, watching his son running, playing, giggling, learning new words —
and getting to know a tall man he called Daddy. Shy at first, Chester Jr.
quickly bonded with the man who delighted in reading to him and tickling
him as he ran past.

October 21, 1945
LA CROSSE TRIBUNE

For the first time
Chester holds his
son, Chester Jr

I Want You to Meet My Daddy!

Britt, Prisoner Of Japs 3 Years, Greets Family

"Hello Daddy," Capt. Chester Britt had waited a long time to hear those words.

It was a shy son who greeted him for the first time Saturday afternoon. But Capt. Britt said later in the day that they were "making up."

Taller and weighing more than when he left, Capt. Britt arrived home for the first time in five years. His mother, Mrs A. R. Britt, rushed to the train, holding his son by the hand.

For a second, while Capt. Britt kissed his mother and sister and embraced his father and brother, Kenneth, Chet, Jr., was forgotten. But only for a second.

Amateur With Children

Then the captain was down on his knees, drawing his son into his arms. He's an amateur as far as holding children is concerned, especially a four-year-old who can't be picked up like a baby any longer. But it was with comparative ease that he brought Junior to his shoulders.

Previously, his wife, the former Grace Hanze, had met Capt. Britt in Chicago. Her mother and sisters also were at the train to meet the couple.

"Now that he is here, it seems like yesterday that we saw him," someone said.

But yesterday was a long time ago. For the Britts went to the Philippines in September, 1940. The women and children of Americas stationed there were sent home in May, 1941, and in September, Chet, Jr. was born.

In August, 1942, Britt's family was notified that he was missing in action. It was not until December that they knew he was a prisoner.

Liberated Sept. 3

During his imprisonment he was at military prison camp No. 1 in the Philippines, the island of Honshu and Camp Hoten, Mukden, Manchuria. He was returned to military control Sept. 3.

He was promoted to his present rank after his release, then flown from China to Manila. He was hospitalized there for a month with malaria, then flown to Letterman General hospital in California.

After a week at home, he reports at Vaughn General hospital, Hanes, Ill. Asked how he felt about being back, Capt. Britt said:

"It's wonderful. There's nothing like it."

Chet saw a U.S. Navy fighter shoot down a Japanese aircraft on
September 21, 1944, while at Cabanatuan prison camp. He promised himself that he would try to meet this pilot one day. The military was doing

Victory flyovers over many American cities to celebrate our people and nation. The U.S. Navy pilot that shot that plane down, Commander Bill Dean, did a Victory flyover at La Crosse on October 24, 1945. Chet drove to the local airport and met Commander Dean that day, 13 months after the event and a world away from the Philippines. Commander Dean and more details on this extraordinary encounter can be found on our website.

Thanksgiving was a joyous occasion as the Britt family gave special thanks that Chet was now home and out of harm's way. The family had much to be grateful for, including the safe return home of Edgar and Franklin, who also saw combat. They feasted on a massive turkey dinner with all the trimmings, the most food Chet had seen since before the war. He was thankful to be home with his wife and son and remained hopeful for the future. That hope would come in a few days with news that Grace was pregnant with their second child.

In November, Col. Delbert Ausmus finally fulfilled a deathbed promise to his friend and fellow prisoner, Col. Paul D. Bunker — Chet's first commander — who died in March 1943 at a Japanese prison camp in Taiwan. On the day American forces were ordered to surrender on Corregidor, Colonel Bunker had cut a remnant of the American flag that had flown over the post and hid it behind a patch on his shirt. When he realized, he wasn't going to survive the war, Colonel Bunker ripped a red swatch from the remnant he had and asked Colonel Ausmus to deliver it to the Secretary of War upon his return home. He'd hidden it in the cuff of his shirt for 29 months until his rescue in August 1945. As he sat in the outer office of the Secretary of War at the Pentagon, he fingered the precious piece of fabric, remembering his friend's words. At the appointed time, he was escorted into the office of Secretary of War Robert P. Patterson and formally presented him with the only remaining piece of the flag that flew over Corregidor. Mission accomplished.

On June 14 — Flag Day — Secretary Patterson unveiled the beautifully framed flag remnant to the nation. It was subsequently presented to the museum at West Point, where it has been on display ever since.

Chester and Grace's friend from Fort Wint. November, 1945 wirephoto caption: "EXAMINE CORREGIDOR FLAG FRAGMENT Secretary of War Robert Patterson (left) and Col Delbert Ausmus of Schenectady, N.Y., examine a fragment of the American flag that was lowered at Corregidor, May 6, 1942, at the War Department in Washington, D.C., Nov. 14. Col. Ausmus was entrusted with it by a dying soldier (NOTE: Col Paul D Bunker), and he had kept it hidden in a false shirt cuff for three years while he was a prisoner in a Jap prison." Map behind them shows Luzon. Wirephoto of the authors.

Some former prisoners held by the Japanese felt shameful as they made their way home following the war, wondering if they'd be treated as heroes or cowards. They had been ordered to surrender and had no choice but to do so. Still, fellow survivors from the POW camps and hell ships found readjusting to peacetime was tougher than they'd imagined. Some had been subjected to harsh criticism by new superiors or outright rejected by co-workers. One survivor reported being told by the superior officer of his new unit after the war that he "did not want a coward working for me." Those who'd suffered the most so far from home were subjected to unwarranted taunts and insults, forced to overcome even more anguish and pain at home. Chet never mentioned being the recipient of such comments, and if he was, kept it to himself.

During his convalescence over the spring and summer months, Chet was making good progress physically. He had enjoyed plenty of rest, and his stamina had increased. But the recesses of his mind, where his darkest memories and images haunted him, still played out in agonizing nightmares. He talked about the issues he was trying to overcome with Grace, his parents and oldest sister without burdening them with the details. It helped ease the painful memories to acknowledge them, and he kept reminding himself what the doctors had told him: what he was experiencing was normal, and it would take time to readjust. His adjustment included sharing stories of imprisonment with old friends who must have asked about life in the prison camps.

One story he related to old friend Ewald McCoy, from Logan High School, was when he spent an entire day watching a caterpillar through the barbed wire prison camp fence. He watched it all day in the hope that it would get close enough to the fence for him to reach it so that he could eat it. There must have been many other stories lost to history. This story was provided by Ewald's son Pete through his grandson Matt McCoy.

Chet's letters from the Army hospital in the Philippines are provided on the web site for the reader's to read and give a true sense of his mental condition and longing to be with his family.

CHAPTER 10

Return to Active Duty
(August 1946 – December 1949)

In August 1946, the Britt brothers returned home for a small family reunion before Chester departed for his next duty assignment in Texas. It was the first time the five brothers were together since before Chester and Grace sailed to the Philippines in September 1940.

The four Britt brother WWII veterans together in 1946
L-R Chet, Edgar, Archie, Franklin

"My best guess on location. The Britt family usually had picnics in
the park in Onalaska (small community north of La Crosse), as
there were tables enough for everyone and they played softball,
etc. together and visited in the shade of the big elm trees there."
- Dave Britt

Fortunately, all of Chester's and Grace's brothers returned home from the war in overall good health. A new-found peace filled their homes with optimism, and they looked forward to the opportunity to resume their lives after putting them on hold to fight for the nation's survival. Like all American families with men who served during the war, they looked forward to rebuilding their careers and expanding their families. Edgar remained in the Navy as a pilot and retired in the late 1960s. Ultimately, he enjoyed a successful career in Real Estate for one of the largest Realty companies in northern Virginia. Archie Jr. fulfilled his active-duty commitment as a Navy physician and returned to La Crosse where he practiced medicine for more than 40 years, retiring in the 1980s. Franklin, a B-24 tail-gunner who visited big brother Chester while he was recovering from his years as a POW, returned to the La Crosse area and built a house in nearby Onalaska. He worked as a lineman and foreman for the Northern States Power Company for 40 years, retiring in the 1970s. Throughout the ensuing years, their families grew, and at a family reunion in Virginia in 1996, more than 70 members of the Britt family attended.

Ironically, youngest brother Kenneth was absent for the 1946 family reunion due to his service as a member of the Army's allied occupying forces in Japan following the war.

circa June 1947   Dad AR Britt, five year old son Chet Jr,
brother Ken, and Chet as Ken heads for Japan

Chester and Grace stayed in La Crosse the first half of 1946 and lived with his parents while he convalesced. It was the perfect place to rest. He needed to decompress from his war-time experiences as his body continued to heal. The variety of activities available in the area provided ample opportunity to help him heal and regain his health and strength. The Mississippi, La Crosse and Black rivers provided options for fishing, swimming, hiking, boating and picnics along the shoreline. Such activities reinvigorated not only Chester's spirits as he transitioned back into a peaceful routine but reconfirmed his faith and solidified his marriage as the family worshipped together.

With proper nutrition and exercise, Chester steadily regained the weight he'd shed as a POW. His body no longer was ravaged by diseases primarily caused by starvation — malaria, beriberi, dysentery, dengue fever — and his wounds had healed, miraculously overcoming infections contracted in the filthy, unsterile condition of the hell ships and prisons.

During his convalescence, Chet finally received his delayed promotion orders, his rise in rank retroactive to his original promotion date, which occurred while he was a prisoner. Captain Britt was declared fit to return to active duty in the summer of 1946, around the same time Grace gave birth to their second son, Donald. The captain was assigned to White Sands Missile Proving Grounds and Test Range in New Mexico, about 45 miles north of Fort Bliss in El Paso, Texas. Chet reported to his new duty location while Grace stayed behind a few months to care for her newborn and toddler. Near the end of 1946, she and the boys joined Chester, and they moved into family housing at the Army post.

Captain Britt quickly adapted to active-duty life once again and concentrated on succeeding in his delayed Army career. He quickly impressed his superiors and was assigned to the 384th Anti-Aircraft Artillery (AAA) Battalion, Headquarters Battery at Fort Bliss. Given his leadership and knowledge, Chester was given command of the battery, which came with a promotion to major, a position he held for 18 months until the end of January 1948.

Chet 3rd from right above

1946, Chester center
2nd row with cap,
384th AAA unit, Fort
Bliss, El Paso, Texas

pre-WWII Philippine Department sealion patch on Chester's
shoulder signifying he was there at the start of the war, and
a sign of what he had endured as one of those first men

Life at Fort Bliss was good for the Britt family. They became close friends with Bob and Rita Payne, who lived in the other half of their duplex, a converted barracks building. On their off-duty time, they frequented the post's swimming pool, played cards, and enjoyed picnics, ball games, archery contests and other outdoor sports — a throw-back to their high school years and simpler times. Rita developed a close attachment to baby Donald, fawned over him at every opportunity and watched him grow into a rambunctious toddler while Bob enjoyed swimming with Chet Jr. Grainy, black-and-white home movies — the high-tech way at the time to record the family's happy, playful memories for posterity — served as a reminder of how good their lives were in a world without war. After more than three years of fear and worry, the Britts grew closer together as a family, leaving behind the trials that stalked them during the early years of their marriage.

In early 1948, due to his proficiency in math and his experience calculating bomb trajectories on the fly as an artillery officer, Major Britt was reassigned to work with German scientists, engineers and technicians who were secretly relocated to the United States following the war as part of Operation Paperclip. They had developed the lethal and feared V-2 rockets for Adolf Hitler that rained down on London and other European cities, causing untold death and destruction. Chet worked closely with Wernher von Braun; the famed aerospace engineer responsible for developing the notorious V-2 rocket. Dr. von Braun would later lead the development of the massive Saturn V rocket, which launched former U.S. Navy pilot Neil Armstrong into space on a peaceful mission, making him the first man ever to walk on the moon.

Regardless of his professional standing, Grace remembered von Braun as a good dancer with bad breath.

She possessed a wry sense of humor and eagerly showed off her talent on the dance floor with Chet. At West Point, cadets were required to be proficient at dancing in order to graduate, and the couple moved about the dance floor at the Fort Bliss Officer's Club with ease and elegance.

The Germans also lived at Fort Bliss, which proved to be ironic. The most brilliant men in their scientific fields, who also were former enemies, were housed together and given a singular mission — to collaborate on a variety of projects to advance America's fledgling missile and space programs. Major Britt worked as a ballistics engineer and manager of test projects at White Sands Missile Range from mid-1948 to 1949. It was a dream job where he was allowed to think outside the box and use his intellect and creativity much as he had done with the gliders he built in his early teens.

His love of flying inspired him to experiment with new concepts and designs to produce and test various rocket capabilities at a newly formed Army development department. Instead of the basic materials he used to build his gliders, Chet had access to state-of-the-art facilities, materials and technicians who could produce whatever he needed or imagined. It was a big playground, and Major Britt reveled in it. He finally felt fulfilled using his knowledge and skills as a mathematician and was proud of his contributions to his country.

circa 1948 photo of a V-2 rocket at White Sands, New Mexico, in
the Britt family collection.
"German V-2 rocket, Dad worked on them" - Dave Britt

Settled into a successful and promising military career, Chet and Grace were the perfect picture of the military family. They enjoyed raising their two sons and their marriage finally matched their dreams. The war that had torn them apart was overtaken by the peace that brought them back together. The challenges and obstacles they'd overcome were buried away in their minds but always close enough to the surface to remind them how truly thankful they were for the blessings of life they enjoyed.

Easter 1949 offered the opportunity for the Britt family to celebrate their faith and enjoy one of the family's most anticipated traditions — the annual Easter Egg hunt. The day before Easter Sunday, Grace boiled a few dozen eggs and the family dyed them in vivid colors. After the boys were in bed, Grace and Chet took great care and deliberation to hide the eggs, placing a few that were easier to find for their youngest son, Donald, and tucking a few away in harder-to-locate places that would challenge 8-year-old Chet Jr. Early the next morning, each of the boys searched for their personal Easter baskets and hunted in earnest for the eggs. When all were retrieved, the family enjoyed a small breakfast, then headed off to church wearing their Easter best. After a big lunch, Grace and Chet would hide the eggs again — once or twice more to the boys' delight — and took pleasure in watching them romp and giggle with each new discovery as if it was the first egg hunt of the day. The simple joy of just being together as a family and creating new, fond memories to replace years of heartache was priceless to the couple who had sacrificed so much.

Easter Sunday April 17, 1949 Donny holding an Easter basket.
Chester Jr and Chester Sr Photo at their home at Fort Bliss, likely
taken by Grace, pregnant with baby David soon to be born on
May 9, 1949. Photo of a happy and proud dad.

On May 9, 1949, the couple's third son — David L. Britt — was born in El Paso, Texas at the General Beaumont Hospital. The following month, Chet's parents, Archie and Hazel and his youngest sister Hazel Jean — Jean to friends and family to avoid confusion with her mother — traveled by train from Wisconsin to California to visit relatives then headed to Texas to see the newest addition to the Britt family. Jean had just graduated from high school, and the trip was part of her graduation present. Fortunately, as a railroad engineer, transportation by train for Archie and his family was practically free, which allowed Archie and Hazel to travel extensively with their seven children.

Mr. and Mrs. A. R. Britt, 1508 Wood, announce the approaching marriage of their daughter Jean to Merle E. Buehler, son of Mr. and Mrs. E. Buehler, Niagara, Wis. An August wedding is planned.

June 26, 1950
wedding announcement for
Chester's little sister (Hazel) Jean

Chet's parents headed back to Wisconsin after a few days in Texas, but Jean stayed behind to help with the new baby for a month. With three boys under the age of eight, Grace was grateful for the extra pair of hands to corral the two older boys and keep them entertained while Grace cared for her third — and last — child. The life and family Chet and Grace wished for was complete. But once again, their lives soon would be overshadowed by the ravages of war.

May 16, 1949   Chet Sr, Donny in Chet's arms, Grace, Chet Jr holding newborn baby brother David

In August, only three months after Grace gave birth, Chet began to experience periodic headaches. He ignored them, thinking they might be temporary and go away. On December 1, while awaiting a train to take him home following Army business in California, he collapsed on the platform at Los Angeles' Union Station. He was taken immediately to Long Beach Naval Hospital and then later transferred to Lettermen Hospital in San Francisco. Major Britt never lost consciousness, but he experienced short-term memory loss, difficulty speaking, brain fog and weakness on his left side.

Grace, alone in Texas and caring for her three sons while worrying about her husband's condition, traveled to California to be at Chet's side as soon as she was able to arrange for friends at Fort Bliss to care for the boys. As much as she didn't want to leave them behind, her priority was to do whatever was needed to help her husband get well.

Doctors conducted extensive exams and tests on his brain function and physical abilities to determine what had caused his medical emergency. In layman's terms, they said Chet had suffered a stroke. He was 34. Doctors noted in their initial report that Major Britt, who had been in the Army less than 10 years, was "well-developed and well-nourished male who appeared older than his stated 34 years."

The same could be said for any of POWs who experienced the inhumane punishment dispensed by their Japanese captors. Three-and-a-half years of starvation, injuries, dehydration, tropical illnesses, and brutality had taken an immense toll, resulting in irreversible damage to their bodies. Missing limbs, blindness, deafness, and other outward medical problems were easily observed and diagnosed. It was the unseen, internal damage from innumerable blows to the head and body from rifle butts and the lack of nutrition that affected organs from functioning properly that proved elusive to doctors who had no knowledge of the myriad injuries they'd sustained.

After a week of intense rehab, Chester was not progressing with his physical therapy as well as his doctors had hoped. His memory problems persisted, his left arm was paralyzed, and he was unable to dress himself.

He was able to walk slowly with the help of a cane, but his gait was unsteady. Unable to lift his leg even a few inches to take a decisive step, his left foot shuffled across the linoleum floor of his hospital room.

Excerpt from medical report on Chester K Britt Sr.

On Dec 1, 1949 while enroute from San Francisco to Texas, he suddenly collapsed in the Union Station in Los Angeles. Did not lose consciousness but developed a left hemiplegia and left facial weakness of the control type and had difficulty talking. He was admitted to Long Beach Naval Hospital where the facial weakness almost disappeared but he thought more slowly than before and had some difficulty with recent memory.

An electro-encephalogram on Dec 7, 1949 reported an abnormal focus in the right partial and occipital region. A cerebral arteriogram on Dec 13, 1949 showed excellent filling of the middle cerebral artery branches but poor filling of the anterior cerebral on the right. He was transferred to Letterman Army Hospital in San Francisco on February 10, 1950 for further diagnosis and treatment.

This patient is a 34 year old Major with 9 ½ years of service in the regular Army, who was admitted to Letterman Army Hospital on February 20, 1950 as a transfer from U.S. Naval Hospital in Long Beach California with a transfer diagnosis of thrombosis, middle cerebral artery, cause undetermined.

Patient was well until August 1949 when he suddenly felt a numbness , first in his right extremities, later in his left and was weak, dizzy and apprehensive. He recovered in a few days but thought his left arm and leg were weaker than usual. He had another similar episode in November 1949 which lasted for ten days and was associated with severe headaches. He also had Tinnitus which he had off and on for two years and his tongue felt thick and swollen. He was treated with injections of Thiamine and electro-encephalogram was reported as borderline.

Examination on admission revealed a well developed and well nourished male who appeared older than his stated 34 years.

Report on Chester's medical condition beginning with his collapse on December 1, 1949, to being send to Letterman Hospital in San Francisco in February 1950

Faced with the possibility of having to raise three boys and serve as her husband's caretaker, they had many crucial decisions to make. Fortunately, Chet had not lost his ability to communicate. They spent long hours discussing their uncertain future, weighing the pros and cons of potential outcomes.

Christmas 1949 was a somber holiday for the Britt family. Chester was stuck in a hospital room in California, and Grace was nearly 1,200 miles away in Texas. She struggled to make Christmas as normal and cheerful as possible for the boys while trying to answer the unending, pestering questions of her two older sons, who kept asking where their daddy was. She was strong in the face of yet more adversity, but the impact on her life was stressful and unsettling. At one point, Grace was so desperate for even the slightest bit of respite from the dreadful circumstances she once again found herself in, she thought she was going insane. Her sons relied solely on her for love and support, and although her close friends at Fort

Bliss were more than helpful, she was exhausted with worry not knowing whether Chester would ever recover enough to care for his personal needs without assistance.

Not knowing how long it would be before Chet was well enough to leave the hospital, they decided their best option was to move the family back to Wisconsin. Both sides of the family — especially her mother and mother-in-law — offered to help care for the boys, which allowed Grace to spend more time with Chet as he continued his treatment on the West Coast.

As the new year began, they trusted their faith to see them through whatever challenges and crises arose on Chet's journey to recovery. The journey, they discovered, would be filled with hardship and heartache.

CHAPTER 11

The Rest of the Story
(1950 – 1954)

Following the holidays, Chet continued his rehabilitation, but his doctors determined he needed continued, specialized care unavailable at the Long Beach Naval Hospital. On February 10, 1950, he was transferred by ambulance to Letterman Army Hospital at the Presidio in San Francisco. Once again, Grace left her boys in the care of the extended Britt family while she traveled to northern California to be with her husband. She made the arduous three-day trip by train several times in the ensuing eight months, alone in her thoughts, always concerned what the future might hold and praying for strength to see them through whatever challenges confronted them.

She thought about the four years they'd waited to get married while Chet attended West Point. Cadets were prohibited from being married until after graduation, and they didn't waste a day, marrying the day after graduation as many cadets did. And after all that time, they enjoyed only 11 months of married life together before their lives were interrupted by World War II. When America entered the war, most of the time she had not known if Chet was alive or dead. And when she learned he'd been taken prisoner, the War Department's information was so outdated, she never knew where he was or how he was being treated. Letters marked "undeliverable" were returned two or three months after being sent. Each time, her heart was broken just a little more.

About February, 1950, Major Chester Britt post-stroke at Letterman

Happy he'd come home whole in body, Grace rejoiced at the birth of two more sons in the four years since he'd returned from captivity in Japan. Chester's relentless hope of surviving and his determination to return home to his wife and son had sustained him through unbearable circumstances. Their war-time nightmare was over, but another one was beginning. Seeing him struggle to walk, to speak, to merely button his shirt —- unable to care for himself — plunged her into a valley of dark emotions. Grace's love for him was tested beyond human endurance while he was a POW, and she was being tested once again. She tried to stay positive and encouraging, especially when she was with him. She saved her tears and worry for when she was alone. An amazingly strong and resilient woman, she was given the perfect name as she was indeed, a woman of unlimited grace.

Despite intense physical, speech and occupational therapy, Major Britt's condition improved only slightly. Repeated attempts to regain any use of his left arm proved futile. His ability to walk was still limited to shuffling along slowly. He suffered continual headaches, and his memory began to fail. His brain's ability to process information became slower as did his speech. Once a strapping cadet, agile athlete and math whiz, Chet was now a shell of what he once was — hunched over, his left arm in a sling and walking unsteadily with a cane. More than three years of inhumane treatment, starvation, dehydration, disease, and torture had affected his body's ability to overcome the damage caused by his stroke. Yes, he was alive, but he still was suffering significantly from his years as a POW.

On March 31, 1950 Major Britt was granted convalescent leave, and the couple traveled back to La Crosse by train. Doctors hoped being at home with his wife and sons would help reduce Chet's stress and offer him more opportunity to rest and recuperate from his stroke. For two-and-a-half months, Chet and Grace adjusted to their new lives, making the best of their current, uncertain circumstances. They enjoyed having the family under the same roof once again, and Grace had help not only with the boys, but with Chester.

They returned to San Francisco on June 10 and enjoyed a small, summer picnic on the grounds of the Presidio, with its expansive views from the cliffs overlooking the Pacific Ocean and Golden Gate Bridge. Because Chester's medical condition had not improved, Army officials directed doctors to convene a medical review board to determine the major's fitness to carry out his military duties. Chester appeared before the board on June 30 and was questioned about his duties and physical condition. His attending physician testified there was no hope of recovery from the stroke he'd suffered seven months earlier. He stated that Chet's left side — in particular, his left arm — was permanently paralyzed and his left leg would never recover enough to walk unaided. His recommendation to the board:

medical retirement and separation from the Army. They were harsh words for Chet to hear, and at that moment, the somber reality — the permanence of his paralysis — felt like yet another rifle punch in the gut from his Japanese captors. And in truth, it was.

Following an intensive, six-week, review of his case by doctors and military officials up through the chain of command, Major Britt received the Army's final determination. By order of the Secretary of the Army, Chet was officially relieved of duty and medically retired, effective on August 31, 1950.

SPECIAL ORDERS   DEPARTMENT OF THE ARMY
No.   149   Washington 25, D. C., 2 August 1950

E X T R A C T

39. MAJ CHESTER K. BRITT (Capt) 023078 Ord C having been determined
to be perm unfit for dy by reason of phys disability of 160 percent in-
curred while serving on AD his ret from active svc 31 Aug 1950 with grade
and ret pay of Maj as prov by sec 402 and 409 Act Congress approved 12 Oct
1949 (PL 351 81st Cong) is announced. He is rel from asg Medical Holding
Det Letterman AH, Presidio of San Francisco, Calif, 31 Aug 1950 and at
proper time WP his home. PCS. TDN. 2110425 1-22-222 P 431-02, 03, 07 S99-999.

BY ORDER OF THE SECRETARY OF THE ARMY:

J. LAWTON COLLINS
Chief of Staff, United States Army

OFFICIAL:

EDWARD F. WITSELL
Major General, USA
The Adjutant General

A CERTIFIED TRUE EXTRACT COPY:
Reproduced at Ord Res & Dev Div SubO (Rkt),
Fort Bliss, Texas, 17 Aug 1950.

R. J. MOORE
CWO, USA
Adjutant

Medical retirement of Major Chester K Britt as of August 31, 1950

Grace and Chester traveled home from California a final time and purchased a home on the north side of La Crosse a few blocks from his parents. Being home full-time with Grace and his sons, Chet focused on maintaining the mobility and mental capacity he had regained by creating aircraft models using light-weight balsa wood. His love of flying never waned, but instead of making the life-sized gliders he enjoyed making as a teen, his joy now came from making detailed models for his sons to "fly" around the house — or an occasional ship to float in the bathtub. Because he had use of only his right hand, each model required utmost patience to cut, assemble and paint. His new-found hobby not only challenged his fine motor skills, but it also kept his brain engaged and active. That Chester's one-year-old son, David, sat on his lap while he created his treasures was a bonus.

TOP Chester's LR (Long Ranger) B-24 model for brother Franklin

INSET and BOTTOM A mission by Franklin on the B-24 named MARRYIN SAM with the 307th Bomb Group, the Long Rangers

Chet, Grace, and the boys gradually settled into their new lifestyle as did the entire Britt family. Chet's limitations became a matter of routine, and the boys enjoyed helping their dad when he needed it. They felt special because, unlike their friends, daddy was home full-time. No more long hours at work. No more extended hospital stays. He and Grace always were available to guide, love, and nurture, teaching them the Midwest values passed down from their parents: hard work, respect for others and an abiding faith.

Due to Chet's condition, the family never ventured far from home. Summer vacations to distant locations were out of the question, but the family enjoyed daytrips up the steep and winding narrow road to Grandad's Bluff overlooking the Mississippi River, from where Chet had attempted to fly his homemade glider. Grace packed up a bountiful picnic lunch, and they'd enjoy the scenic view across the river as barges and pleasure boats cruised past. Some days they'd fish along the banks of the Black River with Chet teaching the boys how to put a worm on a hook and watch for the red and white bobber to dip into the muddy-brown water indicating a fish was nibbling on the bait.

1950 - 2003 the Britt family home in La Crosse, Wisconsin

Last family photo. Easter Sunday, April 5, 1953
Front to back - David, Donny, Chet Jr, Grace, Chet Sr

Best of all were trips to the local A&W drive-in where they devoured tasty hot dogs and frosty mugs of root beer on a warm, summer's day. And if the boys were especially good, a trip to the Sweet Shop — a favorite of every kid who lived on the northside of La Crosse — resulted in the agonizing decision of whether to indulge in their favorite homemade chocolate candies or choose a sundae, soda, or ice cream cone from one of the dozen or so homemade ice cream flavors made that very morning. It was a tough choice as the boys peered through the glass cases filled with sweet treasures and watched the soda jerk behind the counter concoct various ice cream treats for the unending line of patrons. Simple pleasures were the order of the day. In the evenings after dinner, Grace corralled the boys for their baths and put them to bed. Then she and Chet sat on the rattan couch she'd brought back from the Philippines when she was evacuated in 1941. Chet puffed away on his pipe while Grace read the paper, or they'd just sit together quietly, Grace's head gently resting on Chet's shoulder as he draped his right arm around her. Soft music from the radio wafted through the living room, filling the silence as they remembered the happy times they'd enjoyed together.

As the months passed, Chet ever so slightly became weaker and began to experience pain throughout his body. The unseen, internal damage he'd sustained from years as a POW — and especially on the torturous hell ships — slowly began to emerge. His headaches had become more intense, and he was experiencing abdominal pain, kidney problems and pain in his legs and joints. His brother Archie, a doctor, had been monitoring his symptoms, but was stymied by what might be causing so many problems at once. On Chet and Grace's 13th wedding anniversary on June 12, Archie admitted his brother to a local hospital with uncontrolled bleeding in his liver, kidneys, and spleen. After a series of X-rays, biopsies and lab tests, doctors were unable to determine what was causing Chet's multiple organ failures, and Archie immediately arranged for Chet to be transferred by ambulance to the Fort Snelling Veterans Administration Hospital near Minneapolis, Minnesota, about three hours away.

Grace's brother Bill Runice drove Grace and her two older sons, Chet Jr. and Don, to Minneapolis, trailing behind the ambulance. David, only four years old, was too young to make the trip and stayed behind with Grandma Hilma Runice. The next day, Chester's 38th birthday, the family enjoyed a quiet, Saturday afternoon celebration in his hospital room with

Bill, Grace, and the boys, who presented their dad with a card. It was the last time Chet Jr. and Don would see their father alive as they had to return to La Crosse on Sunday in order for Bill to return to work. Unknowingly Chet had less than a month to live.

June 13, 1952 Final birthday card from the sons to their dad

During the next few weeks, doctors worked feverishly to stop the hemorrhaging. Grace, along with Chet's brothers Edgar, Archie, and Franklin, made several trips to be with Chester as he once again battled for his life. On the Fourth of July weekend, with three of his brothers at his bedside, Chester recounted the horrors he'd experienced as a POW. Like most veterans, he rarely talked about his war-time experiences, preferring instead to keep them cordoned off in the deep recesses of his memories.

He talked of the torture and inhumane treatment at the prison camps in the Philippines, described the suffocating and freezing days in the hold of the hell ships, the hunger, the thirst, the ever-present threat of imminent death and the horror upon realizing he and his fellow prisoners were being attacked by friendly forces. Most of all, he was sickened watching men he'd served with being torn apart by bombs and bullets. His feelings of unending despair, which he'd overcome through his relentless hope and force of will, returned to haunt him once again as he re-lived the loss of so many close friends, especially those in his lifeline circle. Sharing his experiences and memories of the war with his true, blood brothers in arms — who also served their country during World War II — lifted the burden of survivor's guilt he carried with him, knowing as veterans they would understand. It was a delayed, emotional outpouring of grief, yet cathartic to impart.

On July 5, Bill once again drove Grace to visit Chet. One by one, his organs were failing, and doctors were helpless to stop the bleeding. She joined Chet's brothers at his bedside waiting for the inevitable. Sweethearts since 1932, their love for each other was unbreakable. The family vigil continued overnight, and as Chet's blood pressure declined slowly, he lost consciousness. Surrounded by family, he slipped away peacefully on July 6. The bugle boy who became a soldier and went to war was home for good.

Because doctors knew so little about what caused Chet's organs to fail, they requested Grace's permission to conduct an autopsy. She agreed in hopes of advancing research to discover a treatment and possible cure so other lives potentially could be saved.

Chet was buried at Oak Grove Cemetery in La Crosse with full military honors. As the last notes of "Taps" floated across the gravestones, Grace prepared for the next chapter of her life without the love of her life by her side. Her full-time focus immediately shifted to raising her three sons — alone. She soon realized that wouldn't be necessary. Her family, and the Britt family — who accepted her as their own sister — wrapped their arms around Grace and became surrogate parents to Chester Jr., Donald, and David.

On August 12, Dr. Martin Segal, a Veterans Administration pathologist, wrote to Grace explaining the findings of Chet's autopsy. He apologized for the delay and explained Chet had died of an extremely rare condition called periarteritis nodosa (now commonly known as polyarteritis nodosa, which better describes the autoimmune disease). "This is an illness about which very little is known," he wrote. "It has not been until recent years that this illness has been recognized and diagnosed correctly … it is felt to be in some way related to an unusual allergic sensitivity of the individual." He further explained it was not contagious or hereditary adding, "The examination revealed many clots in the blood vessel walls in many areas of the body, including the heart, liver, spleen, kidneys and other organs." But they had no explanation of how, why, or what caused the clots to form.

1929 Boy Scout Bugler
La Crosse, Wisconsin

1941 Army First Lieutenant
Fort Wint, Philippines

The Wisconsin Bugle Boy who became a soldier, standing beside
the Britt home at Fort Wint, Grande Island, Subic Bay, Philippines

In conclusion, Dr. Segal expressed his gratitude, writing, "We wish to thank you most sincerely for granting permission for this examination. It is only through such examinations that we can determine the exact cause of death and study the changes occurring within the body in disease conditions. The findings we obtain help us improve our methods of diagnosis and treatment and will undoubtedly be of great assistance in similar cases in the future." Although disappointed regarding the lack of an explanation about how Chester acquired the disease, she was comforted by the letter knowing medical researchers would further expand their knowledge to help others in the future.

A widow at 37 with three young sons, Grace had no job or financial means to support her family. To help with expenses, Grace's brother and sister moved in with her. She obtained a job as a clerk at Mr. Heslip's Grocery and the three siblings shared child-care duties between their work hours. In the meantime, Grace enlisted the help of the American Legion in La Crosse to apply for death benefits for her and the boys, 12, 7 and 4 years old. To her astonishment, the claim was denied. The reason: Major Britt's death was not service-connected — an unbelievably routine finding at the time for servicemen who died after hostilities had ceased. Undeterred, Grace enlisted the help of the American Legion in La Crosse to appeal the claim. Together, they compiled additional evidence and statements from doctors and Chet's personnel records at the suggestion of a claim's processor at the Veterans Administration in Milwaukee.

On December 29, 1954 — more than 18 months after Chet's death — the three-member Veterans Administration appeals board sent Grace a detailed letter outlining the case, a review of the evidence, their findings — and their decision. As she read through the letter, Grace became apprehensive and her heart skipped a beat as she reached the end of the letter, which stated "… a reasonable doubt exists as to the incurrence of periarteritis nodosa during service and its relationship to the service-connected vascular disease, …" And then she read the rest of the letter. "… which doubt is resolved in favor of the veteran and, accordingly, wartime service connection for the cause of death is granted. The appeal is allowed."

As a result, Grace received a small pension for the rest of her life, as well as a monthly benefit for each of her three sons until they reached 18 years of age. Although the family's financial situation had stabilized somewhat, every penny was budgeted. They had enough to keep a roof over their heads, plenty of food and adequate clothing — including hand-me-downs from older brothers and cousins when necessary. Extravagance was not part of their lifestyle.

Grace's sister, Exzilda Runice — everyone called her Aunt Ex — continued to live with Grace and the boys. She worked at the local Autolite spark plug factory and shared her paycheck to assist with living expenses. Grace continued working as a grocery store clerk for several years while the boys were in school.

The sisters were excellent cooks and bakers. Almost every day after school, the boys' friends stopped by the house to devour fresh-baked rolls with peanut butter, homemade grape jam, and glasses of cold milk. The boys' uncle, Dr. Archie Britt, provided healthcare for the family, which helped stretch Grace's finances. Both sides of the family — Chet's mother Hazel, brother Frank and his wife, Deloris, and Grace's siblings Bill, Exzilda and Helen May — became their nearby "village," raising the boys not only to survive, but thrive.

In early 1960, Grace wrote to the doctors at the VA hospital in Minneapolis and, out of curiosity, inquired whether there had been any advances in their research regarding the disease that took Chet's life. She received a reply dated March 31 from Dr. H.L. Vogl. "It is somewhat disappointing for us to have to tell you that very little new information has been obtained," he wrote, explaining that periarteritis nodosa was a very rare disease. For some unknown reason, patients with the disease developed an allergic reaction much like people with food or pollen allergies. Except in people with periarteritis nodosa, small arteries and blood vessels became inflamed, and the interior walls developed small nodules, blocking the flow of blood to the organs and extremities, which need a rich blood supply.

The doctor further stated that current treatments were unsatisfactory. Drugs used for allergies and other hypersensitive diseases had little effect, although very rarely, adrenal corticoid drugs provided some relief. "Very, very rarely," he wrote, "a patient is cured by these drugs. Also, very rarely the hypersensitivity disappears, and the patient gets well without treatment. In the great majority of cases, however, the disease proves fatal in spite of all our efforts."

To this day, no known treatment or cure has been found, although some research has suggested it could be linked to a lack of vitamin C. Inadequate amounts food and the absence of a balanced diet — with no access to vitamins and minerals needed to sustain the body — indicated a very likely connection regarding how Chester might have acquired the disease. A robust athlete, more fit than most due to the strict, physical demands of West Point cadets, Major Britt could've been the poster boy for the military academy's recruiting efforts. But after 42 months as a prisoner of the Japanese, Chet was barely able to stand let alone walk.

Grace never remarried and instead concentrated on raising her sons, providing them the best life she could. She never felt closure for the contempt shown POWs following the war. While soldiers returned home to countless victory parades and celebrations immediately following Japan's surrender, Chet was too ill to travel and returned to the States nearly two months after the war ended. There were no parades or celebrations. Instead, the POWs held captive by Japan remained overseas, struggling just to regain the strength to travel as the country paid tribute to the returning troops. And upon Chet's return, it wasn't unusual for prisoners of Japan to be ridiculed for surrendering.

But in 1988, 35 years after Chester had died, the Department of Defense established the POW medal for all military personnel who had been prisoners of war. Her youngest son, David, an Air Force lieutenant colonel serving at the Pentagon, applied for a medal on behalf of his father. Following approval, he arranged a small award ceremony. His boss, Maj. Gen. Chuck Boyd — himself a Vietnam POW — agreed to present the medal to Grace in his office.

With the precious medal in her hands, Grace finally felt the sacrifice Chet and his fellow Japanese POWs endured so many years ago finally had been recognized and honored. The ceremony proved especially meaningful, knowing the medal had been presented by a military man who had experienced the horrors of being a prisoner of war firsthand. She had the closure she so desperately sought.

Grace added the medal to all the mementoes she had collected throughout their marriage — Chet's Legion of Merit, Purple Heart, his personnel and retirement papers and government correspondence. Most of all, she cherished the family photos and letters Chet wrote after she was evacuated from the Philippines and following his rescue in Mukden. Together, they highlighted a life interrupted too many times by tragic circumstances.

Over the years, Grace had become a true sister to Chet's six siblings. They adored the woman who had remained his strong, loving wife through trying circumstances and had raised their three sons with the values they treasured. They included her in family celebrations and holiday gatherings as if she were a blood relative. In 2002, the ever-expanding Britt family enjoyed a reunion dinner in La Crosse. Siblings, children, and grandchildren shared an evening of laughter, memories, and an abundance of family photos. It would be the last time the entire Britt family would be together.

The following spring, Grace suffered a massive heart attack. Doctors determined her heart was damaged extensively and held out little hope for her recovery. Donald, who lived closest to her, rushed to her bedside at St. Francis Hospital. The next day — May 2, 2003 — as Chet Jr. and David were on their way to La Crosse to be with her, Grace passed away as she and Donald listened to the lilting notes of "Amazing Grace" being played on a harp. Chet Jr. and David arrived the following day to grieve with Donald as they honored the woman who raised her sons to be the successful family men they'd become.

After 50 years, Grace and Chet were reunited once again to rest in eternity beside each other. She lived as she had died, with dignity — and grace.

CHAPTER 12

Comrades & Unknown Heroes

A s we began this book it was to be about Chester Britt and his life. Early on we knew of some men Chester was friends with during the war and at other points in his life. However, upon finding the small diary he was able to write as a POW, that number quickly grew as we set out to find out more about the men in the diary, not an easy task with many simply listed as a name. As we continued that quest and made progress in our book, more names came to light, some we are certain Chester knew, and others that are simply fascinating people lost to history.

We will have a website where much more will be documented about them, and so what we have here are the barest of summaries. We encourage the readers to find out more about these people. Our simple goal is to honor them here.

First, we honor the only two survivors of Chet's WW II experience as a POW who knew him, Paul Phillips, a 1940 West Point graduate, and Ben Skardon. Then we provide cameo summaries in alphabetical order of the other 20 men from the West Point class of 1940 who were in the Philippines when WW II began. This is followed by a group we can directly associate with Chester, a group who may have known Chester, and a group which did not know Chester but who are noteworthy in their own right.

If we have missed including anyone whose relatives we contacted in the process of writing this book, we sincerely apologize, but will be sure to add them to the website if you contact us.

To all the family members who graciously provided us with family photos, letters, diaries and so much more about their relatives who served in the armed forces or on the home front, and to experts who have shared so much of their knowledge and information with us, thank you. It has been one of life's great pleasures to get to know you all and through you to get to know these men and women who brought this period to life for us.

Brigadier General (Ret) Paul David Phillips

2nd Lt Paul Phillips graduated from West Point on June 11, 1940. He married Rita Ruzicka in Baltimore on June 15, 1940 and they went to Ft Sill, Oklahoma for Field Artillery school for the basic course, prior to sailing to the Philippines for his first real operational assignment in the 24th FA Regiment, arriving in Manila in early 1941. The winds of war forced the evacuation of his new bride and 4-month-old baby girl back to the U.S. in August, 1941.

Paul D Phillips   West Point 1940 HOWITZER yearbook page 207
horsemanship was an important part of training for Cadets at the academy

Lieutenant Phillips was transferred to the newly formed Visayan-Mindanao Force on the island of Cebu about 375 miles south of Manila where he served as Secretary of the General Staff and Aide to General William Sharp Commander of Army forces in the Southern Philippines. Paul fought the Japanese until he was surrendered along with all other army personnel, winning a Silver Star for his bravery. He was promoted early on to Captain then Major, before capture by the Japanese and began 39 months of captivity, first at Davao prison camp. He survived the rigors and deprivation of five prison camps and the hells ships the Oryoku Maru, Enoura Maru, and Brazil Maru, then time as a POW in Japan and finally Mukden, Manchuria. He was rescued by parachutists from the forerunner to the CIA, the Office of Strategic Services (OSS) and the Russian army in Mukden. He was promoted to Lt Col after his return to U.S. control. Later as a graduate of the Army's Advanced Field Artillery course he was assigned as an instructor there before attending Command and General Staff College in 1951. Then he served as battalion commander in the 1st Armored Division, with follow-on assignments to Germany and the Armed Forces Staff College. Later he had an assignment to the Pentagon with jobs in the Department of the Army and Joint Staff. He was promoted to Colonel in 1957 and attended the National War College. A tour in Korea came next, and when he returned to the U.S he was assigned to the faculty of the Army War College and received promotion to Brigadier General in 1964. He was needed on the Army staff and served there from 1964-66, retiring May 31, 1966 from that last military assignment. He was the Deputy Assistant Secretary of the Army for Manpower and Reserve Affairs for about 10 years. He finished his contributions to national defense as the head of the Economics Department for the Research Analysis Corporation.

He retired for good in 1979 and moved to Colorado with his bride Rita, with whom he had three children. She passed away in 1992 after over 50 years of marriage.

General Phillips remarried in 1992 to his second wife, Dorothea (Spallone) Evans, who passed away in 2002. They too had a wonderful and loving life together, enjoying the hard-earned retirement years they so richly deserved.

During his life Paul Phillips has excelled at most everything he ever attempted. He is a man of self-determination and focused ability, the same stuff that contributed to his survival as a POW of the Japanese. He celebrated his 103rd birthday in March 2021.

Paul Phillips and Ben Skardon are the last two survivors of the 1,619 men who boarded the hell ship the Oryoku Maru on December 13, 1944, and whose numbers were steadily whittled away through to the Enoura Maru, then Brazil Maru, then a POW camp in Japan, finally Mukden, and who finally experienced the joy of liberation by the OSS team on August 16, 1945.

You can read about Brigadier General Paul Phillips' life on our website, as he has graciously given us permission to put his written account of his life there.

Colonel (Ret) Beverly N "Ben" Skardon

1LT Lieutenant Beverly "Ben" Skardon was a 1938 graduate of Clemson College, South Carolina.

He arrived in the Philippines in October of 1941 and was immediately assigned to a training battalion in the Philippine Army. As a commander of Company A, 92nd Regiment of 91st Division Philippine Army, he travelled north from nearby Samar Island to Manila, then on to the front lines where he was ordered to lead his minimally trained and poorly equipped soldiers against the battle-hardened and well-equipped Imperial Japanese Army. Problems experienced in training with multiple dialects of Philippine tribal regions caused added challenges for the young lieutenant. Ben led and managed his men as well as could be expected. He moved and maneuvered his company as directed by the regimental commander. The Filipinos were brave though not technically adept at soldiering and fought hard and courageously in a losing battle for ground. The 91st Division fought a delaying action as they moved south, being pushed back by superior Japanese forces. Their final line of defense was just north of Mount Samat and west of Abucay on the Bataan Peninsula. The 91st Division held its defensive positions until early April 1942.

On April 9, 1942, 1LT Skardon and his men were surrendered to the Japanese by their commanding General E.P. King, thus beginning a horrendous 41-month ordeal at the hands of their savage and brutal Japanese captors. Captain Skardon survived the Prisoner of War camps in the Philippines and Japan as well as the hell ships the Oryoku Maru, Enoura Maru and Brazil Maru, finally released from the POW camp in Mukden Manchuria, along with Paul Phillips, Chester Britt, and the other survivors of the Oryoku Maru.

Following the WWII, he remained in the Army, later fighting in the Korean War and was promoted to Colonel. Colonel Skardon retired from the Army and went on to teach at Clemson University in the English Department, retiring as Professor Emeritus. He received the coveted Clemson University Medallion.

Ben Skardon ID card issued after being repatriated after Mukden

Ben Skardon   34 Ben Skardon 35 Paul Phillips   16 Chester Britt
August 19, 1945 MUKDEN 3 days after liberation

He will be 104 years old in July of 2021 and is believed to be oldest survivor of the Oryoku Maru, just nudging out Paul Phillips for that honor.

He has lived a blessed and remarkable life and he is a joy to talk to, full of wit and humor, a trait that served him well as a Prisoner of War. He tries to walk a mile a day to maintain his health and has become a fixture, leading "Ben's Brigade" on the Commemorative Bataan Memorial Death March held in the Spring at White Sands, New Mexico.

Classmates of West Point Class of 1940 who fought in the Philippines

We encourage you to get to know more about these men on our website. It is impossible to properly chronicle the lives of all these men in our book, each had a rich life, and a book could easily be written about every one of them. Every man from West Point from the West Point class of 1940 who was in the Philippines when the war started saw combat, some of it the most brutal imaginable. Half of them died. Half went on to continue to serve their country in uniform after WWII. They all deserve our highest respect and gratitude.

Raw statistics of the 22 men (20 below plus Paul Phillips and Chester Britt) from the West Point class of 1940 who went to the Philippines and were there when the war started for them on December 8, 1942, local time.

- Killed in Action: 2
  (Herb Pace, Jerry Toth)

- Executed for fighting with Filipino guerrillas: 1
  (Vicente Gepte)

- Killed in hell ships: 4
  (Bob Cooper, Joe Murphy, John Presnell, Izzy Wald)

- Died in POW camp due to hell ship conditions: 3
  (Gus Cullen, Joe Iacobucci, Bob Wheat)

- Died after the war due to POW-related illness: 1
  (Chester Britt)

- Survived the war and went on to lead a long life: 11
  (Felicisimo Castillo, Silvio Gasperini, Paul Krauss, Paul Phillips,
  Mel Rosen, Morris Shoss, Harry Simpson, Warren Stirling,
  John Wright, Jules Yates, Fred Yeager).

About 40% of the POWs of the Japanese Empire perished before the end of the war, and this closely matches with the death rate of this West Point class.

It's important to note is how often we found the survivors doing what they could to remember and keep the memory of their friends alive, not just fellow West Point graduates, but all the men and women they served with in the Philippines. They talked about them, wrote about them, and contacted the families of their departed friends, always to do whatever they could to honor them. Paul Phillips and Ben Skardon, even now more than 75 years later, and with robot vehicles on Mars, are still doing this in their own way.

We have tried to give these men their most appropriate rank for the book. Some men's promotions missed them because they were in the thick of fighting, others got their promotions because they were worked closely with senior officers who took the initiative to get the men the promotions that they were due. While they were POWs, most for 3-1/2 years, their ranks were frozen by the U.S. government while they endured their torment as captives.

Generally, for men taken prisoner we refer to them at their known rank at that point they were taken prisoner. Then, after the war, everyone taken prisoner was given an automatic increase of one rank after they were liberated. We hope we have made no mistakes about their ranks.

CASTILLO   1LT Felicisimo Sulit Castillo WEST POINT 1940

From the city of Malolos, Bulacan Province, in the Philippines. A March 1942 article about Aviation Cadet Thomas Abellera states Lt Castillo was on Bataan. Beyond that we know little. He survived the war and passed away Sept 11, 2007. If anyone has knowledge about his WWII service please let us know. It may be found under first names of Felicisimo, Felicismo or Felicimo

1940 West Point HOWITZER yearbook writeup by roommate
Felicisimo (literally the "happiest one") was a rare specimen of an "ultra-specoid" who "understood it;" so much so that he earned his stars second class year by a very comfortable margin. Much to the soniferous discomfort of his less lyrical roommate, Casti swung a mean violin — incidentally, self-taught. Deliberate, but not slow, and meticulous to the smallest detail in everything he undertook, he maneuvered his chessmen with a far-sightedness that was hard to equal and harder to excel. Nickname "Casti"

CULLEN   Capt Augustus GUS John Cullen WEST POINT 1940

Born July 12, 1915, Columbia City, Indiana. Graduated 1933 Bucyrus High School, Ohio. Served on Corredigor where he was taken prisoner May 6, 1942. **Died February 9, 1945 in Fukuoka #3 POW camp, Kyushu, Japan, of Acute Enteritis due to the appalling conditions in the camp, with Chester Britt near him.**

1940 West Point HOWITZER yearbook roommate writeup
Carefree, completely likeable, blessed with the ability to make and keep many friends, Gus came to West Point from Ohio and an "O.A.O." The T.D. was impressed and academic departments indifferent as Gus proceeded to make his stay enjoyable to himself and for everyone knowing him. No basketball or squash game was complete without his encouragement both physically and verbally. All these characteristics plus a determination to do things correctly and precisely will assure him success as an officer.   Nickname "Gus"

COOPER   Capt Robert Gibson BOB Cooper WEST POINT

Born January 1, 1918, New Haven, Connecticut. Graduated 1935 Roosevelt High School, Honolulu, Territory of Hawaii. Served with distinction on Corredigor with the 59th Coastal Artillery where he was taken prisoner May 6, 1942. **Killed January 9, 1945 in the hold of the Enoura Maru bombed by U.S. Navy dive bombers in Takao, Formosa**

1940 West Point HOWITZER yearbook writeup by roommate
From the time he entered West Point, Coop worked diligently and had stars to show for it. However, that did not indicate that he was a bookworm or a "specoid" because he definitely was not. He had a playful, bubbling humor that evidenced itself in many pranks and incessant teasing, but that did not detract from his popularity with his classmates. At times, he was shy, though his bold manner did not indicate it. He did well here and should keep doing so. Nickname "Coop"

GASPERINI   1LT Silvio Emil Gasperini Jr WEST POINT 1940

Born January 5, 1918, Stambaugh, Michigan. Graduated Stambaugh, Michigan, High School. Served on Bataan where he was then taken prisoner April 10, 1942. Was among an early group sent to Japan where he spent most of the war as a POW. Died August 28, 1986, in Colorado Springs, Colorado.

1940 West Point HOWITZER yearbook roommate writeup
If there was a gathering of the gang to absorb a little wit the center was Gasso. As originator of jokes and pranks and leader of discussions he was a mean man to cross verbal swords with. Seriously, he was always straight from the shoulder in his dealings, and no one needed ever to debate as to what opinion he held on matters of discussion. The State of Michigan sent a good man to West Point, and the hands which receive him will gain a good officer. Nickname "Gasso"

GEPTE   Capt Vicente Ebol VINCENT Gepte WEST POINT 1940

Born May 29, 1917 to a Filipino military family in Zamboanga, Philippines. His father was a sergeant in the Philippine Scouts. Fought on Bataan and taken prisoner April 9, 1942. Freed with all Filipinos by the Japanese. He then joined Filipino guerrillas to fight against the Japanese and was captured. **Executed by beheading on August 30, 1944. His remains were never found.**

1940 West Point HOWITZER yearbook roommate writeup
"Mr. H'epte, sir!" Five feet two inches, and every inch a man!" We remember that thunderous voice reverberating clear across the Area whenever Hep was stopped by curious flankers, and later, when he stopped the flanker plebes. He was a "hive" in his own right, coming within a hair's breadth of wearing stars second class year. A mind of varied interests, he quoted technical formulae, historical dates, vital statistics, or poetical quotations. He wielded a mighty pen, and a mightier "bolo punch." Nickname "Hep"

IACOBUCCI   Capt Joseph V JOE Iacobucci WEST POINT 1940

Born March 23, 1916.   Served on Bataan, escaped when it fell and swam to Corregidor where he then served until it fell and he was taken prisoner May 6, 1942. **Died March 14, 1945 from of starvation, dysentery and exposure at POW camp Fukuoka #1 on the island of Kyushu**

1940 West Point HOWITZER yearbook roommate writeup
If at first you don't succeed, then ask Yako. From the beginning of plebe year Joe passed out approved solutions to everything we studied. First class year saw him with both stars and lieutenant's chevrons, but neither the T.D. nor the Academic Board could reward him for his most valuable qualities, a ready wit, a cheery smile, and a boundless generosity. His first and only love, the Air Corps, received a valuable man.   Nickname "Yako"

KRAUSS   1LT Paul H Krauss WEST POINT 1940

Born January 5, 1916 in Newark, New Jersey. He served in the "45th Infantry (Philippine Scouts) of the Philippine Division." Paul was "one of the first American infantrymen in combat in World War II." Lt Krauss was taken prisoner when Bataan fell on April 9, 1942. He passed away on January 6, 1986

1940 West Point HOWITZER yearbook roommate writeup
Conscientious, determined, and ambitious—thAT is our Paul. You have all heard his stories of Panama—the Infantry is the only branch, A little slow in penetrating the first line of resistance offered by the academic departments, Paul changed his method of attack, gave up reasoning, and took up "specing." His files show the results. Paul's excess energy was devoted to gymnastics. What a physique! Not a "dragoid," Paul, is one of the few ever-faithfuls. The Infantry is getting a good man. Nickname "Paul"

MURPHY   Capt John Joseph JOE Murphy Jr WEST POINT 1940

Born January 7, 1916 South Bend, Indiana. He served in the Field Artillery in several units on different islands, and was captured on the island of Mindanao. **He was killed on September 7, 1944 in the torpedoed hell ship the Shinyo Maru**

1940 West Point HOWITZER yearbook roommate writeup
An introduction to the F.A. at Purdue inspired Murph to come to the "cradle of future generals." Well prepared to technical subjects the only reason he didn't wear stars was that he was more interested in keeping them off other men's "B-robes." He proved himself to be a master of "British Science" the moment he started on the subject of diesel engines. A tribute paid to this "fighting Irishman" from South Bend is that he remained a staunch Hoosier throughout his four years in the East. Nickname "Murph"

PACE   1LT Herbert Edward HERB Pace Jr WEST POINT 1940

Born March 19, 1918 in Panama.
Killed in action April 28, 1942 on Corregidor when his anti-aircraft Battery Chicago was hit by Japanese 105 mm artillery fire from Bataan after he risked his life to direct his men to safety.

1940 West Point HOWITZER yearbook roommate writeup
Herbert was a misanthrope who believed in studying lessons, hazing his roommate, and writing daily letters to a young lady. This last habit, a sad slip from the practices of a true bachelor, was caught on furlough while away from the sheltering influences of U.S.M.A. As a result, as wager was made which will leave someone ten dollars poorer in June 1941 than he might otherwise have been. It seems certain Herb won't get his hands on that "tenner" even if it is paid.   Nickname "Herby"

PRESNELL   Capt John Finzer JOHNNIE Presnell Jr WEST POINT 1940

Born November 2, 1914 in Portland, Maine. Graduated from Portland High School in 1932.   He was an officer in the 14th Engineering Regiment (PS), Philippine Scouts, taken prisoner when Bataan fell on April 9, 1942. **He was killed by conditions in the hold of the hell ship the Brazil Maru on January 19, 1945**

1940 West Point HOWITZER yearbook roommate writeup
Being a Phi Beta Kappa graduate of Bowdoin College, Johnnie experienced no difficulties with the academic departments. Always an energetic worker, he played plebe and "engineer" football, and helped reorganize the wrestling squad. Johnnie's "All right, you are at attention," kept many of us out of trouble, especially his "goat wife." With Spring the inevitable feminine touch penetrated our "fat" John's stern military heart. His weakness was woman, for no hop was complete without John and his hop manager's sash. Nickname "Johnnie"

ROSEN   Capt Melvin Herbert MEL Rosen WEST POINT 1940

Born June 8, 1918   On Bataan he commanded E Battery, 2d Battalion, 88th FA (PS) and became a prisoner when Bataan fell on April 9, 1942.   He survived the war and died peacefully on August 1, 2007

1940 West Point HOWITZER yearbook roommate writeup
Mel came to" USMay" from Massachusetts. He started as a "buck" and carried on the good work for three years. These years were spent in dreams of day when he would become an indifferent first class "buck." However, on that fateful day when the "make list" was published, his castles in Spain rumbled - he was made a sergeant along with the rest of the "bucks." He hasn't been the same since. Mel never searched after glory or responsibility, but when it came he handled it well.   Nickname "Jeb"

SHOSS   1LT Morris Loeb Shoss WEST POINT 1940

Born April 10, 1915. Served on Fort Wint, Bataan, and Corregidor where he was taken prisoner when it fell May 6, 1942. Survived the sinking of the hell ship the Shinyo Maru. Survived the war and died August 4, 2004

1940 West Point HOWITZER yearbook roommate writeup
This Texan quit the plains for the Hudson Valley to wear the gray. As a plebe, he refused to succumb to the red comforter but started early to develop himself. Active for a time on Corps Squad, minor injuries forced him into intra-mural league where he won his scars. His foremost achievement, however, was on the academic front. Never over-studious, Maury nevertheless garnered an enviable rank in his class. Nickname "Maury"

SIMPSON   1LT Harry Thompson H.T. Simpson Jr WEST POINT 1940

Born June 10, 1913   Attended William and Mary College in Williamsburg before West Point.   Served in the 59th Coastal Artillery "A" Battery on Corregidor, taken prisoner on May 6, 1942.   Survived the war and died on July 8, 1988

1940 West Point HOWITZER yearbook roommate writeup
"A Virginian, suh," - his "out" and "house" were quite indicative of his birthplace. Although an exponent of our disciplinary system he still insisted that West Point is more than a four-year course, Debonair, devil-may-care, his greatest fault was thinking aloud, his greatest virtue, constancy. Despite academic hardships and T.D. troubles he contrived to master the game of bridge. His ready counsel always was, "Mister, take a fool's advice." A very hard but an aspiring man, he decided on the Coast Artillery. Nickname "H.T."

STIRLING   Capt Warren Curtis Stirling WEST POINT 1940

Born November 13, 1914 in Philadelphia. Led infantry on Bataan, recovered the body of an American Lieutenant while under fire from the enemy.   Taken prisoner when Bataan fell. Survived time as a POW, and died December 5, 2005 in Austin, Texas.

1940 West Point HOWITZER yearbook roommate writeup
An agreeable disposition won for Warren the friendship of his classmates. Where his nickname, Goon, originated is somewhat of a mystery, it is certainly no detriment in his relations with the fair sex. Always nonchalant and never seemingly in a hurry he invariably managed to turn up at the right time and place. Although his class standing was not particularly high, academics have never interfered with his peace of mind. His ability to realize his ambitions should ensure him a successful career in the branch of his choice. Nickname "Goon"

TOTH   Capt Jerry Geza Toth WEST POINT 1940

Born March 17, 1915 in Michigan. **Killed in action, April 6, 1942 on Bataan during the last chaotic days before surrender. He was hit by a 47 mm shell fired by the Japanese which hit him in the chest. He died instantly.   His body was never recovered.**

1940 West Point HOWITZER yearbook roommate writeup
Jerry came to West Point the hard way, through the Army. This mighty mite battered his way through the plebe year despite "gal trouble" and found the rest of the way fairly easy. Though a "runt", he soon earned the name Toughy and took down many a "flanker" in football, boxing, and track. West Point ironed out most of his rough spots, leaving him with an inclination for cartooning, music, and getting into scraps. Nickname "Toughy"

WALD   Capt Walter Israel IZZY Wald WEST POINT 1940

Born November 2, 1914 at Fort DeRussy, Hawaii. He was with the 61st Field Artillery fighting on the island of Cebu when he was taken prisoner after the fall of Corregidor. **Killed September 7, 1944 in the sinking of the hell ship the Shinyo Maru**

1940 West Point HOWITZER yearbook roommate writeup
A "regimental buck" without a "buck's" personal indifference—God bless him. His philosophy of "live and let live" prevented his "boning" tactical files with the rest of the boys. His tactical indifference was more than balanced by his academic assiduity. Behind those eyebrows lurched a walking dictionary and encyclopedia—most of which was in Spanish. With his broad knowledge, infallible logic, and convincing obstinance that defeated even his little redhead he mowed down the best of them in arguments. Nickname "Iz"

WHEAT   1LT Robert Ila BOB Wheat WEST POINT 1940

Born March 6, 1918 in Arkansas. He was an officer with the 92nd Coast Artillery (Philippine Scout) Regiment on Corregidor and takne prisoner when it fell on May 6, 1942. **Died February 22, 1945 due to the aftereffects of his three hell ship voyages and the conditions in Kokura Military Hospital on the island of Kyushu**

1940 West Point HOWITZER yearbook roommate writeup
Rev. Trigo, or Lil' Abner; they serve as an introduction to one and the same—that happy-go-lucky, carefree chap from Arkansas. We heard his voice above the roar of every gathering and remember him as one who enjoyed most his own sense of humor. And as his witticisms and friendliness drew him toward his classmates, so an active, calculating brain sustained him well in the classroom. No matter what the occasion, he was there in the thick of the fight and invariably on the winning side. Nickname "Trigo

WRIGHT   1LT John MacNAIR JACK Wright WEST POINT 1940

Born April 14, 1916   He fought on Corregidor with a battery of fixed and finally a roving 155 mm gun until Corregidor fell and he was taken prisoner. He survived his time as a POW and died on January 27, 2014

1940 West Point HOWITZER yearbook roommate writeup
"Cette vie militaire, it gets me." Whether coming in from hours of playing ghost, putting books away for early taps during "cow deadbeat," or entering the room disgusted with a deficient grade, this was Jack's standard comment throughout four years of cadet life. Never an admirer of the genus "file-boner," his ability to get along with people kept him at the top in spite of an engagement with the T.D. second class year. Graduation brought the Coast Artillery and a chance to live again beneath California skies. Nickname "Jack"

YATES Capt Jules David YAT Yates WEST POINT 1940

Born Novemer 2, 1916   He was with the Coast Artillery on Corregidor and taken prisoner when it fell on May 6, 1942,   After spending years in POW camps he was freed during the Great Raid by Army Rangers at Cabanatuan POW camp January 30, 1945. He died on August 10, 1996

1940 West Point HOWITZER yearbook roommate writeup
The population of Yardville dropped to 259 when Yat came to West Point. However, this metropolis was responsible for instilling in Yat many characteristics that stayed with him for four years. There he developed a fondness for reading that led him to our library daily. A desire to teach was manifested here in his coaching of underclassmen. Yat was for his two first years an "area-bird," but when he took up golf and liked it so much, he decided to stop walking and he did. Nickname "Yat

YEAGER   Capt Frederick Jacob FRED Yeager WEST POINT 1940

Born November 19, 1915 in New York City. Commanding Officer of Company A, 57th Infantry Regiment, Philippine Scouts on Bataan.   Taken captive when Bataan fell. He spent much of the war at POW camps in Japan.   He survived the war and died February 20, 2009

1940 West Point HOWITZER yearbook roommate writeup
The seven-league boots that carry the athlete, scholar, gentleman, and friend combined through West Point in a four year bound are as titanic as they are rare. These encased the feet of Tiger who not only wore them but filled them well. Fred took his work seriously, his honors humbly, his injuries smilingly, his "femmes" lightly, his fan mail laughingly, and our respect and admiration always. Both his constant punning anD his "barracks-shaking" jitterbug activities added laughs which made our cadet days more enjoyable. Nickname "Tiger"

People who knew Chester are listed in three groups on our website.

Some knew him well and were good friends, some only fleetingly and some we are unsure of the relationship. Their names were in Chester's diary, or were associated with actions in which Chester was involved. We simply want to honor them by listing their names.

Epilogue

This story of Chet and Grace is our family story, unique in many respects from other family stories and similar to only a hand full of others for only 271 men survived the war and all the things that Chet had experienced. Fewer men had a wife like Grace that stayed with them regardless the challenge that life presented to their marriage.

There are some things that we can learn from their story.

Chet and Grace were people of faith, and they were at peace with God, the Creator of all things, because they knew who they were, and they knew who He is. Though they did not understand why the war happened and why they were subjected to the nightmare of separation and the uncertainty of life itself, they knew always that God was in control. They were the clay and God was the potter.

Every war causes families to be separated, torn apart, and wounded, relationships bleed with the cuts of a thousand moments of uncertainty, emotions are lifted high with hope only to be dashed by tragedy.

The circumstances Chet and Grace faced and the patience they had created endurance to withstand whatever came next as the war unfolded. They endured the years of uncertainty and extreme hardship. Chet's character was forged by the fire of death and fight for survival; Grace's character by the need for a life with Chet, who would return home alive and whole, but shadowed by the possibility that he would not live, and she would be a single mother.

The trials they faced created perseverance in their faith, and this created character to withstand whatever came and led to their hope for a future together.

Love perseveres when it is real, Chet and Grace, the young newlyweds, were committed to life with each other and no other. This love gave them strength when they no longer seemed to have any strength or reason to live. Their love was hard work, but it did not prevent tragedy from entering their lives. This love provided the endurance to continue on, despite the circumstances.

Love shared has life-giving value.

Hope comes from within.

Their belief that you are loved and that by persevering in hope you will once again experience love, served them both as life sustaining nourishment. We should follow a code of honor to continue to remember and respect what our parents and their generation have done for us. A people without a past to remember have little basis for knowing who they are as a people.

We continued to honor Chet with the award of a POW medal in 1989 while providing Grace with closure from the tragedy of war.

We honored Grace on her 75th birthday in 1990 with a "This is your life" type venue with her sons, daughters-in-law and grandchildren playing the leading roles in period costume for different periods of her life reenacted as they must have been.

On April 11, 2021, a national ceremony was held virtually to award the Filipino Veterans of WW II Congressional Gold Medal to Major (Ret) Chester K. Britt for his honorable service and selfless sacrifices in the Philippines. Receiving the award on his behalf was his son, LtCol USAF (Ret) David L. Britt and members of his family. America must not forget the members of the WW II generation who gave so much for our freedom.

June 11, 1989 at the Pentagon, Grace Britt received the POW Medal on behalf of her beloved late husband, Chet

"Left to right, my wife Gail's mother Betty Hastings, my dad's brother, Uncle Edgar Britt (Ret. Navy Cmdr) and his wife Eileen, Maj. Gen. Chuck Boyd, our mother Grace, me (Lt. Col. David Britt USAF)" - David Britt

September 6, 1990   Grace's 75th birthday
L-R Dave, Don, Chet Jr with Mother Grace

April 11, 2021 Army Major (Ret) Chester K. Britt's Filipino Veterans of WW II Congressional Gold Medal for his honorable service and selfless sacrifice in the Philippines.   In attendance: (L-R) Lt (USN) Gary Doss, Great Grandson Grant, Granddaughter Lindsey Doss, Great Grandson Dillon, LtCol, USAF (Ret) David Britt who received the award on his behalf, Dave's wife Gail

Acknowledgements

Lincoln was humbled by the sacrifices his men made in Pennsylvania in 1863. His words in the Gettysburg Address, reflect our feelings of inadequacy as we created this offering to the memory of the men whose names are in this book. The first half of his address talked about the Civil War; the second half laid out the sacrifice of those that fought the battle. His words still apply to every man, every woman, every race, every creed, to anyone whoever sacrificed for our country anywhere.

"But, in a larger sense, we cannot dedicate—we cannot consecrate—we cannot hallow—this ground. The brave men, living and dead, who struggled here, have consecrated it, far above our poor power to add or detract. The world will little note, nor long remember what we say here, but it can never forget what they did here. It is for us the living, rather, to be dedicated here to the unfinished work which they who fought here have thus far so nobly advanced. It is rather for us to be here dedicated to the great task remaining before us—that from these honored dead we take increased devotion to that cause for which they gave the last full measure of devotion—that we here highly resolve that these dead shall not have died in vain—that this nation, under God, shall have a new birth of freedom—and that government of the people, by the people, for the people, shall not perish from the earth." - Abraham Lincoln, November 19, 1863

We are indebted to our ancestors for so much. They gave us life, they protected our liberty and ensured that we have a future as Americans, and it is only fitting that we thank them before others for providing a story worth sharing. Thanks Dad and Mom for your example of how to live and how to die. We love you and will never forget you.

Special recognition for my co-laborer on this book and high school friend, John (Jack) Duresky, a wizard at on-line research and it turns out, someone who lived in Japan in the 1970s and speaks some of the language. John spent countless hours researching for information on so many different subjects related to this book, organizing the collected volumes of information on relationships of the classmates, on their families and friends, without which the book is incomplete. Jack found and worked U.S., Filipino and Japanese historians as well as with a U.S. Navy historian, to glean details related to attacks on 2 of the 3 Hell ships that took the POWs to Japan, which allowed us to tell history from the U.S. Navy point of view. He also found many of the family members of men written about in the book to get the background information on Chet's fellow warriors. John has become a member of my family through the research as the intensity of it laid his soul bare and he embraced our parents. You are a brother now.

Special recognition for Vickie Graham our professional editor. A classmate from Logan High School and friend for over 55 years, she had a career as a professional journalist and editor. Working on our draft narratives, between stints at a food bank during the COVID pandemic, she graciously agreed to read and fix what we wrote and made silk out of a sow's ear. Without her skills and the rewriting of our narratives, so that our high school English teacher would be proud, we would have nothing to offer as a tribute to so many deserving people, especially my parents. Vickie is now a sister that I never had. Thanks, from the bottom of my heart, for helping John and me to complete this book.

Thanks to my older brother Don Britt who did research on-line, in interviews with survivors, including Dad's fellow warriors, Al D'Arezzo, Morris Shoss and Dad's closest friend on Bataan, Bill Lewis and by obtaining some books used to build this story. Don also travelled to the Philippines to retrace some of the journey of the Death March. Thanks for your inputs brother.

Thanks to Patricia Labounty who provided us with an invaluable source document. Patricia is the widow of Marshall Owens who authored a Master of Arts Thesis on "The American POWs in the Philippines During World War II." September 1989. This extensively researched and well written narrative of the POWs and the captors provides documented insight into many things about the POW experience from POW testimonies and has enriched our book with details lost to history. His work has helped us see Lt Britt in the unbelievably horrible and unspeakable environment that he and only the few survived. The POW survivors had great moral courage and relentless hope, Supermen.

Thanks to Manny Lawton, who Dad knew personally, for his valuable record of the experience of the Death March and Hell Ship journey chronicled in *"Some Survived,"* and Sidney Stewart, who Dad also knew, who recorded his experiences in "Give us this Day." Their accounts live on and coupled with family documents and the other historical books, that allowed me to find truth in the legends and stories of our family.

Thanks to Tim Hampton, Historian for Air Group 11, USS Hornet. We accurately depicted the U.S. naval action through documented history and aerial photos as well as after action reports from the pilots who flew in those raids. Amazing stuff that helped us tell the U.S. Navy story as a participant in the real lives of men desperate to survive.

Thanks to our high school friend Jeanne Beeler, who took photos and researched information for us in La Crosse, WI. Jean has been a friend for over 52 years and over 67 years for John Duresky.

Special shout out for Brigadier General (Ret) Paul Phillips and Colonel (Ret) Beverly "Ben" Skardon, surviving warriors of the POW experience who turned 102 and 103 years old, respectively, on March 9 and July 14, 2020. They experienced everything my Dad went through: the same camps and hell ships. They are still firecrackers, sharp as tacks and both have a sense of humor. We enjoyed laughing together, for even in dark places and the difficult times we discussed, irony brings humor and keeps us human.

Acknowledgements from John Duresky

"It is impossible to adequately acknowledge and thank everyone who has helped with our book. We hope to do a **better job of acknowledging** all the family members and experts **in our website**. This is only the barest list of those who have helped us so much. Thank you all."

Our sincerest hope is that this book honors the sacrifice and memories of these men and their families who saved our nation. There is a saying that "Freedom is not free" and these men paid the price.

David L. Britt, Lt Col, USAF (Ret), Residing in Odessa, FL. Privileged to be the youngest son of Major (Retired) Chester Sr. and Grace Britt.

Bibliography

ABRAHAM, Abie, "Oh, God, Where are you?," 1997, Vantage Press, Inc,
516 West 34th St, New York, NY 10001

ALLEN, Oliver, "Abandoned on Bataan," 2002, Crimson Horse Entertainment
& Publishing, 103C Parkway, Boerne, TX 78006

BANNING, Kendall, "West Point Today," 1937, Funk & Wagnalls Company,
New York, NY

BRITT, Captain Chester Kieser, "War Crimes Affidavit on Hell Ships,"
San Francisco, CA, November 1945

BRITT, Captain Chester Kieser, "War Crimes Affidavit pertaining to
Fukuoka#3 and Hoten Camp, Mukden, Manchuria"

BRITT, Lt Chester K., assorted letters, documents, photos, and other
family records

BRITT, Grace R., assorted letters, documents, photos, and other family records

BROKAW, Tom, "The Greatest Generation," 1998, Random House Inc.,
New York, NY

BROUGHER, Brig. Gen. W.E., "South To Bataan, North To Mukden," 1971,
University of Georgia Press, printed by the TJM Press, Baton Rouge, LA 70821

BROWN, Lt Col Charles M., "The Oryoku Maru Story," 1983, taken from
legal proceedings, war crimes testimony

BUNKER, Paul D., "Bunkers War," edited by Col. Keith A. Barlow US Army, 1996, Presidio Press, 505 B San Marin Drive, Suite 300, Novato, CA 94945-1340

CALDWELL, Donald C., "Thunder on Bataan," 2019, Stackpole Books, 4501 Forbes Blvd, Ste. 200, Lanham, MD 20706

CALHOUN, S. W., "Duty, Honor, Country the Long Gray Line in the Pacific," Pub 281, June 2012, Lauderdale County Dept of Archive and History, Inc., PO Box 511, Meridian, MS 39302

CHUNN, Maj Calvin Ellsworth, "Of Rice and Men," 1946, Veteran's Publishing Co L.A and Tulsa

DAWS, Gavan, "Prisoners of the Japanese: POWs of World War II in the Pacific," 1996, Harper Collins

ENGELHART, Col E Carl, "TRAPPED ON CORREGIDOR," from a PDF file

FORTIER, Col., Malcolm Vaughn, "The Life of a P.O.W. Under the Japanese in caricature," 1946, C.W. Hill Printing Co. W. 920 Riverdale Ave. Spokane 8, WA

GELB, Ludwig, "My Third Escape," 1993, Rossel Books, Berman House Inc., 235 Watchung Ave., West Orange, NJ 07052

GRADY, Frank J., and Dickson, Rebecca, "Surviving the Day — An American POW in Japan", 1997, Naval Institute Press, Annapolis, MD

GRAY, Isabel McReynolds, "Florizel," with a dedication to her son Harry McReynolds Gray, 1910, Los Angeles, CA

GRIFFIN, Lt Col Robert A edited by, "SCHOOL OF THE CITIZEN SOLDIER", 1942, D. Appleton-Century Company, Inc.

HASTINGS, Max, "Inferno — The World At War 1939-1945," 2011, Vantage Books, A Division of Random House, New York

HEISINGER, Duane, "FATHER FOUND, Life and Death as a prisoner of the Japanese in World War II", 2003, Xulon Press

HINES, Walter, "AGGIES OF THE PACIFIC WAR — New Mexico A&M and the War with Japan," 1999, Yucca Tree Press, 2130 Hixon Dr., Las Cruces, NM 88005

HUDSON, J. Ed, "A History of the USS Cabot (CVL-28): A Fast Carrier in WWII," 1986, Deluxe Printing Co.

IND, Lt Col Allison W., "BATAAN THE JUDGEMENT SEAT," 1944, The Macmillan Company, New York

JACOBS, Col. Eugene, C., "Blood Brothers," 1985, Eugene C Jacobs, Carlton Press NY, NY

JAMES, D. Clayton, "South to Bataan, North to Mukden, The Prison Diary of Brig. Gen. W. E. Brougher" 1971, University of Georgia Press, Athens, GA 30601

JONES, Betty B., "The December Ship, A Story of Lt. Col. Arden R Boellner's Capture in the Philippines, Imprisonment, and Death on a World War II Japanese Hellship," 1992, McFarland & Co., Inc., Box 611, Jefferson, NC 28640

KNOX, Donald, "DEATH MARCH: THE SURVIVOR'S OF BATAAN," 1981, Harcourt Brace Jovanovich, 757 Third Avenue, New York, NY 10017

LAWTON, Manny, "Some Survived," 2004, Algonquin Books, Chapel Hill, NC 27515 @1984

LOGAN HIGH SCHOOL, La Crosse, Wisconsin, "WINNESHIEK yearbooks," years 1933, 1934, 1942~1945, 1967

MICHEL, John J. A., "MR. MICHEL'S WAR," 1998, Presidio Press, 505 B San Marin Drive, Suite 300, Novato, CA 94945-1340

NORMAN, Michael and Norman, Elizabeth M., "Tears in the Darkness," 2009, Farrar, Straus, Giroux 18 W 18th St NY, NY 10011

OFFICE OF THE JUDGE ADVOCATE GENERAL, U.S. War Department War Crimes

OLSON Colonel (Ret) John E., "USMA in the Philippines 1941-42," July 1993, Assembly Magazine

OWENS, Marshall, "American POWs in the Philippines World War II," September 1989, Master's Paper submitted to History Dept, U of Wyoming toward Master's degree

PEARSON, Judith L., "Belly of the Beast," 2001, New American Library a division of Penguin Putnam, Inc., 375 Hudson St., New York, NY 10014

PHILLIPS, Claire "High Pockets" and Goldsmith, Myron B., "Manila Espionage," 2017, Enhanced Media Publishing, Los Angeles, CA

REYNOLDS, Robert V., "Of Rice and Men, 1949, Leicht Press, Publishers, Winona, MN

ROBERTS, Frank R., "The Last Big Gun," July 1994, Assembly Magazine

ROMULO, Col Carlos P., "I Saw the Fall of Philippines," 1942, Doubleday

SCHULTZ, Duane, "Hero of Bataan," 1981, St. Martin's Press, 175 Fifth Ave, NY, NY 10010

SLONE, William Reuben, "The Light Behind The Clouds," 1992, Texas Press, Waco, TX

SOMMERS, Stan, "The Japanese Story," 1980, Marshfield, WI. https://www.axpow.org/medsearch/packet10converted.pdf

STAKES, Benjamin F., "Shadows of Bataan," 1940 (reprint 2013), Inknbeans Press

STEWART, Sidney, "Give us this Day," 1956, W.W. Norton & Co 500 Fifth Ave. NY, NY 10110

TENNEY, Lester I., "MY HITCH IN HELL," foreward by James B. Stockdale, 1995, an imprint of the University of Nebraska Press

ULANOWICZ, Col. Emil M., "Early World War II Events in the Philippines," 1944

UNITED STATES MILITARY ACADEMY at West Point, NY, "HOWITZER yearbook", years 1906, 1923, 1924, 1925, 1929, 1931, 1932, 1933, 1937, 1938, 1939, 1940, 1941

UNITED STATES NAVAL ACADEMY at Annapolis, MD, "THE LUCKY BAG yearbook," years 1939, 1940

USS HORNET, "The United States Ship HORNET First War Cruise 1943 — 1945," 1945, Lithographed on board the U.S.S. Hornet

TODD, Ann, "OSS Operation Black Mail," 2017, Naval Institute Press, 291 Wood Rd., Annapolis, MD 21402

WHITMAN, John W., "Bataan our Last Ditch," 1990, Hippocrene Books, 171 Madison Ave, NY, NY 10016

WILLOUGHBY, Amea, "I Was On Corregidor," 1943, Harper & Brothers Publishers, New York

WODNIK, Bob, "Captured Honor," 2003, Board of Regents Washington State U. WSU Press Pullman, Wash 99164

WRIGHT, John MacNair. Jr., "Captured on Corregidor," 1988, McFarland & Co., Inc., Box 611, Jefferson, NC 28640

ZIMBLER, Sheldon, "Undaunted Valor- The Men of Mukden," Tri-State Publishing, 71 Tenbrook Ave. Kingston, NY 12401

Index

for ordinary people in this book

This book is about friends and others Chet and Grace Britt knew; famous people have their own books.

Britt family member are not listed as they appear periodically throughout the book.

Name-Chapter(s)